BUDGET AUTO RESTORATION

Low cost, step-by-step tricks for rejuvenating your '50s and '60s cars

Burt Mills

Motorbooks International
Publishers & Wholesalers ®

First published in 1990 by Motorbooks International Publishers & Wholesalers, P O Box 2, 729 Prospect Avenue, Osceola, WI 54020 USA

Motorbooks International books are also available at discounts in bulk quantity for industrial or sales-promotional use. For details write to Special Sales Manager at the Publisher's address

Library of Congress Cataloging-in-Publication Data
Mills, Burt.
    Budget auto restoration / Burt B. Mills.
      p. cm.
    ISBN 0-87938-405-0
    1. Automobiles—Conservation and restoration.
    I. Title.
TL152.2.M5414 1990   90-5700
629.28′72—dc20   CIP

On the front cover: This beautifully restored 1961 Impala is owned by Darel Luster of White Deer, Texas. *Jerry Heasley*

Printed and bound in the United States of America

Contents

	Foreword	5
	Acknowledgments	5
	Introduction	6
1	Choosing the right car	7
2	Buying the car	12
3	Preparing for work	20
4	General troubleshooting	24
5	The engine	28
6	Engine rebuild, top end	33
7	Engine rebuild, bottom end	42
8	Engine replacement	52
9	Electrical systems	59
10	Fuel system	73
11	Cooling system	82
12	Exhaust system	90
13	Transmission and clutch	96
14	Drive shaft and differential	106

15	Rear suspension system	115
16	Front suspension system	122
17	Steering system	131
18	Brakes	139
19	Body rebuilding and repair	151
20	Convertible top	167
21	Upholstery	186
22	Carpets	201
23	Trim items	207
24	Preparing for painting	216
25	Painting	225
26	Serious show car restoration	231
27	Caring for your car	235
	Appendix	238

Foreword

Be Careful, Please

Rejuvenating an old car can be fun, but if care isn't taken when making some repairs, injuries can happen. Working with flammable substances as well as operating machinery can be hazardous. While every effort has been made to advise and describe safe procedures, the reader will have to use common sense and follow accepted safety precautions.

Acknowledgments

Acknowledgment is gratefully made to the following individuals and companies, who either furnished information or allowed their cars to be photographed for this book, or allowed photographs to be taken on their premises.

Antique Auto House, Loveland, CO
Accurate Rebuilders, Englewood, CO
Archives, Old Cars Weekly, Iola, WI
Auto Trim Specialists, Denver, CO
Colorado Cars and Parts, Englewood, CO
Colorado Classic Cars, Denver, CO
Empire Radiator Service, Littleton, CO

Englewood Driveshaft, Englewood, CO
G & S Automotive Parts, Englewood, CO
Genuine Automotive Parts, Englewood, CO
Marvin Hall, 1954 Mercury, Denver, CO
Jerry Lips Collection, Englewood, CO
Mag-Co Transmissions, Englewood, CO
Merle's Alignment, Littleton, CO
Midas Muffler & Brake Shop, Lakewood, CO
Platte Canyon Restorations, 1965 Mustang, Littleton, CO
Sam's Reconditioning, Englewood, CO
Soneff's Classic Auto Sales, Denver, CO
Joe Stengel, 1951 Buick, Englewood, CO
The Carburetor Shop, Englewood, CO

Introduction

Budget Auto Restoration is written for the men and women who like old cars; the would-be hobbyists, who may have but little to average mechanical ability and can invest but a minimal amount of money and time. It is a general introduction to what is involved—including problems to expect—when rejuvenating a car of the 1950s, 1960s and early 1970s.

This book is intended to be used as a guide through a thoroughly acceptable mechanical and cosmetic renovation, rather than a complete frame-off restoration for serious show car competition, though that, too, is outlined. It is a source book for complete information on the rejuvenation and repair process.

The basic functions of the major components, how to diagnose needed repairs, repair and replacement procedures and money-saving tips, all are explained on the following pages. Emphasis is on doing most of the work yourself, *which you can,* and save money, too. Most repair and rejuvenation jobs can be done evenings, or on weekends, leaving the car for everyday use.

The appendix lists, chapter by chapter, sources of information on specific makes and models produced during these years; parts interchange resource information; technical and general resources; hobby periodicals; and major automobile makers.

You've probably seen repaired or rejuvenated beauties at car shows, or advertised at fantastic prices. You may feel the old car hobby is out of your reach.

Not so!

There is a wide variety of restorable cars of these years at affordable prices, many well below $1,000. You may already have such a car that you've put off rejuvenating.

Perhaps you've felt that parts are unobtainable, or that the cost would be too high.

Not true!

For all but a few exotic, low-production or long-orphaned makes, new, rebuilt or used replacement parts are easily obtainable, and at reasonable prices.

Maybe you've shied away from rejuvenating one of these cars because you felt the work would be too difficult and take too long.

Wrong!

There is no reason why the average man or woman can't make an excellent rejuvenation. Sure, certain heavy jobs may require the efforts of two people. Their gender doesn't matter. All but a few jobs can be done by the beginning restorer, and in your own garage. You can farm out jobs like plating and welding. If planned properly, most jobs won't put the car out of service for more than a weekend, allowing you to drive your project car on a regular basis.

Leave yourself some options when deciding which make, body style and year you want. Decide on a general price range, then look around. Inspection techniques and bargaining tips are all covered in this book. They'll help you locate a surprising variety of cars you can rescue and rejuvenate for a reasonable amount of money and time.

Join the fun!

Good luck,

Burt Mills

Chapter 1

Choosing the right car

Rescuing and renovating a car from the fifties, sixties or early seventies can be fun and it makes a lot of sense. Whether you choose a perky compact, an exciting convertible, a handy station wagon or a roomy family sedan, you and your family can enjoy the project.

These are capable cars that will hold their own on today's fast and crowded highways. They have sufficient pickup and speed to satisfy most drivers.

Price

Of course you'd *like* an Auburn Boattail Speedster, Cadillac V-16, Franklin Roadster or Packard Dual Cowl Phaeton. Who wouldn't? There are but few of these left and they command fantastic prices. In fact, most restorable cars made through the forties are owned by collectors.

The low prices, wide selection and large number of cars of the fifties, sixties and early seventies still

Handsome 1967 Chevrolet Impala SS convertible with Strato-bucket front seats holds five passengers. The 283 ci V–8 develops 195 hp, giving the large car plenty of pickup and power. Upholstery and carpeting are color coordinated for contrast.

available give you the opportunity to find the right car in your price range. Cars of these years can only increase in value, if they are well maintained, giving a substantial increase.

Styling

Fifties styling broke away from the carried-over pre-World War II designs used through the forties. Studebaker's Loewy-designed coupes, Buick's Roadmaster Skylark, Ford's retractable hardtop and Thunderbird, Edsel's distinctive front end, Cadillac's fins and Chrysler's Virgil Exner designs are but a few examples.

Longer, lower cars were fashionable in the sixties, their sleek lines usually accented by chrome trim. Chevrolet's Camaro, Chrysler's 300 Series, Dodge's Charger, Oldsmobile's Toronado and Studebaker's Avanti styling all bespeak power and speed.

Then in the early seventies, before gasoline shortages forced downsizing, huge sedans, station wagons and convertibles offered by the "Big Three" (General Motors, Chrysler and Ford) made the scene.

Cars of this era give plenty of passenger room. Even the low-priced cars are roomier than many of today's cars. Most have large luggage compartments, which hide a full-size spare wheel and tire.

Interiors are attractive, comfortable and often colorful. They're well finished, with a minimum of plastic knobs. Many used plated interior trim on dashboard and panels. Most were equipped with radios, heaters and defrosters. As the sixties progressed, stereos and tape decks were added. Power seats and other assists added to driver and passenger comfort.

Parts and repair

Cars of these years are easier to repair than later models. There is more working room around the major components, and engine layout is simpler, making troubleshooting much easier.

Brakes, steering, and front and rear suspension systems are not complex, computer-controlled components as are today's systems, and can be repaired by the average person without great difficulty.

Many of these cars used brake, clutch, transmission, steering and other mechanical components supplied by the same company. Often specifications were the same, making it easier to locate needed parts.

In fact, many cars manufactured by the same parent company used the same basic engines, mechanical parts and body stampings in their various makes for several years. Sharing of many body parts makes the search for replacements easier. Sources of parts interchange information are listed in the appendix.

Major automotive supply chains have specifications of interchangeable parts. Some car clubs maintain libraries of important information. You can take a part with you to an automotive supply store or salvage yard for identification and match-up. In addition, new, rebuilt or good used parts, and rebuild kits for many components, are readily available at reasonable cost.

Structural integrity

Cars of this era also offered a great deal of structural strength. These were the years before metal was pared away from engines, frames and other components in an effort to save weight. They were built of solid steel and heavily reinforced at all stress points. In other words, they were built to withstand tough treatment. Body stampings, welded into a strong unit, gave stability and passenger protection.

Considered by many to be Ford's most handsome car of the fifties, this 1959 Ford Fairlane Galaxie 500 adapted Thunderbird's roof styling and tasteful use of plated trim, providing elegance and understated class. The 292 ci V–8 developed 200 hp. A fine family car.

The stylish 1964 Lincoln Continental four-door convertible sedan offers top luxury and comfort combined with excellent performance. Its quality construction ensures that a *minimal amount of time and money will be necessary to put these cars in first-class condition.*

It's your decision. So, there's no reason to postpone enjoying the old car hobby. Choose almost any car of these years and join the fun.

It's important that you decide to what degree you want to restore your car. This makes a big difference in what car you choose.

You can go for a complete, frame-off restoration, one in which everything is brought back to original specifications. This will give you a car you can enter in serious show car competition. For this type of project you'll have to be prepared to spend a lot of time and money. Once you've finished, though, you may have a car you feel is too good to drive every day and risk the dings and scratches of parking lots.

You may decide to customize the car you choose, changing it from its original body style, making it into a personalized vehicle. This could include making mechanical alterations, too, such as installing a different make engine or updating the transmission, lowering front or rear suspension, even changing axles to allow wider wheels and tires. This choice can require a lot of time and money, and leave you with a fun car that may be difficult to sell some day, and not be practical for everyday use.

The most popular and practical decision is to renovate a car to dependable and safe condition, so it can be used every day, if necessary. This may require adjustment, repair or replacement of certain mechanical components. It may also mean some body and fender repairs and painting, as well as interior refurbishing.

The finished project will produce a car you can be proud of and enjoy. It's the easiest and most economi-

American Motors muscle car, the 1968 AMX two-seater sports car is fitted with a 290 ci OHV V–8 developing 225 hp. The taut suspension system gives excellent cornering *and handling. Fastback styling has allowed the car to retain its appeal.*

9

Extremely rare, this 1952 Chevrolet sedan delivery uses Chevy's dependable OHV six-cylinder engine developing 108 hp. There is front seating for two in passenger car comfort, plus tremendous carrying room. The rear door makes loading easy.

cal entry into the old car hobby. Initial prices will be lower, as will repairs, since you can do most of the work yourself.

Decide what you want in the completed car and make your choice accordingly.

How to choose your car

Decide on several cars that you'd like. Don't set your mind hard and fast on just one car, unless you're willing to pay what it'll take.

Follow advertised prices on these cars for a reasonable period, so you'll have a good idea what you should pay. There are periodic publications listing average prices of old cars by make, year and body style in various conditions. There is usually at least a twenty-percent difference between the asking price and final selling price.

You may see ads for cars in other cities at lower prices than local cars. While these may be worth looking into, remember you'll have to add roundtrip travel costs to the final selling price.

Get as much information on the car's condition as possible; get it in writing, when considering a car some distance from your home. Ask for pictures, which you should return if you're not interested. This will help you decide if you want to invest the time and money necessary to investigate further. You should never buy a car based solely upon telephone conversations with the owner. Too many misunderstandings can arise, which could be disappointing to you and cost you a lot of money.

There are some generally accepted classes commonly used to describe a car's condition. You should become familiar with them.

Class 1   *Excellent:* Restored to current professional standards of quality in every area; or original with all components operating and appearing as new.

Class 2   *Fine:* Well restored; or combination of superior restoration and excellent original; or extremely well maintained original showing minimal wear.

Class 3   *Very good:* Completely operable original or older restoration showing wear; or amateur restoration; presentable and serviceable inside and out. Also, combinations of well-done restoration and good, operable components; or partially restored car with all parts to complete and/or valuable NOS (new original stock) parts.

Class 4   *Good:* A driveable vehicle needing no or only minor work to be functional; or a deteriorated restoration; or a very poor amateur restoration. All components may need restoration to be rated Excellent, but mostly useable as is.

Class 5   *Restorable:* Needs complete restoration of body, chassis and interior. Not driveable, but is not weathered, wrecked or stripped to the point of being useful only for parts salvage.

There are standard abbreviations used in car literature and ads you'll come across, as you look for your car and later pursue the hobby. Here is a list of the more commonly used terms.

AC	Air conditioning, or alternating current
AT	Automatic transmission
BHP	Brake horsepower
BxS	Bore times stroke
CID	Cubic inch displacement
C/R	Compression ratio
Cust	Custom
DL	Deluxe
Def	Defroster
F-Hd	F-head engine: Intake valve in head, exhaust in block
GR	Gear ratio
GVW	Gross vehicle weight
Htr	Heater
H&D	Heater and defroster
HD	Heavy duty
LWB	Long wheelbase
MPG	Miles per gallon
MPH	Miles per hour
NOS	New original stock
OD	Overdrive
Ohv	Overhead valve engine
OL	Overall length
PB	Power brakes
PS	Power steering or power seats
PT	Power-operated top
R	Radio
RPM	Revolutions per minute
SR	Sunroof

Std	Standard
SWB	Short wheelbase
Tr	Transmission, 3-Spd, 4-Spd, 5-Spd
VIN	Vehicle Identification Number
WB	Wheelbase
WSW or WW	White sidewall tires

The want ad departments of many magazines and newspapers also publish a list of their commonly used abbreviations, which will help you clarify some ads.

Things to consider

Most manufacturers have marketed at least one model they've regretted and had to correct. This may have been because of faulty engineering, poor design, styling not accepted by the public, insufficient testing, bad publicity or other reasons.

Some examples are: the position of Pinto's gas tank; the early Corvair's tendency to overturn when cornering fast; the Vega's engine problems; the Tempest's driveline difficulties; the Cadillac's first air suspension system; and the Pacer's styling.

Makes and models with generally known problems should be avoided, unless you really want that car and are willing to put up with associated problems, which will probably come up during your renovation.

Wraparound windshields during the mid 1950s can be difficult to locate and expensive to replace, especially on orphaned makes and low-production models. The same goes for curved glass used on certain hardtops. Some interior and exterior hardware used on low-production makes may be almost nonexistent. Take these things into consideration when choosing your car.

It's easy to get carried away in your renovation efforts and invest far more in the project than you planned. For this reason, set a tentative budget. Record expenses and check closely.

1950s cars

These were the years known for the consolidations and eventual demise of well-known independents. Sales were good in the early 1950s, as post-World War II designs evolved, keeping individual makes easy to identify. These were solid automobiles, built to give increased performance with surprising fuel economy.

There was a wide selection of body styles and choices of interior and exterior trim. There was often a choice of engines, and power-operated options were common.

By the middle of the decade, the Big Three made an all-out push to knock out weaker competition. Their financial capabilities allowed them—Chrysler, Ford and General Motors—to dominate the business. They offered new and different body styles, new high-power engines and engineering advances.

1960s cars

With competition narrowed to the Big Three, a weak fourth and one, on-the-ropes independent, the 1960s became an all-out race. There was great model proliferation, with manufacturers adding new makes, submakes, models and nameplates.

Mechanical and comfort options multiplied, allowing the customer to personalize a car. Prices kept increasing, but that didn't hurt overall sales. Sales of foreign-made cars at each end of the price scale continued and started US manufacturers rethinking their products.

Manufacturers kept their engineering staffs going full speed, working on engine and transmission refinements, and steering and suspension improvements. Styling departments presented futuristic prototypes to tease customers, while finding new places to add chrome trim. Advertising people spent millions promoting the new cars.

All in all, the 1960s was a decade of extremes, during which new models were introduced and later discontinued, and some respected names were lost. The top-of-the-line models grew larger and more luxurious, while compacts, subcompacts and midsize makes all found their niche. Emphasis was on economy at one end of the scale, with brute power and high speed combined with luxury and comfort on the other. The 1960s produced some beautifully designed and engineered cars that will be in demand for years to come.

1970s cars

The 1970s was a decade of change in US automobile production. Government safety regulations, some of which were pushed by insurance interests, caused changes in roof supports, front and rear bumpers and the installation of seatbelts. Environmental interests caused regulations concerning engine emissions.

Inroads by foreign cars continued to chip away at US car sales. Low-price cars from Japan were finding ready buyers, as were high-priced imports from England and Germany.

During these years gasoline prices increased and shortages appeared in some areas, adding to the demand for smaller, more fuel efficient cars in all price ranges.

Manufacturers started downsizing some models and increased the use of unit body/frame construction, giving a substantial savings in weight, with increased rigidity.

Prices increased, as manufacturers passed along tooling costs to the customer. A slight economic recession in the early 1970s put all manufacturers in a bind, adding to the necessity for hurried changeovers.

After about 1973, electronic ignition and other gadgetry were added, along with more antismog devices. The increased use of molded plastic interior components and subassembly of certain mechanical parts makes repair and renovation of cars after 1973 much more difficult and expensive. Their restoration is not covered in this book.

Sources of information on specific makes and models produced during these years, including engine and drivetrain options, are listed in the appendix.

Chapter 2

Buying the car

When you've found a car you think you'd like to own and enjoy, and are satisfied that the person you're dealing with has the legal right to sell it, you should make a careful visual inspection and road test.

Make copies of the checklists and so forth included in this chapter. Attach them to a clipboard when you inspect the car. There's some implied psychology here, as the seller will be impressed with your thoroughness. These reports will give you an excellent basis for judging what repairs and restoration will be required. They're a good bargaining chip, too, when you get around to talking dollars.

Most cars of these years were built with strong, channel steel frames. Reinforced frame rails and extra bracing were used on convertibles to compensate for the lack of top bracing.

Mustang and other compact and midsize cars used a unit body/frame. On these cars you must look for rust-throughs on floor pans and frame rails. This may require putting the car on a lift or an oil change pit, during your road test.

Preliminary checklist

Start at the front and follow the Preliminary Checklist included at the end of this chapter, working your way completely around the car. Check each item on the list. Look for paint blisters indicating under-surface rust. Check for obvious rust patches along the bottom of the cowl, doors, body and fender panels and rocker panels. Check the area around the headlights. On cars with unit body/frame construction, look for sagging doors and uneven cowl panels—sure signs of weakened frame rails.

After checking the outside, make a complete inspection of the inside, using the Preliminary Interior Checklist. Open and close each door and the luggage area lid. Stain on upholstery around windows means leaks, and leaks can mean eventual rust from inside panels.

Don't let dirty, torn upholstery or headliner unduly upset you. Their condition, along with that of

instruments and interior hardware, can be repaired or refurbished, but they should affect the price you'll pay.

Lift the carpets and floor mats to learn the condition of the floors. If they are damp, or rusted, expect to repair them, as they're often a structural part of the car's body.

Pay particular attention to the windshield and rear window glass. Wraparound windshields can be expensive to replace. Rear curved glass on some hardtops may be hard to find and expensive. Straight side glass is no problem.

While checking the inside, look at controls for the air conditioner, heater and defroster. Often these plastic vent controls are broken. Check the operation of window cranks and door handles, as well as each electrically controlled window.

An overall appraisal of the car's interior will give you a good idea of how the car has been used and the importance the owner(s) has given to maintaining it.

Directions on repairing, replacing and refurbishing trim and upholstery parts are included later in this book.

Pre-road test

You can tell a lot about the car's condition by looking at the way it stands on level ground. As you look at the car from the front, it should be level. You can often tell by the bumpers; the left and right ends should be the same distance from the ground. If one side sags, it can be because of a weak coil spring or a badly adjusted torsion bar.

Look at the front wheels. They should be perpendicular to the ground. If not, there may be problems with the steering or suspension systems. Check the tires on both front wheels, looking for uneven wear, indicating possible misalignment or a damaged front wheel.

From the side, check if the car sits level. If it appears to be down on the front or rear, there may be weak or broken springs.

From the rear, check that the car doesn't lean to one side, indicating weak springs.

To check the shock absorbers, push down hard, one corner at a time. The car should return to its former position without further bounces, as these indicate badly worn shock absorbers. If the car has rear coil springs, check for uneven tire wear, meaning the trailing arm bushings may need replacing, or the springs are weak.

If the car has stood for some time in the same place, look for spots underneath, indicating oil, transmission fluid or brake fluid leaks. A spot under the middle of the rear axle means leaking differential oil.

These checks take but a few minutes and can tell you a lot about the car's condition before you drive it.

Under the hood

Before starting the engine, check the oil. It should be within marked limits, and there should be no water drops on the dipstick. The radiator or spillover tank should contain coolant. The automatic transmission dipstick should show within the "cold" limits and should be red, not brown. Plan on making another "hot" check after the car has been running, and note the color and consistency.

Check the battery. There shouldn't be white, chalky build-ups around the terminals. Check the water level in each cell. Check the fan and other belts. They should all be tight and not frayed or cracked. Though easily repaired, these things are another expense. Look for badly worn wires, or signs of wires being spliced and repaired with tape.

The engine compartment, though dirty, should show no signs of leaks around valve covers. There shouldn't be an accumulation of oil-soaked dirt around the block, heads, firewall or starter.

Look for sooty marks around the manifolds, indicating exhaust leaks. There should be no puddles of gasoline, and no signs of leaks in the radiator or around hoses. The hoses or tubes from the power steering pump should be free of abrasions and signs of leaks around the couplings.

Directions on how to correct these conditions are covered in later chapters.

Road test

Use the Road Test Report included in this chapter as a guide. When you start the engine, see how quickly the oil gauge shows pressure, or how quickly the indicator light turns off. Notice if the ammeter gauge shows a charge, or if the warning light turns off quickly.

Listen for loud knocks, or clunks, deep in the engine. These can indicate worn or burned-out bearings. Knocks higher up in the engine can mean a worn camshaft, valve-operating mechanism, or wristpin wear. Overhead valves often clatter until oil gets to the rocker arms, but the noise should stop in a short time.

Starting an engine that hasn't been running in some time may require a jump start. Once started, it may run unevenly for a while. This could be the automatic choke, worn points in the distributor or worn, dirty spark plugs. None of these are difficult to adjust, repair or replace.

Test clutch action on manual transmissions by releasing the clutch slowly, to notice at what point the car starts to move; if over halfway out, the clutch needs adjusting, possibly replacement. Set the handbrake and release the clutch slowly. If the engine begins to stall, this means the handbrake is holding.

Automatic transmission cars shouldn't crawl or creep when in park or neutral. The handbrake should hold, when you put the car in drive, but don't accelerate. Some vibration should be felt, as the engine wants to move the car, but the brake holds it, before stalling the engine.

Drive through the gears slowly. Listen for unusual clunks or grinding, when accelerating or decelerating. On an automatic, if you feel engine speed increase with slow response and grabbing on up-shifting, it needs attention.

With the car moving slowly, apply the brakes. Notice pedal travel before the brakes take hold. Try a hands-off stop, pushing the pedal hard. If the car pulls to one side, it could mean worn brake linings or pads in one wheel. If the pull is severe, it could mean the car is out of line. To check this, have someone drive behind you and check if the wheels track. If the brake pedal creeps, there's a leak in the hydraulic system.

More than an inch play, either way, in the steering wheel can indicate worn bushings. Wheel shimmy often means worn kingpins or ball joints. A shuddering feeling toward the end of the steering wheel turns can indicate low fluid in the power steering reservoir, a loose drive belt or worn pump and leaking hoses.

Chucking movement at slow speeds and a rumbling noise underfoot indicate probable universal joint wear. Vibration, which increases with speed, can mean the drive shaft needs to be balanced. A high-pitched, whining noise, which increases with speed, usually means worn differential gears.

During the road test, try to put the car on a lift so you can examine the underparts (use the Undercar Inspection Checklist included in this chapter). Look for welding seams on the chassis, or platform on unit body/frame cars. Check for rust damage on floor pans and luggage area. Examine the exhaust system for rust-throughs and damaged muffler and pipes.

Check the engine/transmission area for oil leaks, as well as welding seams on the engine block.

Follow the drivetrain from the back of the transmission along the drive shaft to the differential and rear wheels. Oil leaks in these parts can mean extreme wear, or merely leaking oil seals. Look for signs of brake fluid leaks on the brake backing plates and on the inside of the wheels.

If you plan to tow your car home, rent a substantial tow bar, which has safety chains, as well as strong bolts to attach the clamps to the bumper. Make sure the bumper arms are firmly attached to the car's frame. Test light connections before moving the car.

Check the front suspension and steering systems. The gearbox must be bolted tightly to the frame. Though the tie-rod and antisway bar bushings may be worn, there should not be much movement you can make by hand.

Directions to adjust or repair the problems you may have discovered on the test drive are covered in following chapters, and sources for additional information on these subjects are listed in the appendix.

How to bargain

Compare your notations on the preliminary checklists, road test and undercar examination. If you decide this is the car you want, start negotiations.

By following advertised prices of similar cars in newspapers and magazines, you should have a good idea of what the car you're considering is worth.

Make an initial offer well below the price you've decided upon. Expect the owner to make a counter offer, higher than he or she expects to get. From then on, it's a battle of wills. Use your test results to defend your offer, and continue bargaining until you've reached an agreement.

How to pay

You knew the asking price before you looked at the car. You also knew how much you could afford to pay. Seldom will a seller sign the bill of sale and endorse the registration and title to you upon receipt of a personal check.

Take a bank draft made jointly to the owner *and* you, for at least twenty-five percent less than the asking price. Bring the rest in traveler's checks or cash. You can endorse the bank draft and add to it from the checks or cash for the final price, if necessary.

Be certain all documents are signed and notarized. Also be sure to get all the spare parts that should come with the car.

Getting it home

Once the car is yours, you have the responsibility for transferring the title, licensing and insuring it. You can learn in advance from your motor vehicle bureau what is required for bringing a car into your state.

If you tow the car, rent a strong tow bar with safety chains. Check connections for lights and turn signals. If the car has an automatic transmission,

Disconnect the universal joint at the differential when towing a car with an automatic transmission. Make a sling to keep the drive shaft from dragging on the road. If you cover the car with a tarpaulin, be sure all the edges are secured to the car.

When using a trailer to bring your car home, choose one that is long enough to balance the car evenly. Avoid excess down-pressure on the tow car, as this can make your headlights worthless for night driving. Block the wheels and use tie-down chains for security.

disconnect it and secure the drive shaft universal joint at the differential.

Take the car through a coin-operated car wash. Use the soapy spray to clean the engine, under the fenders and as much of the underside as you can reach. A few coins will save you hours of work later.

Preparing your workspace

You should have the workspace planned before you go after the car. This, of course, depends upon the amount of room you have and how much work will be required.

For the average project, half of a two-car garage will suffice. More room is handier if available, especially if you plan to remove the engine or body. You may want to staple a sheet of heavy, clear vinyl sheeting dividing the garage to protect your other car.

Your work area should have natural light, a cement floor and at least one electrical outlet and good overhead lighting. A source of heat depends upon your climate and the time of year you'll be working on the car.

A workbench, which you can build, will be handy. Mount some shelves for storing parts. A sheet of peg-board helps keep tools where you can find them. If there's room, nail some planks or plywood across garage rafters for extra storage area. Get a large, galvanized trash can with lid to hold throw-aways. Plan to empty it regularly.

You should plan to rent or borrow tools you'll only use occasionally, or for special jobs. A torque wrench, valve grinding tool and coil spring compressor are examples of tools you'll use so seldom, they're not worth buying.

Some car clubs own sets of tools that are used mostly on their own models, which they'll loan or rent to club members. Some hobbyists chip in to buy certain tools. This works out pretty well, unless more than one person wants the same tool the same weekend.

When you've completed your project, keep the tools you feel you'll need and sell the others, recouping some of your tool cost.

Either buy a "Car in Tow" sign, or print it on the back window to warn drivers behind you that they'll need to allow extra passing space. Check motor vehicle regulations when bringing a car from another state, and be sure your insurance covers a towed vehicle.

15

Preliminary Checklist

Date _____

Owner's name _____ Address _____

_____ Make _____

Model _____ Body style _____ Year _____

Price _____ Accessories _____

Title? _____ Licensed? _____ Last used? _____

General Appearance _____

Stored inside? _____ Visible damage? _____

Check before starting motor

Oil in base? _____ Coolant in radiator? _____

Water drops in oil? _____ Oil in coolant? _____

Visible oil leaks? _____ Visible coolant leaks? _____

Visible cracks in motor block? _____ Cylinder head? _____

All belts tight? _____ Hoses tight? _____

Check before driving car

Does brake pedal creep? _____ Handbrake hold? _____

Any signs of leaking brake fluid? _____

Oily spots under transmission? _____ Differential? _____

Grease leaks around rear wheels? _____

Air in tires? _____ Horn work? _____ Lights? _____ Wipers? _____

Visible leaks on power steering pump or hoses? _____

Power steering reservoir full? _____

Checklist for body and fenders

	Excellent	Good	Fair	Poor	Repairable
Grillework					
Front-end metal					
Hood					
Windshield glass			Molding		
Left upper cowl					
Left lower cowl					
Left front fender					
Left front door			Glass		
Left rocker panel					
Left rear door			Glass		
Left quarter panel					
Rear panel					
Deck lid			Molding		
Rear apron					
Rear bumper					
Right quarter panel					
Right rear door			Glass		
Right rocker panel					
Right front door			Glass		
Right front fender					
Right lower cowl					
Right upper cowl					
Front bumper					
Headlights	Left		Right		
Turn signals	Left		Right		

Preliminary Checklist (continued)

	Excellent	Good	Fair	Poor	Repairable
Taillights	Left _____		Right _____		
Door handles	Left _____		Right _____		
Chrome trim	_____				
Accessories	_____				

Preliminary Interior Checklist

	Excellent	Good	Fair	Poor	Repairable
Front cushion	_____				
Front seatback	_____				
Rear cushion	_____				
Rear seatback	_____				
Right front door	_____				
Right kick panel	_____				
Right rear door	_____				
Rear shelf	_____				
Left rear door	_____				
Left front door	_____				
Left kick panel	_____				
Headliner	_____				
Dash padding	_____				
Visors	Left _____		Right _____		
Mirror	_____				
Front ashtray	_____				
Lighter	_____				
Window shades	Left _____		Right _____		Rear _____
Window cranks	Left _____		Right _____		
Door handles	Left _____		Right _____		
Radio/Tape deck	_____				
Air conditioner	_____				
Heater/defroster	_____				
Other	_____				

Road Test Report

Motor

	Yes	No		Yes	No
Start easily?	_____	_____	Pull evenly?	_____	_____
Run evenly?	_____	_____	Any knocks?	_____	_____
Idle evenly?	_____	_____	Emit smoke?	_____	_____
Noise-cold?	_____	_____	Noise-warm?	_____	_____

Other _____

Instruments (work properly?)

Oil pressure _____ Fuel _____ Temp. _____ Speedometer _____ Tach _____ Other _____

Clutch

Motor stall with brake on? _____ Clutch slip? _____

Clutch grab when pedal is released slowly? _____

Road Test Report (continued)

Automatic transmission

Creep in neutral? _____ Pull smoothly from start? _____

Grab as gears change? P _____ R _____ N _____ D-1 _____ D-2 _____ L _____

Downshift smoothly? _____

Does park hold car? _____

Clunking or grinding noises? _____

Does gear selector move evenly? _____

	Acceleration	Deceleration
Low	_____	_____
Second	_____	_____
High	_____	_____

Universal joints

Thumping or clunking noise from the middle of the car when accelerating? _____ Decelerating? _____

Other noises under car? _____

Differential

Whining noise at moderate speed? _____ High speed? _____

Chucking noise when accelerating? _____ Decelerating? _____

Noise when cornering right? _____ Left? _____

Steering

	3 in.	2 in.	1 in.	½ in.
Amount of play in steering wheel:	_____	_____	_____	_____

Front wheels shimmy? _____ Steer easily? _____

Pull to one side? _____ Wheel center after corners? _____

Squeal from power unit on corners? R. _____ L. _____

Shuddering at end of sharp turns? R. _____ L. _____

Brakes

Amount of pedal pressure? _____ Quick pedal return? _____

Stop quickly at moderate speed? _____

Hands-off-wheel (10 mph) stops even? _____

Brakes grab? _____ Squeal? _____ Grinding noise? _____

Pedal creep to floor under pressure? _____

If power assisted, can you feel pedal depress slightly when engine starts? _____

If engine dies, do you feel loss of brake power? _____ Does handbrake hold car? _____

Wheels and tires

Any wheels bent? _____ Wheels match? _____ Spare wheel? _____

Complete, matching hubcaps or wheel covers? _____

Tires? L.F. _____ L.R. _____ R.F. _____ R.R. _____ Spare _____

Additional comments on road test _____

Undercar Inspection

Use flashlight or extension light. Start at the front.

Steering system

Wheel movement on vertical plane?	Right _____	Left _____
Wheel movement on horizontal plane?	Right _____	Left _____
Hand movement on ball joints?	Right _____	Left _____
Hand movement on kingpins/spindles?	Right _____	Left _____
Hand movement on tie-rods?	Right _____	Left _____
Hand movement on drag arm?	Yes _____	No _____

Undercar Inspection (continued)

Front suspension system

Turn-in spacers in coil springs?	Right _____	Left _____
Weakened, compressed coil spring?	Right _____	Left _____
Visible wear on upper bushings?	Right _____	Left _____
Visible wear on lower bushings?	Right _____	Left _____
Bent or loose torsion bar?	Right _____	Left _____
Worn, leaking power steering hoses?	Yes _____	No _____
Loose bushings on antisway bar?	Right _____	Left _____

Engine/transmission unit

Weld marks on engine block?	Right _____	Left _____
Oil leaks around engine pan?	Yes _____	No _____
Weld marks on bellhousing?	Yes _____	No _____
Fluid leaks on transmission case?	Yes _____	No _____

Drive shaft/differential

Oil drips around front universal?	Yes _____	No _____
Balance clamps on drive shaft?	Yes _____	No _____
Oil drips around rear universal?	Yes _____	No _____
Oil drips from differential?	Yes _____	No _____
Oil or fluid drips on backing plates?	Yes _____	No _____

Exhaust system

Soot marks on pipe joints?	Yes _____	No _____
Damaged lead-in pipe?	Yes _____	No _____
Damaged, rusted muffler?	Yes _____	No _____
Damaged lead-out pipe?	Yes _____	No _____
Damaged, rusted resonator?	Yes _____	No _____
Damaged, rusted tailpipe?	Yes _____	No _____

Chassis/frame

Weld marks along side rails?	Right _____	Left _____
Weld marks on cross-members?	Yes _____	No _____
Rust damage to body supports?	Yes _____	No _____

Unit body/frame cars

Rust damage on side frame rails?	Right _____	Left _____
Rust damage to lateral body braces?	Yes _____	No _____
Rust where stub frame joins cowl?	Right _____	Left _____
Rust-throughs on front floor pans?	Yes _____	No _____
Rust-throughs on rear floor pans?	Yes _____	No _____
Rust damage on lower cowl?	Right _____	Left _____
Rust damage to luggage area floor?	Yes _____	No _____
Signs of welding repairs to frame?	Right _____	Left _____
Rust at rear trailing arms and body?	Right _____	Left _____
Other visible damage or repairs?	_____	

(Save for use when you make a later, more complete inspection.)

Chapter 3

Preparing for work

Cleaning the car

Probably the dirtiest job in your renovation project is getting rid of twenty to thirty years of grease and grime from your car. Years and miles build up an almost impenetrable coating around nuts, bolt heads and other undercar components. Hopefully, some of this washed away or was loosened by the high-pressure spray before you got the car to your work area.

Spread layers of newspapers on the floor to catch dirt and make cleanup easier. Wear goggles to protect your eyes and gloves to protect your hands. Use one of those new hand lotions that allow you to wash away dirt and grime, so you can go to work Monday with clean hands.

Don't let all this scare you. Once the car is clean, parts can be repaired or removed much easier.

Some cars of these years have areas that have proved to be rust prone, as dirt holds moisture in seams. Floors hold water from occupant's shoes, soaking into carpets, and are further dirtied by water, chemicals and dirt thrown up from the road. This moisture from above and below keeps steel floors damp, allowing dirt and grime to cling and rust-throughs to start.

On many of these cars, their slab-sided design makes rocker panels and door bottoms more vulnerable to rust formation. Often this starts on the inside,

You'll save hours of scrubbing and scraping if you rent a steam cleaning machine. You may live in an area where a steam cleaning outfit can come to your garage to do the job. It doesn't take long to get the chassis, engine and undercarriage clean.

A little practice holding the wand and adjusting the nozzle can make you an expert in degreasing. You won't damage anything other than insulation on some wires, which should be replaced anyway. When the job is done, spray the pavement or garage floor clean.

between the inner and outer skin, allowing rust to get a strong start before telltale paint blisters appear. Wheel cutouts, lower cowl sections and areas around the headlights and grilles are potential danger spots.

Even if you have only a few projects planned, it's wise to clean the engine, chassis, drivetrain and body cavities at one time. This makes it much easier for you to work on individual jobs you've planned for later.

Degreasing

You have some choices as to how you'll remove the rock-hard accumulation of dirt and grime around the steering arms, tie-rods and kingpins. You'll find the same build-up on front suspension systems, as well as on parts of the engine/bellhousing assembly.

Douse these areas with Gunk or kerosene and let it soak in. Spray small areas with WD-40 to soften grease. Chip away at the accumulations with a putty knife and follow up with a steel-bristled brush.

Consider renting a steam cleaning machine, which mixes steam with hot water and kerosene and sprays it under high pressure, removing grease and dirt. In many areas, a steam cleaning outfit will come to your garage and do the job for you. High-pressure wands

Common spots to find rust-throughs are around the headlights and grilles, because of dirt being thrown against these spots and holding moisture. This 1957 Ford is no worse than other cars without inner fender panels. Hooded headlights are another danger spot.

Shop for body and fender repair tools. You may have some already. It's better to buy good quality used tools, than inexpensive, poor quality new ones. You may be able to borrow some from friends. If not, rent those you'll only use occasionally.

When working under the car, always place jack stands under the axles or frame. There are several kinds from which to choose. Each stand should be stamped to support at least twice the weight it will be required to hold. Don't scrimp on these.

You'll find an undercar creeper great for those jobs where you'll need to be flat on your back and looking up. Also very handy is a combination stool and tool tray for mechanical work and bodywork along the lower parts of the car. These are easy to store.

with canisters attached mix kerosene or heavy-duty cleaners containing Trisodium Phosphate (TSP) with water to wash away heavy, greasy build-ups in hard-to-reach places.

For frame-off restorations, or degreasing particular mechanical components removed from the car, mix a solution of 3.5 oz. lye, or caustic soda, to every gallon of very hot water in the amount necessary to cover the part.

Caution: Always wear goggles and rubber gloves when working with lye, TSP or any caustic solution. Keep the kids away from the action.

After degreasing with any caustic solution, the parts must be thoroughly washed with clear water to remove all traces of the solution.

Protect the surfaces with a light coat of oil, or use an aerosol spray can of rust-inhibiting primer.

Part of the cleanup operation may include removing rust from small, removable parts (not to be confused with removing rust from floor pans or body panels).

Rust removal

Rust can be removed from small parts by soaking them in phosphoric rust remover, marketed under several brand names. Mix one part remover to two parts water in a plastic container large enough to hold the part. It doesn't take long to remove an average coat of rust, so keep checking. After soaking, the item must be thoroughly rinsed in clear water. Protect against future rust with a light coat of oil or primer.

Naval Jelly is an excellent rust remover for badly rusted and pitted parts. However, it works so fast, it takes careful watching to make sure the jelly doesn't eat away too much metal. Careful rinsing with clear water is a must. Protect the freshly cleaned metal from future rust.

A strong solution of a household detergent and water is great for washing sheet steel body parts, as well as many small plastic and plated pieces. An overnight soaking, with a followup scrubbing with a soapy, fine steel wool pad does the job. Rinse well and protect against future rust.

Beadblasting

Beadblasting is a replacement for sandblasting that uses small glass beads to cut away paint, plating and rust. It's great for wire wheels and frame-off chassis cleaning. Use this method carefully, though, as you can't replace any metal you may have cut away. Although you can buy, or rent, small glass bead

A common reason for a malfunctioning power top and electrically operated windows is that debris has accumulated behind rear cushions and quarter panel upholstery. Debris often holds moisture against the inner and outer skin, inviting rust.

equipment, it's less expensive to take the parts to a specialist in the field.

Compressed air

Compressed air is an excellent way to clean away dirt, loose grime and scale. Rent or buy a unit that will deliver from 150 to 200 psi (pounds per square inch). Wear goggles and point the nozzle to direct the powerful stream of air where you want it. Of course, the loosened dirt will settle on everything around it, so be prepared for a thorough cleanup of your work area when you've finished the job.

Chapter 4

General troubleshooting

Having decided how you plan to use your car, once it is completed, you need to know what must be repaired, replaced or refurbished to bring the car to the standards you've set.

Though troubleshooting the components that make up each system in the car is outlined in the appropriate chapters, you should understand the purpose of these operational tests. As you understand the functions of the components in each system, and how these systems interact, you'll find that what once may have been confusing and intimidating will become much clearer and simpler.

Troubleshooting, after all, is the logical method of identifying a problem so it can be corrected. How you make the tests depends upon the symptoms, location, function and conditions under which the problems occur.

When troubleshooting any system, a basic rule is to start by checking the obvious first, then work from component to component, until you've located the problem. You'll save time and money by using a systematic approach to testing.

The following chapters outline the function of components within each system and suggest tests you can make to determine if each is functional. They also explain how to interpret results of the various tests, include directions on how to adjust, repair or replace malfunctioning items and walk through repairs that

EVALUATING CYLINDER LEAKAGE TESTS		
Sound of air escaping	Reason	Causes
At radiator	Air leaks to water jacket.	Leaking head gasket cracked head or block.
Around heads or spark plug hole.	Air leaks past head gasket.	Faulty head gasket.
Around oil filler cap.	Rings not sealing.	Worn rings, cylinder walls, worn piston.
At carburetor	Air leaks past intake valve.	Faulty intake valve.
At tail pipe	Air leaks past exhaust valve	Burned or faulty exhaust valve.

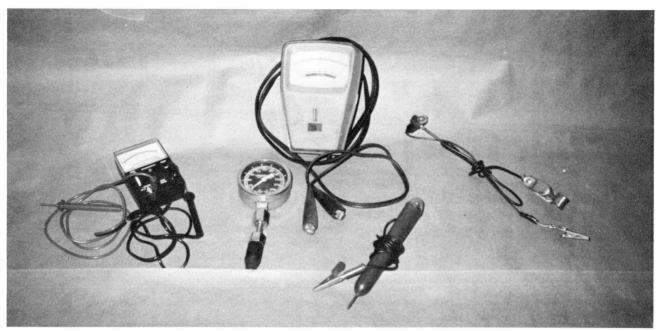

You don't need a large assortment of expensive gauges for initial troubleshooting. A voltage meter (voltmeter), compression gauge, dwell-tach, vacuum gauge and test lights are a great help. You can make a simple test light, and may be able to borrow the gauges.

are unique to cars produced during these years.

Because of the wide variety of makes, submakes and models produced during the 1950s, 1960s and early 1970s, not all repair procedures and specifications can be covered in detail. For this reason, sources for repair of individual makes and models, wiring

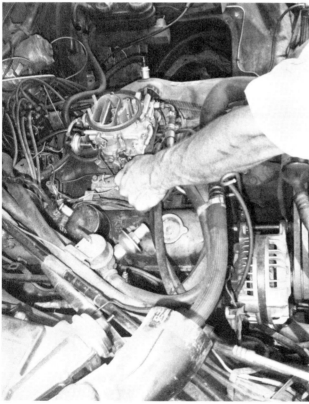

With the air cleaner removed, you can control engine speed by operating the throttle manually. This will help when finding at what engine speed range certain noises or irregularities appear and disappear. Be careful of moving fan and belts when engine is running.

If there is fuel and the car won't start, disconnect the fuel line from the tank and blow through it to check for a clogged line or filter. Disconnect the line to the carburetor. Run the starter to see if the fuel pump is furnishing gasoline to the carburetor.

Remove and examine the spark plugs for initial check on engine condition. Look for oily, gummy deposits and burned electrodes. Note the position of each plug for future repairs. With spark plugs removed, run the starter to check the compression in each cylinder.

Refer to your car's wiring diagram when using your test light to check circuits. Use your voltmeter to check generator or alternator output, as well as the amount of current the starter draws. Inspect the insulation and connections on wires.

diagrams, specifications and repair manuals are listed in the appendix.

Some adjustments and repairs of mechanical components can be made visually. You can spot a frayed fan belt, worn wires, a shock absorber that's hanging down because of a broken mounting bracket, or a leaking radiator. More difficult to determine is the condition of the pulleys in which the belt rides, what damage has happened to the components connected by the worn wires, why the shock absorber mounting bracket broke and if any other damage was caused, and the extent to which the loss of coolant may have damaged other parts of the engine.

You can hear some defects that you know must be corrected. The clatter of badly adjusted valves, the grinding of second gear in a manual transmission or a rapping sound deep in the engine that increases with acceleration are all unmistakable warnings of components that need attention.

Not so easy to be aware of, but equally important, are the results of wear. You may believe that a slight slippage in the clutch can be taken up. But the clutch plate may already have been adjusted to the limit. You won't know this until you make a visual inspection of the clutch.

Lack of power on hills and sluggish acceleration may seem to be problems that can be corrected by carburetor adjustment or overhaul. But unless you make a compression check of each cylinder, you can't rule out worn piston rings or badly adjusted valves.

Very important in troubleshooting is the process of elimination. You'll save a lot of time and make eventual repairs easier, by making note of where, when and at what intensity and frequency problems

Remove spark plugs, and have a helper operate the starter to check compression in each cylinder against factory specifications with the compression gauge. Place spark plug wires so they won't short on the engine. Watch out for moving belts.

To check engine vacuum to the power brake unit, disconnect tubing from the manifold to the booster and attach the tube to the vacuum gauge. Manufacturer's specifications state

what vacuum the engine should pull. First check the condition of the tube, if below the recommended figure.

appear and disappear. This applies to the chassis and running gear, as well as to engine components.

When troubleshooting the various components and systems, you should determine which jobs affect the car's handling and safe operation. These should be done first, of course.

It makes sense for you to combine certain jobs to save duplicating labor and costs. Removing carbon deposits on pistons, valve heads and from combustion chambers, and adjusting valve clearances is but one example. If you do these jobs separately, you'll have to buy replacement gaskets twice and do much of the work a second time. Checking the dwell and adjusting the breaker points in the distributor are other jobs that should be combined for best results.

Throughout the car, you'll find that many systems interact and work closely with each other. Troubleshooting in one system may turn up problems in a related system. Both of these should be corrected at the same time.

For these and other reasons, careful scheduling of all adjustments, repairs or replacements should be made, taking into consideration their necessity, relationship to each other and the time and money involved.

If the car continues bouncing up and down after the first push downward on any corner, it's an indication that that shock absorber is worn out. Look under the car. If the shock absorber is west, it is probably leaking fluid. Tubular shocks cannot be repaired, only replaced.

27

Chapter 5

The engine

The fifties continued the revolution in engine design started by General Motors in 1949, with its new OHV V-8 for Cadillac and Oldsmobile. Public acceptance was immediate. These smaller, lighter-weight, higher-powered engines made the long-stroke, inline eight-cylinder engines obsolete.

Other manufacturers saw the light. They switched to similar high-revving, large-bore, short-stroke engines, and their engineers worked as feverishly as finances permitted.

Metallurgical developments allowed lighter weight and stronger engine blocks. These new, high-compression engines gave more power, pickup and economy from the same, or even less, cubic inch displacement. They used considerably less gasoline than their predecessors, too.

Valve-in-block, also called L-head engines contain intake and exhaust valves in the cylinder block. The valve-operating mechanisms are accessible through removable plates on the side of the engine. Intake and exhaust manifolds are on the same side.

The familiar valve-in-block, also known as the flathead and L-head six-cylinder engines, continued for a few years, but as new six-cylinder overhead valve engines were developed, they were replaced. They were gone by the mid-sixties.

The few four-cylinder engines in use during the fifties were either carried over as L-heads, or the newly developed F-heads. In the sixties a new breed of OHV four-cylinder engines was developed, and later some four-cylinder engines that were literally one half of a V-8, with modifications.

As compact and midsize cars increased in popularity, four-cylinder engines became more powerful. V-6s were used in some downsized makes, as the need for more power in less engine space was solved.

Because of cramped engine space and bolt-on accessories, such as air conditioning compressors, power brake diaphragms, power steering pumps and more complex car heating systems, working on engines is more difficult. Often, large air cleaners, with ducting to the front, hide much of the engine.

With increased heat in the tighter engine compartments, space-taking shrouds were installed to help the fan do its job. To conform to lower front-end styling, lower, wider radiators were used, combined with a pressure system and space-taking spillover tanks.

Increased heat from the large displacement V-type engines, many with a front crossover pipe, caused some to stall from time to time, because of vapor lock. This excess heat often caused quicker failure of underhood placed batteries, as the water would evaporate.

The increased use of accessories, often driven by two or more belts, makes disassembly for repairs more complex. This also makes maintaining belt tension more difficult.

How engines work

Whether V-type or inline, F-head, L-head or overhead valve, all engines work the same. Fuel and air are

The pre-World War II designed Continental L-head six-cylinder 226.2 ci engine developed 118 hp at 3650 rpm. It was used in Kaiser-Frazer cars until 1954, when a su-percharger was added, boosting horsepower to 140 at 3900 rpm.

compressed. As compression peaks, the mixture is ignited in a tightly controlled container and produces the power impulse.

When power impulses are controlled and directed, they produce a revolving motion. When that motion is controlled and directed, it causes the vehicle, in which the container is installed, to move. It's that simple!

All US engines are four-stroke. The container in which the air/fuel mixture explodes is the cylinder. A piston moving downward in the cylinder in its first stroke draws in the air/fuel mixture. On the second, an upward stroke, it compresses that mixture. At the peak of this stroke, the mixture is ignited and the explosion forces the piston down in its third, or power stroke. On its fourth, an upward stroke, it pushes the burned mixture into the exhaust system.

The piston is connected to the crankshaft and its downward motion makes the crankshaft turn. The rotation of the crank on its shaft turns a heavy flywheel. The momentum of the flywheel keeps the crankshaft turning.

Combining the advantages of L-head and OHV engines, F-head engines fit the exhaust valves in the block, with the intake valves in the cylinder head. This allows bigger valves in the combustion chamber in a more compact engine block.

Compact and lighter than inline engines, V-types may fit the valves in the block or in the cylinder heads. Since the midfifties, most US engines have overhead valves. Some manufacturers fitted the valve-operating camshaft in the block, others in the cylinder heads.

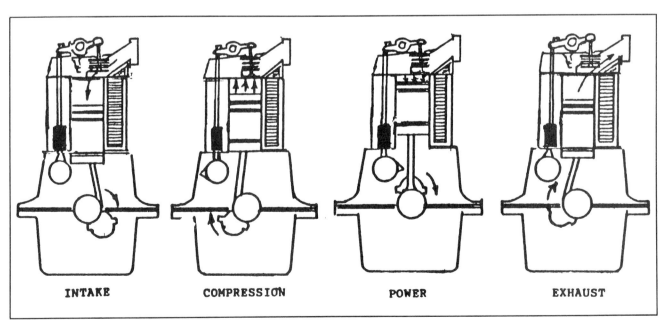

INTAKE   **COMPRESSION**   **POWER**   **EXHAUST**

How engines work: The first, downward stroke sucks in the air/fuel mixture. A second, upward stroke compresses the mixture. At the peak of compression, the spark plug explodes the mixture causing the third, downward power stroke. The fourth stroke expells the burned gases into the exhaust system, and the cycles start again.

After the fourth stroke, the series starts again.

The more cylinders, the more power impulses. The higher the compression ratio, the more power produced by a given-size piston.

The camshaft, driven by a gear on the crankshaft, operates the valves. These allow the air/fuel mixture to enter the cylinder and hold it there during the compression stroke, and allow the spent mixture to clear the cylinder.

The distributor, operating from a gear on the camshaft, sends the electrical spark igniting the air/fuel mixture to the correct cylinder at the correct time.

The carburetor combines fuel and air, which is drawn into the cylinder on its first downward stroke. The driver controls the amount of this mixture through the gas pedal.

The coordination and timing of all these components and their functions make the engine run.

Troubleshooting

There are some simple tests you can make to determine which of the engine's systems or compo-

This spotlessly maintained 1964 Oldsmobile Ninety-eight V–8 is strictly stock. The 394 ci engine, fitted with a four-barrel carburetor, turns out 330 hp. By keeping dirt-holding oil from wires and electrical connections, the owner has prevented many problems.

Chrysler's famous Slant Six valve in head engine allowed a lower hood line for straight-ahead vision as well as giving stylists more leeway. It was fitted in some Dodge and Plymouth cars and their sub-models in 170 and 225 ci sizes, giving 101 or 145 hp.

nents need adjustment, repair or replacement. Have your owners manual and manufacturer's specifications on hand when you make these checks.

If the engine runs hot, first check the coolant level. Look for leaks in the radiator and hoses. Check the condition of the fan belt; it should not be frayed or loose. The hose to the spillover tank must not be crimped or damaged. (Further troubleshooting tests are covered in chapter 13.)

If the engine runs unevenly, look for a worn or loose wire from the coil to the distributor, or from the distributor to the spark plugs. Make a compression test on each cylinder by removing one spark plug at a time and holding the conical rubber end of the tester into the spark plug hole. Have your helper press the starter. Compare the dial figure with the spec sheet. Release pressure on the valve stem and check the next cylinder. All cylinders should have equal compression.

Examine the bottom of each plug to see if it is clean, or has a gummy, oily or wet deposit, indicating possible internal engine problems.

Because an uneven-running engine can be caused by both the fuel and electrical systems, refer to chapters 9 and 10 for further checks and their remedies.

If there are deep-down knocks in the engine that get louder as engine speed increases, refer to chapter 7 for specific information on main and connecting rod bearings.

If there are knocks and clatter high up in the engine, refer to chapter 6 for further checks you can make on the valvetrain, with recommended adjustments and repairs.

If there's just a lot of noise, with no particular location, refer to chapter 12 for suggested causes and remedial action.

Locating engine parts

Because the same engines were used in so many cars, and the number of years engines were used with only minor changes, there's little problem finding new, rebuilt or used parts for cars of this era.

Though some engines in the same family of cars have different horsepower ratings, cubic inch displacement and other dissimilarities, many of the basic components are interchangeable. Sometimes the cylinder heads, camshafts and carburetion are the only changes made to give an engine more power.

Many parts suppliers originally furnished identical components for several makes of cars. Automotive supply stores have lists of interchangeable parts. Refer to the manufacturer's specification sheets for adjustments, settings and tolerances for your car's engine.

Sources for specific information on engine repairs and rebuilding, parts suppliers and interchangeability of parts are included in the appendix.

Chapter 6

Engine rebuild, top end

To get maximum performance from your car's engine, the tops of the pistons, valves and combustion chambers need to have carbon build-up removed periodically. If you noticed hard starting and sluggish performance during the test drive, that time may have come. If valve clatter continued after engine warm-up and there was uneven running and hesitation in pickup, it could be because of dirty, poorly seated or adjusted valves.

A simple test to determine the condition of the valves and combustion chambers, as well as wear on piston rings and other mechanical components, is to remove and examine each spark plug. Note the cylinder from which each plug is removed for any necessary repairs.

Normal plugs will have a fine, light gray or tan deposit on the insulator and electrodes. These can be cleaned, gapped and reused. If the gap is more than 0.01 in. (25 mm) from the original, the plug should be replaced.

Wet, black deposits are caused by oil leaking past worn piston rings or valve guides, as well as transmission fluid leaking past the modulator, or brake fluid leaking past the booster diaphragm.

Dry black sooty deposits are caused by an overly rich fuel mixture. These can also be caused by poor compression, faulty timing or the wrong heat range (too cool) plug.

Red, brown and yellow deposits are caused by anti-knock fuel additives. Don't confuse these foul-

Examine the condition of each spark plug as you remove it for a top engine rebuild. Note which cylinders have plugs with gummy, oily deposits. These cylinders may need new rings on the piston, or n ew oil seals around the valve guides.

After removing any bolt-ons that are in the way, use a torque wrench to remove initial pressure on the cylinder head. Follow the pattern advised by the manufacturer on the first full turn, before removing any nuts. Fit the socket tightly to avoid stripping the nuts.

It isn't necessary to remove the engine for a carbon and valve job. However, if it is part of a complete engine overhaul, disconnect everything connecting the engine to the frame or firewall. Rent a chainfall to lift the engine from the car.

smelling deposits with rust spots which are caused by water in the cylinders.

Spots on the insulator are caused by overheating and by overly advanced timing. These can also be caused by vacuum leaks, too lean a mixture, or the wrong heat range (too hot) plug.

Eroded electrodes and blistered insulator are caused by extreme and continued plug overheating.

If you found other than normal plug wear, you should check the causes indicated and plan the necessary repairs.

Because you'd have to do much of the same work twice, and buy some of the same parts a second time, it's easier to clean the carbon and grind and adjust the valves at the same time.

To do the job properly and with the least effort, have tools and replacement parts on hand. In addition to sockets, open-end wrenches and your regular assortment of hand tools, you'll need a hardwood chisel, putty knife and wire-bristled brush. You'll also need a torque wrench, which you can rent. This gauge/wrench combination fits ½ in. drive sockets and shows the torque being applied. Factory specifications give the recommended torque figures.

You'll also need a valve compressor and valve grinding tool, which you can rent, as well as a feeler gauge.

Have the necessary gaskets, a can of valve grinding paste and gasket cement before you start. If the upper radiator hose shows wear, plan on replacing it with this job. You'll probably want a new set of spark plugs. Check factory specifications for the correct heat range and gap setting.

Removing carbon

Removing carbon is a simple and common job complicated only by certain parts that have to be removed to get at the carbon. Squirt WD-40 or cutting oil on nuts and bolts for easier removal.

Disconnect the negative battery cable and remove the spark plugs. Either prop the hood full open, or remove it. While the coolant is draining from the radiator, remove the air cleaner for working room. Remove any bolt-on components and disconnect any cables or control rods that are in the way. On some

Lift the cylinder head straight off the studs to avoid damaging the threads. It will be heavy, so handle it accordingly. On overhead valve engines, the valves and valve-operating mechanism will be part of the head. Disassemble the head at your workbench.

With the cylinder head removed, lift the old gasket from the studs. You won't reuse it. With the gasket removed, you can see carbon deposits on the heads of the pistons, as well as on the combustion chambers in L- and F-head engines. Examine the block for cracks.

Use a wire brush and putty knife to remove carbon from the cylinder head and valve faces. Use solvent and compressed air to clean the water passages. Be sure mating surfaces for water pump and other bolt-on accessories are clean. Always use new gaskets.

cars you may have to remove the upper radiator hose. Be sure to tag wires for later match-up.

On V-types, work one bank of cylinders at a time.

Remove the valve covers on OHV engines, exposing cylinder head nuts. Use a wire-bristled brush to clean rust or grime before fitting the correct socket. Follow the manufacturer's "de-torquing" sequence when releasing pressure on the cylinder head to prevent cracking or warping. Normally a half or one turn is enough to remove the pressure; then nuts can be removed in any order. Store nuts and washers for future use.

Lift the cylinder head straight off the studs to avoid damaging the threads. There are simple T-shaped threaded rods that fit spark plug holes, making the job easier. The head will be heavy and is quite fragile, so handle it carefully.

With the head removed, lift the gasket from the block. Don't plan to reuse it.

Clean the block first. Stuff rags in water passages around the cylinder you'll be working on to prevent carbon particles from entering the cooling system. Use a putty knife, wooden chisel and wire-bristled brush to chip and brush away carbon deposits from pistons, valve tops in valve-in-block engines, and the block's combustion area. Be careful not to scratch or gouge any part. Wipe any remaining carbon particles to keep them from entering the cylinder bore.

Use a wrench to turn the crankshaft pulley to push the next piston to the top. Complete all the pistons, block and valve tops before starting on the cylinder head.

Lay the cylinder head on a flat metal surface. If it is warped, it can often be ground back to level at a machine shop. The operator will tell you how many thousandths of an inch can be removed, and to what degree the mating edge can be leveled.

35

Unless you're making a complete engine rebuild, you won't see this part of the engine. The large gear on the end of the crankshaft drives the smaller gear attached to the camshaft. Valve-operating rods ride against the camshaft to open and close the valves when the pistons are in the correct position.

When removing carbon deposits from the cylinder head, rely more on the wire-bristled brush than the chisel or putty knife, so you won't gouge the irregularly shaped combustion chambers.

If the water passages in the head or block show a lot of scale and sediment, use a stiff wire or thin blade to scrape this away. Turn the head over to free the loosened scale. If you have access to an air compressor, blow any remaining particles out of the head. Any scale you loosened in the block must be flushed out before you connect the top hose to the radiator to prevent clogging.

The top camshaft is from a six-cylinder engine, the lower two from a V–8. In a complete rebuild, the lobes on the camshaft must be examined for wear. Though camshafts can be repaired at a machine shop, it is usually less expensive to buy a replacement.

Following up on checks of spark plug condition, this is the time to check cylinder and piston ring wear. If you found wet, gummy deposits on piston tops, valves and in combustion areas, these indicate piston ring wear, oil leaking past seals on valve guides, brake fluid from the power brake booster or transmission fluid from the modulator in automatics.

A definite ridge around the top of the cylinder bore means wear, since this is the area that takes the brunt of the mixture's exploding force. Directions for correcting these and other conditions are covered in later chapters.

Grinding valves

With the pistons, valve tops and combustion chambers in the head and block cleaned, it's time to

View from below of intake manifold for a four-cylinder L-head engine. Note the flange to which the carburetor attaches, and the heat transfer chamber to which the exhaust manifold attaches. All mating surfaces must be clean and new gaskets used when it is installed.

Use this handy tool to compress valve springs after the washers and retainers have been removed and the valves pushed out of the way. Note from which cylinder each spring was removed. Intake and exhaust springs may be different, but those in a set should be the same height.

grind the valves. Because of differences in engine design, details may vary. The job consists of releasing the coil springs that hold the valve in tension, then removing the valves from their guides. Each valve must be ground against its own valve seat for a close fit. There are handy valve grinding tools that make the job simple. Valve grinding compound, a mild abrasive,

Before . . . an intake manifold from an OHV V–8 engine. Note where the two-barrel carburetor bolts to the manifold. Remove any fittings for bolt-on components before using solvent and compressed air, to remove years of accumulated grime. The unit is heavy . . . lift carefully!

After . . . the thoroughly cleaned OHV V–8 intake manifold is ready for installation. Turn-in threaded fittings carefully. A close examination of this heavy casting will indicate the firing order, rotation of distributor shaft, even where and when the casting was made.

Clean springs, spacers and retainers in solvent before fitting them back in their original positions. Use a valve grinding tool and compound to seat cleaned valves in their original valve seat. Only a couple of minutes of grinding should be necessary on each valve.

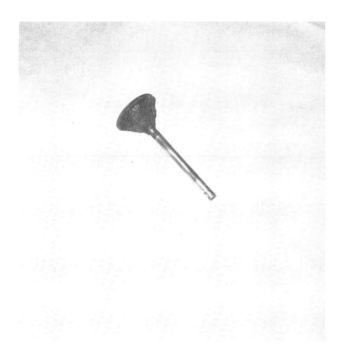

Sludge accumulations such as this on valve stems are caused by dirt and additives in the gasoline. In most cases, this can be removed by soaking in solvent. Future accumulations can be prevented by using a better gasoline and changing the filter regularly.

smooths away pits and helps the valve fit tightly against its valve seat.

Most engines of these years have overhead valves, that is, the valves are fitted into the cylinder head, instead of in the engine block. Valve heads face down and the stems up in these engines, the opposite of the L-head, valve-in-block engines.

A pliers-like spring compressor releases tension so the valve can be freed. Remove the nuts and retainers holding the spring. The nuts on valve lifters allow for adjustment with a feeler gauge. The tappets, which are also called buckets, are short rods that ride against the lobes on the camshaft. They fit against the ends of the valve stems to open and close the valves, as the camshaft lobes move them.

Some engines are fitted with hydraulic valve lifters for quietness. Tiny orifices in the tappets allow oil to pass to operate the valves. These must be kept open.

When removing valves, note their original position, as they should be returned to their original seat for grinding to ensure a closer fit.

The valve grinding tool allows you to hold the valve against its seat. A few minutes of rotating action with valve grinding compound will be all that's normally required to fit the average valve. Any valve with a burned, cracked or warped head must be replaced and ground to fit into its valve seat.

Compare the height of the valve springs on the bench. All intake springs must be the same height to give the same tension. All exhaust valves must be the same height, but intake and exhaust valves may be different height and diameter. If one spring is a different height than its mates, the valve may not open high enough, or close tightly enough. Do not use washers or spacers to build up a weak valve spring; replacement springs are readily available. Most auto supply stores can advise you on the correct spring to buy.

Before reassembling the valve-operating mechanism, check for indentations on the ends of cam followers, indicating excessive wear. Small cracks or wear marks on cam lobes show weakening of the metal and possible future failure. Chipped ends on

With water passages cleaned and new valve guides installed, this cleaned OHV cylinder head is nearing completion of rebuild. Use compressed air to blow out remaining grinding dust. For best performance, use new spark plugs, gapped to factory specifications.

rocker arms mean arm wear, making replacement necessary. If the adjusting threads are worn, they'll cause the lock nuts to work loose. This makes valve settings impossible to hold. The worn parts must be replaced.

Seals fitted near the tops of valve stems are important in controlling the amount of oil let into the combustion chamber. In OHV engines, excess oil in the rocker arm housing can leak past faulty seals and into combustion chambers. For longer oil seal life and less oil consumption, replace the rubber O-rings with the newer Teflon umbrella shields. These are inexpensive and easy to install at this time.

Check the valve guides, those little tubes in the head or block, through which the valve stems fit. If they are worn or bent, new ones should be pressed into place.

Reassembly

With the carbon removed from the head and block, the valves ground for a smooth fit against their seats, you're ready to put things together.

Here is a rebuilt overhead camshaft cylinder head with valves and spring assemblies in place. The camshaft will ride in bearing inserts fitted in stanchions. The valve tappets will ride against camshaft lobes. Double overhead camshaft engines are far more complicated.

Coat the threaded part of the exposed cylinder head studs lightly with grease. Spread a small amount of gasket cement around water passage openings, taking care not to use too much, since it could enter water passages. Be careful, when slipping the new gasket over the cylinder head studs, to avoid snagging it on the threads. It must slide on in a level and even

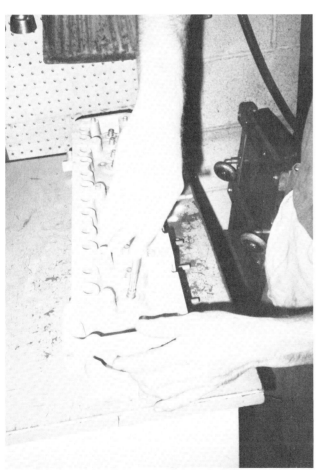

Use a tapered cutting tool to chamfer the edges of valve guides before fitting new oil seals and installing the valves and valve-operating mechanism. Follow the manufacturer's recommendations on tightening sequence and torque, when installing the cylinder head.

Before installing valve assemblies in cylinder heads, clean the heads with solvent and make sure all water passages, which cool the valves, are open. Always use new gaskets when installing cylinder heads, and new valve cover gaskets when heads are in place.

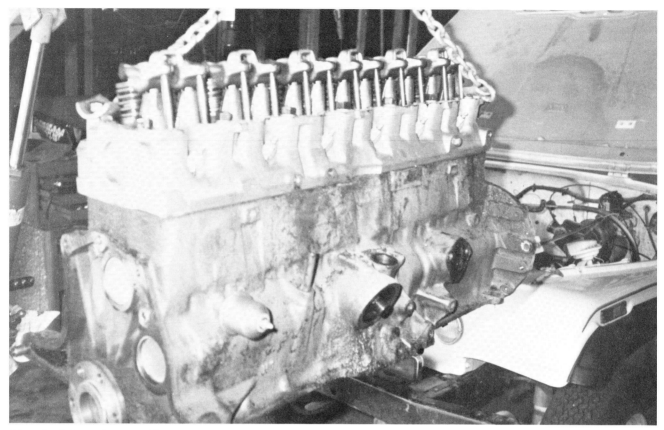

If you had the engine out of the car for rebuilding, attach the cleaned cylinder head with valvetrain in place. Attach the chains securely, so they don't push against the valve-operating mechanisms or other bolt-ons, when lowering the engine in place.

Initial cold valve settings can be made before you attach bolt-on accessories that were removed for the job. Set the intake valves first, then the exhaust valves. A feeler gauge, screwdriver and wrench are all you'll need for this job.

manner. The same applies to the cylinder head. It must slide over the studs without binding or being forced.

Clean the washers and nuts and slide the washers on the studs. Finger tighten the nuts, then snug them with your socket wrench. Following the tightening pattern recommended by the manufacturer, torque all nuts to the required pressure.

Bolt on any components you removed, leaving off valve covers and possibly the air cleaner. Install spark plugs and connect all wires. Connect all cables, tubes and control rods. Be sure all belts are tight against their pulleys. Check the upper hose before filling the radiator with a 50:50 permanent antifreeze and water mixture. Connect the battery to complete reassembly.

Adjusting valves

There are two types of overhead valves in common use. Camshaft in block engines use pushrods riding against a camshaft in the cylinder block. These operate the rocker arms in the head to open and close valves.

Other engines mount the camshaft in the cylinder head, with bucket tappets riding on a camshaft opening and closing the valves. Each type is adjusted differently.

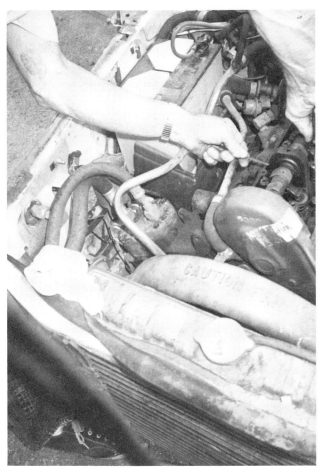

With the throttle set at fast idle, use your feeler gauge and turn the adjusting machine screw to set the correct clearance. Follow factory specifications on valve clearance, which may vary between intake and exhaust valves. Use a new gasket with valve cover.

You may want to increase engine idle speed slightly for initial valve adjustment, but remember to set it back to normal idle around 700 rpm for fine-tuning.

Refer to the manufacturer's specifications as to whether valves should be adjusted cold, or at normal engine operating temperature.

Clearance on pushrod-operated valves is set by loosening or tightening an adjusting nut on top of the pushrod. This raises or lowers the other side of the rocker arm. A lock nut holds the adjusting nut in place. Use your feeler gauge to set the clearance to the manufacturer's specifications.

These are cleaned rocker arms, with pushrods aligned for installation in an overhead valve six-cylinder engine. Do not attempt to straighten any bent pushrod; replace it with a new rod for a better balanced and running engine.

Valve clearance on overhead cam engines is adjusted by adding or subtracting thin steel shims to the bucket tappets against which the valve rides.

Work intake valves first, then the exhaust valves. Insert the correct thickness from the feeler gauge, or the correct thickness shims. Tighten the adjusting and lock nuts, holding the spring retainer to the correct tension to give that clearance. Clearances on intake and exhaust valves may differ. Set the idle speed as recommended, and check valve clearances again for fine-tuning.

There is no adjustment on hydraulic valve lifters, as they maintain zero clearance at all times.

Attach the valve cover(s) using new gaskets, or silicone gasket sealer, if your car has no valve cover gasket.

As with any adjustments on a running engine, take care to keep hands and clothing clear of the fan. You should not smoke during this operation.

References for additional information on specific engines are included in the appendix.

Chapter 7

Engine rebuild, bottom end

Take a special road test drive to help troubleshoot needed engine repairs. By paying careful attention, you can determine the general condition of piston rings, wristpins, and connecting rod and main bearings. You can also determine the condition of some of these parts by listening for certain sounds while the car is standing with the engine idling. Set the handbrake, put the gearshift in park or neutral, raise the hood and operate the throttle by hand. Listen for solid, clunking noises deep in the engine, no matter what speed. These usually mean worn main bearings. Loud rapping and grinding sounds that get louder as speed increases indicate worn connecting rod bearings.

Look in the rearview mirror during the test drive. Steady blue smoke from the tailpipe, coupled with sluggish pickup and loss of power because of poor compression, can mean worn piston rings, which allow oil from the base to bypass the rings and enter the combustion chamber. Distinct slapping noises, well up in the engine, usually indicate worn wristpins.

Before a bottom-end engine rebuild, drain the oil and examine it for shavings and other bits of metal before disposing of it. A few drops of water will be from condensation. Any coolant in the oil can mean a cracked block or head or blown head gasket.

You don't have to remove the engine for a bottom-end rebuild. However, if you do remove it, clean the block and other components with solvent and compressed air once it is disassembled. You can rent an engine stand for an easier rebuild.

You can postpone installing piston rings, if you detected no main, connecting rod or wristpin noises, and are willing to put up with slow starting, sluggish performance and oil consumption. However, if the car uses a quart of oil every couple of hundred miles, it's best to replace the rings. There are no adjustments for worn or burned bearings, as cars of these years did not allow for shims to be added or removed to take up for wear.

You can install piston rings without fitting new main or connecting rod bearings and wristpins, if re-ringing the pistons is all you want to do at one time. However, because you'd have to do much of the same work twice and have to buy a second set of gaskets, it's easier and makes more sense to replace main and connecting rod bearings and wristpins while you fit new piston rings. By careful planning and having supplies and tools on hand, you can do the job over a long weekend.

Tools and supplies

You'll need your socket set and open-end wrenches, assorted screwdrivers and pliers, a punch, ball peen hammer, wooden or rubber mallet, fine-gauge files, a feeler gauge and possibly other commonly used tools. Borrow or rent a torque wrench, ring spreader, groove cleaner and a micrometer, as well as a piston ring clamp. You'll also need a deglazing tool and a ridge reamer.

To do the job in the shortest time, you should plan to have everything on hand. You'll need a set of replacement gaskets, main and connecting rod bearings, wristpins, possibly with retaining clips all in the correct size. You'll need solvent, some short lengths of ½-inch rubber or plastic hose and a screened funnel for examining the drained oil. Have a correct amount of replacement oil and a filter cartridge.

If the oil gauge showed only weak pressure, or the oil light glowed dimly or blinked, you should inspect the oil pump while you have the oil pan removed. You can buy an oil pump rebuild kit for many cars, which can be returned if not used, or buy a rebuilt oil pump if you don't want to rebuild your present pump.

It is helpful to have a factory repair manual and other specifications for your car on hand as reference material.

Don't let the mental image of greasy engine parts scattered over your garage floor, like so many jigsaw puzzle pieces, scare you away from making repairs. It's not necessary to remove the engine for these jobs, though many restorers prefer to do so. If you do, rent a chainfall and engine repair stand. For a frame-off restoration, the engine should be removed. Directions for removing the engine are included in chapter 8.

Starting the job

Place the car solidly on jack stands, high enough so you can slide under easily on a creeper. Drain the

Examine connecting rod bearings, wristpins and pistons. Keep these in the same order as you removed them from the car, since they were balanced at the factory during manu- *facture. Note the worn connecting rod inserts in these Chrysler components.*

This worn connecting rod bearing insert (left) shows scoring and scorching from poor lubrication. The main bearing insert (right) also shows scoring and excessive wear. Tang on bearing insert fits into matching indentation to ensure correct installation.

coolant, and drain the oil through a screened strainer to see if there are any metal shavings, indicating more problems than you may have anticipated. There may be a few drops of water because of condensation. Any coolant in the oil can mean a cracked block or cylinder head, or a faulty head gasket.

Remove the oil pan, examining the sludge as you clean it. Be careful not to damage the oil pump as you remove it. You'll be looking up at the crankshaft and the journals which attach the crankshaft to the block.

The connecting rods and the lower end of the cylinder bores will also be in plain view.

Once the oil is swabbed away from these parts, you'll understand their logical arrangement. If you think there's a chance you'll be confused as to how they should look after your work, take a Polaroid shot before removing any parts.

Connecting rod bearings

Even if you're only going to replace the main bearings, you'll need to disconnect the connecting rod bearings. Remove any cotterpins and the nuts holding the bearing cap to the bottom of the connecting rod. Put them on your workbench in the same order they were removed for later match-up. Initially, each rod and its cap were balanced at the factory, and you should keep them matched as you rebuild the engine.

As you disconnect each rod, slip a short piece of rubber or plastic tubing over the exposed bolts to protect their threads and to prevent scratching the cylinder wall when the piston is removed. V-type engines will have two connecting rods on each crankshaft throw.

When all the connecting rods are free of the crankshaft, remove the pulley from the nose of the crankshaft, as well as the bolts in the flywheel mounting flange. Block the center of the crankshaft for support, as you remove the nuts on the main bearing journal caps. Pull each cap from its studs and the lower half of each bearing insert will come with it. Remove the insert from each cap. With the journals removed, pull the crankshaft from the engine and remove the top half of each main bearing insert from its journal.

Remove connecting rods from the crankshaft, and the nuts holding the main bearing supports to the engine block. Remove the flywheel pulley and timing gear at the front, *and you can pull the crankshaft from the engine. Clean oil passages and examine shaft for wear.*

If you find worn main bearing inserts, you may also find worn connecting rod and main bearings on the crankshaft.

Though you can install new bearing inserts, the crankshaft will have to be turned down on a lathe at a machine shop.

If you're not going to replace the piston rings and wristpins skip the following paragraphs on these jobs, and pick up the directions on fitting main and connecting rod bearing inserts. Assuming you're going to fit new piston rings and wristpins, you'll find it easier to fit the wristpins first, after you've prepared the cylinder walls and sized the rings. Install the rings

before you fit the top half of the connecting rod bearings.

How to buy replacement rings and bearings

You'll get help in determining the correct oversize piston rings and bearing inserts from a knowledge-

A competent machinist can tell you the amount of metal that can be removed from main bearings and connecting rod throws. The crankshaft can then be balanced. When the job is done, make sure the oil passages are open. The machinist can tell what oversize inserts to order.

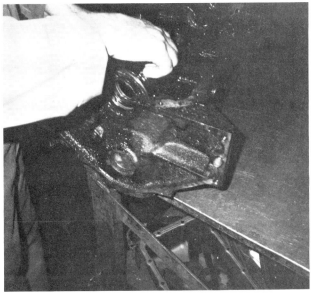

Pry out the worn oil seal at the end of the engine block when rebuilding the bottom end. Clean the recess in which the seal fits. Clean the block with compressed air and solvent before pressing the replacement seal in place. Handle the heavy block carefully.

Fit the oil seal that is required for your car. It may have the split kind, in which two half circles are used. Another is the one-piece, complete ring that fits against a retainer in the block. You may need to press the fiber-strip type into a channel.

able salesperson at an auto supply store. In addition to ordering parts by make, model, year and engine size, tell the odometer reading and general condition of the engine, including oil consumption.

If you have the engine apart, take along a couple of main and connecting rod bearing inserts, wristpins, and a piston with the rings in place. The oil ring will be at the bottom; the others are compression rings.

Your factory repair manual or specification sheets may have information on recommended oversizes based on mileage and other conditions.

In the mid–1950s, some manufacturers changed from a single-slotted oil ring to a slotted ring with a thin, solid ring above and below the slotted middle section. This three-piece assembly fits into the oil ring groove in the piston. It is probably what you'll be sold when you buy the new set of rings, as these have largely replaced the single oil ring.

Oversize is removed by filing a joining edge of the ring. If you're not sure of the size, it is better to get more oversize than you really need, as a couple of swipes with a fine-gauge file will remove the excess

You'll need to use a micrometer to measure the true diameter of each cylinder bore in a complete engine rebuild. Cylinders can be rebored within certain limits. In some cases, cylinder liners can be fitted. Weigh rebuild costs against that of swapping engines.

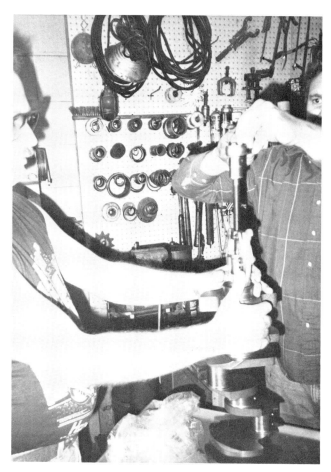

Tap the camshaft drive gear off the crankshaft, once the pin has been removed. You may need to use a gear puller, which you can turn with a socket wrench to remove the gear. Since you won't use a gear puller very often, it's less expensive to rent one.

You can have worn, out-of-round connecting rods trued and made like-new at a machine shop. You will have to fit oversize inserts when mating the rod to the crankshaft. A dial indicates the amount of metal removed, so you can determine the oversize to order.

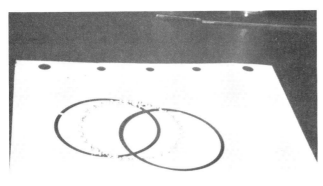

You'll probably remove only a single oil ring from each piston. The new set may contain three thin rings as replacements for the original ring. The slotted ring sits between the other two, and the combination fits into the oil ring slot in the piston.

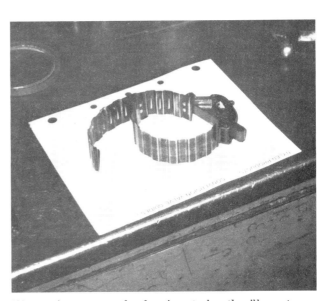

Piston rings are made of spring steel so they'll exert pressure against the cylinder wall. They have to be compressed into their slots when the newly ringed piston is fitted into the cylinder. Rent or borrow a ring compressor for this job.

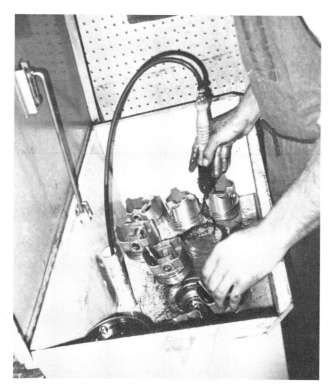

Remove the old piston rings. You may need to scrape some hardened deposits from the ring grooves. Use a brush and solvent to clean pistons before fitting new rings and installing wristpins. Remember to which cylinder each piston should be returned.

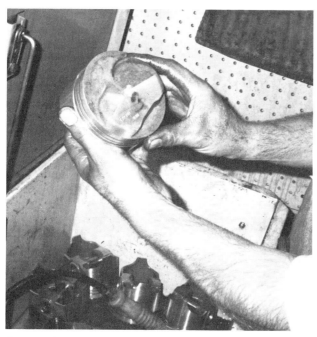

Inspect the top of each piston carefully for cracks and gouges. If the pistons are domed, or have indentations into which valves open, make sure there hasn't been damage from maladjusted valves. Inspect the piston skirts for scorching and cracks.

metal. Be careful when filing not to remove too much metal, as there is no way to replace it.

Installing piston rings

Remove the wristpin attaching the connecting rod to the piston. There may be retaining clips fitted into grooves in the piston, which have to be contracted and removed to free the wristpin. In some engines the pin isn't anchored and can be tapped out, using a small block of wood and a ball peen hammer. If the wristpin must be pressed out of the piston, determine the proper method, as specified in your factory manual; otherwise the piston could become distorted and have to be replaced.

Use a ring spreader to remove the old rings from the piston, or twist a screwdriver between the open ends to pry the ring out of its groove. Once you have the new rings, throw away the old ones, as they can't be reused. With the rings out of the piston, scrape away any carbon deposit on the top, using the flat edge of a putty knife or a wire-bristled brush, making sure not to gouge or scratch the piston. Clean the ring grooves with a groove cleaning tool and solvent, or break an old ring in half, and with solvent, scrape out any accumulation in the groove. Do not use a caustic solvent when cleaning pistons.

Examine the piston carefully. If the top is cracked, chipped or pitted, or the sides scuffed, scored or scorched from the lack of lubrication or excessive wristpin wear, the piston must be replaced. Use a micrometer to check the size of the piston in relation to the other pistons and the size of the cylinder bore.

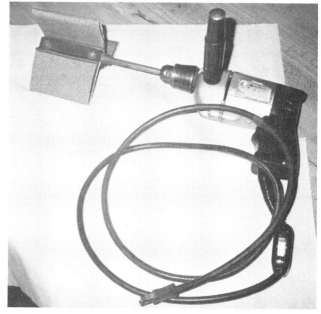

Use this handy tool for removing glaze on the cylinder walls so new rings will work properly. Fine emery cloth strips fit over rubber pads to exert necessary pressure. Only remove glaze to the point where the hatch marks on the cylinder bores show.

Use a deglazing tool to remove glaze on the cylinder walls. Usually six strokes up and down, with a #220 grit bar or emery cloth will remove the glaze so you can see the cross-hatch marks on the cylinder walls.

Use a ridge reamer to remove the ridge, caused by wear, at the top of the cylinder. Work carefully, using a straightedge to make sure you remove only what is necessary.

Push the cleaned piston down in the prepared cylinder and slide one ring at a time into the cylinder bore. You may need to remove some oversize to fit each ring. When each ring is sized correctly, it will fit snugly but won't bind. Size all three rings into the cylinder before pulling the piston from the cylinder. Clean the piston and cylinder wall with solvent to remove any glazing dust or ring filings.

Clean oil passages in connecting rods by using solvent and running a wire through them. Some engine rebuilders also use compressed air after the wire and solvent treatment.

Pistons are marked to indicate the front, as are the connecting rods. Fit the rod to the piston and install the wristpin. There may be a retaining clip on each end that needs to be sprung into place. The pin will usually slide in, or may need to be tapped or pressed into place. If so, follow directions for removing a tight wristpin.

If you're using ring expanders behind the rings, insert these first, though these aren't used too often. Use a ring spreader to fit each ring into the proper groove in the piston. Rings are brittle, so spread them carefully. With the rings in place, space the ring end

When removing glaze, or later trimming away the ridge at the top of the cylinder, spray some solvent into the cylinder bore to make the job easier and help collect the glaze dust and metal shavings. Check cylinder walls for cracks or scorching.

You can feel a ridge at the top of the cylinder. Compare the measurement at the bottom of the cylinder with that at the top. Use a box-end wrench to operate the ridge remover in cylinder bores. It takes only a few turns of the reamer to remove the ridge.

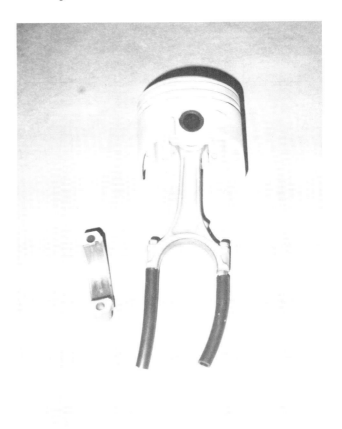

Each piston is marked to show the front for proper match-up with the connecting rod. After installing the wristpin, fit small pieces of tubing over the ends of the studs to protect the threads when you fit the piston rings.

Clamp the ring compressor over the newly fitted rings to hold them in position when sliding the piston into the cylinder. Release clamp pressure as each ring fits in the cylinder. Tubing on rod studs protects threads and prevents scratching the cylinder wall and bearings.

joints equally around the circumference of the piston, as they were originally.

Fit the ring clamp over the piston and carefully push the re-ringed piston into the cylinder, pulling the ring clamp up and out of the way. With all the pistons in place, you're ready to work on the crankshaft.

Installing crankshaft bearing inserts

Run a wire and solvent through the oil passages to make sure they're free of any residue. Insert the front and rear bearing oil seals. These may be in one or two pieces. Insert the top half of the bearing inserts into their journals. Block the center of the crankshaft to support its weight, and bolt the flange to the flywheel.

Fit the lower half of the bearing inserts into their journals. Any filing on the bearing inserts to reduce their oversize must be done with a fine-gauge file, and only on the edges where the two half-inserts meet. *Never* file on the inside or outside of bearing inserts.

Because Plastigage, which is available at auto supply stores, is soluble in oil, be sure there is no oil on the bearing inserts or journals. Place a strip of Plastigage along the full length of each bearing, install the bearing caps and torque to factory specifications. As you tighten the bearing cap, the Plastigage flattens. Remove the bearing caps and compare the width of the Plastigage strips to the scale printed on the envelope. Bearing journal taper is determined by comparing the Plastigage strip near its ends. Turn the crankshaft ninety degrees and retest the clearance to determine journal difference. Be careful *not* to turn the crankshaft with Plastigage in place.

If the bearing journals and inserts are within factory tolerances, prelubricate the surfaces with STP or a similar product before tightening them to factory

The third main bearing cap is yet to be installed in this six-cylinder engine, as well as connecting rod bearings.

Clean the surface against which the oil pan fits for a tight seal.

Remove nuts holding the oil pump to the engine block. Disassemble the pump at your workbench. Check the teeth on the impeller gears in the pump body and the bearing on the shaft. There are rebuild kits for many pumps. Fit a new gasket and clean filter for best pressure.

After cleaning the oil pan inside and out, hammer out any dents before painting. Check the washer on the drain plug. Always use a new gasket when installing the pan to the engine.

specifications. This is to protect them during the initial start-up.

The main bearings have to handle up-and-down and back-and-front pressures. When they're tightened correctly, the crankshaft should spin freely by hand. Too tight, and the engine will barely turn over; too loose, and you're inviting trouble. Take your time and do it right.

Installing rod bearings

Work one crankshaft throw at a time. On V-type engines this will mean fitting left and right connecting rods to the same throw. On the left bank, the rib and boss on the cap face the rear; on the right these face forward. The oil spurt hole on each rod must face up to get lubrication from the crankshaft.

Fit replacement inserts into the rod and matching bearing cap. The tang on the insert fits into a dimple on the saddle. Pull one rod, with piston attached, and mate it with the crankshaft throw. Use Plastigage, as you did on the main bearings. Remove the Plastigage and lubricate the bearing to protect it during start-up, then tighten to factory specifications.

As with main bearing inserts, any filing to reduce oversize must be made on the end of the inserts. It may take two or more fittings to get the correct clearance. Connecting rods transfer the brunt of the terrific pressure of the piston's power stroke into a rotating motion, so must be fitted to the correct clearance.

Oil pump

To be sure the replacement parts you've installed are lubricated properly, examine the oil pump and passages in the engine block. Oil is pulled from the sump and pumped under pressure through the filter and through passages in the block to the main bearings, the crankshaft throws, connecting rods and camshaft, as well as the rocker shaft and arms on OHV engines. Oil passages machined into the crankshaft and connecting rods distribute oil to engine parts having frictional contact.

Clean the screened intake. Check the shaft that drives the pump; it should be free of play. Disassemble and clean the pump case and clean the oil pressure relief valve with solvent. Examine the gears or rotor vanes. If these are chipped or badly worn, they must be replaced.

There are rebuild kits for some pumps. Rebuilt pumps at auto supply stores currently cost about $30; a tested pump from a wrecking yard runs about $15.

Prime a newly cleaned or rebuilt pump. Clean the mating surfaces on the pump and block. Fit a new gasket and tighten any lines when installing the pump. Fit a new oil filter and use a new gasket when replacing the oil pan.

Final assembly

Take one last look at the newly fitted parts. Make sure all cotterpins and lock washers are in place. Fit the fan belt over the newly installed pulley. With new piston rings, wristpins and connecting rod and main bearing inserts replaced, the rebuilt engine will be tight. Plan on a break-in period with light oil, which should be drained and replaced after 500 to 1,000 miles.

Chapter 8

Engine replacement

After a thorough examination of your car's engine and a study of repair expenses and the time involved, you may decide it will be easier, less expensive and take less time to swap it, rather than make a complete rebuild, which may include some machine shop work.

Choosing the right engine

You'll save a great deal of frustration, money and time if you examine all the possibilities before choosing an engine. Decide what engine you'd like in your car, giving yourself some choices. When you locate what you'd like, check its condition carefully to avoid future repairs.

If you buy a rebuilt engine instead of rebuilding your present engine or buying one from a salvage yard, you should get a list of new parts fitted, tolerances to which the crankshaft has been ground and a written guarantee on parts and labor.

Engine swaps can be made by a person with average mechanical ability, if safety precautions are taken and the proper equipment used, giving new power and performance to your old clunker.

You may want a newer, more powerful engine made by the same manufacturer, or you may want to change your present engine for one from another make.

Engine swaps to substitute a better condition engine of the same year and with the same specifications for your present one, do not alter the car's originality. However, changing for a newer, more powerful engine, or one from a different manufacturer, does alter the car's chances in show car judging.

As explained earlier, many cars made by the same parent company shared the same engine. Also, the same basic engine block was used with various modifications to the cylinder bore, heads, camshafts and other components in different models and nameplates within divisions.

A restorer of a fifties, sixties and early seventies car has a wide variety of engine choices. Many manufacturers offered a six-cylinder or V-8 engine in the same chassis. Others offered a choice between a four- and six-cylinder engine. During the muscle car years, most manufacturers' engine options included at least two V-8s with larger cubic inch displacements than their standard model.

You should realize that an engine swap for other than one compatible with your car's chassis and powertrain often requires a lot of changes. If the engine is lighter, or heavier than the original, there can be front suspension and steering problems caused by the different weight placement. You may need to fabricate different engine mounting supports to fit your frame's mounting brackets.

If the engine is longer, there may be problems fitting it between the radiator and firewall. If it is shorter, there may be a cooling problem. There can also be cooling problems if the replacement engine's coolant capacity is more than the radiator can handle.

Problems mating the engine with the bellhousing can arise, as can problems if you plan to install an engine and automatic transmission combination into a car originally fitted with a manual transmission.

These and other problems must be considered when changing engines. They're not insurmountable, but will have to be solved. Check carefully, making a simple sketch as you go along, perhaps taking some photos for later reference.

From underneath, measure the length and width of the chassis rails from the front cross-member, at the rear of the front wheelwells and at the cowl. Note the position of the front motor mount brackets and measure the distance across from one to the other. If there are additional motor mounts at the rear of the engine, instead of only on the bellhousing/transmission casting, get the measurement across. Note what clearance the tie-rods, steering gearbox and other steering and front suspension components require.

Meaure the length from the radiator to the cowl and include the height the toe boards provide. Mark where the exhaust and crossover pipes fit. Note the clearance from the front cross-member and tie-rods

The Mustang V–8 installed in place of the original inline six is an easy change, as these engines were offered as options. More difficult are engine swaps between different families of cars. These often require making new engine and transmission mountings.

Salvage yards have already-removed and tested engines at reasonable prices. They are tagged to show oil pressure, vacuum and compression, so you'll know what you're get- *ting. Buy an engine mated with a clutch assembly and stick shift, or a torque convertor and an automatic.*

to the engine pan. Note the position of the starter in relation to any brace or cross-member. Also measure the room necessary for clutch and brake linkages. If there are any bolt-on accessories, such as air conditioning components or a transmission cooler, attached to the frame, mark their position.

From above, measure the length and width of the engine compartment at the front and at the cowl. Note the position of the battery, power top or brake components, or other bolt-on accessories attached to the firewall. Note positions of the control rods and cables from the firewall to the engine. Determine how much, if any, front-end sheet metal will have to be removed when changing engines.

Technical concerns

If you plan on installing an engine that uses a twelve-volt electrical system, instead of a six, check the position of the alternator in place of the generator. You'll also have additional changes to make, as outlined in chapter 9.

If you intend to attach the replacement engine to your present clutch/transmission assembly, you may have to install an adapter. Check the manufacturer's specifications carefully when making your decision. If you plan to install a replacement engine and transmission as a unit, you'll need to make sure the universal joints and drive shaft will fit. Information on transmissions, universals and drive shafts is covered in chapters 13 and 14. Sources for additional information, as well as engine and transmission specifications, are included in the appendix.

Removing the engine

It's usually easier to remove both the engine and transmission as a unit. Each can be removed separately, if you want. You don't necessarily have to remove the radiator, but it is usually easier if you do. Remove the hood and as much front-end sheet metal as necessary to allow plenty of work room.

Rent a chainfall, if the overhead joists are strong enough to hold the engine's weight. If there is any question, rent an engine hoist to play it safe.

Drain the cooling system. Either remove the battery, or disconnect the cables. Remove the hood and store it out of your way.

Disconnect everything between the engine and firewall, as well as engine and transmission mounting bolts, exhaust pipes and mechanical and electrical linkages. Hook chains securely, so they won't push against any bolted-on components. Balance from side to side before lifting.

While the oil is draining from the base, remove any bolt-on components that aren't included in the swap. These could be an air conditioning compressor, generator or alternator, carburetor, heater hoses and some electrical components.

Tag and disconnect all wires from the firewall to the engine. Disconnect all cables and control rods to the carburetor and distributor. Disconnect vacuum hoses to the power brake booster and any other vacuum-operated components. If they appear to be in the way, or might be damaged in the switch, disconnect hoses or tubes from the power steering reservoir to the steering system, as well as any tubes from the automatic transmission to the cooler or radiator.

From underneath, you must disconnect clutch and manual gearshift linkages, and on some cars the handbrake linkage. The drive shaft must be disconnected at the transmission end. Disconnect the speedometer cable and tag any wiring for automatic transmission operation.

Remove exhaust manifolds, or uncouple the exhaust pipe at the first joint. You may need to remove the crossover pipe on V–8s, if it's in the way.

When the engine is out of the car, use solvent to clean grease and grime from the engine cavity. It is a good time to check power steering hoses, tubing for the transmission cooler and any wires that run along the frame, while there's room to make repairs.

When removing an engine, remove the hood, radiator, shroud and fan, along with the battery—if it is mounted at the front. Unless you remove the air conditioner condenser, use a piece of plywood to protect it as the engine is lifted up and out.

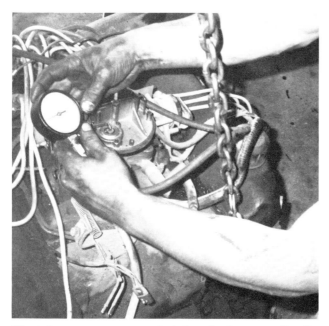

Check the vacuum on an untested engine by connecting the vacuum gauge to the outlet on the intake manifold and running the engine. Compare with manufacturer's specifications. Engines can be run for a short time out of the car for testing, without any damage.

You may need to use a properly jacked block to raise the engine/transmission combination high enough to allow the chain's hooks into the mounting tabs.

Remove the bolts from the motor mounts. Position the chains so they distribute the weight evenly and don't push against any bolt-ons left in place.

If you plan to remove any engine components to use on the replacement engine, or to sell, remove them while the engine is in the car, or after its weight and position are secured.

Because of the length of the engine/transmission unit, it'll have to move forward, as well as up. As the chains support its weight, you and a helper must push it forward until the transmission clears the firewall. The unit can then be lifted from the car.

Because of its weight, don't move the engine any farther from the car than necessary. Either block it solidly, or lower it carefully on one side, making sure no bolt-on component is bearing the engine's weight.

With the old engine out of the car, clean the engine compartment thoroughly, following the degreasing and derusting procedures previously outlined. Use a glazing putty to fill minor dings and scrapes, and feather the edges so they'll blend with the surface.

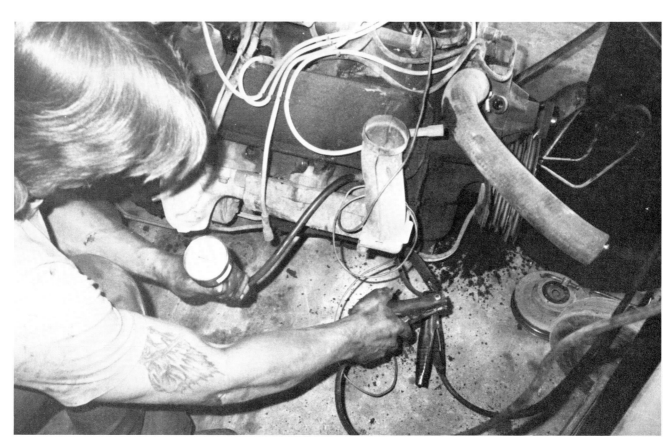

If the engine is out of the car, connect battery cables directly to starter cables for power. Remove spark plugs to check each cylinder's compression, and compare with manufacturer's specifications. Cylinders should be within 5 psi of each other.

56

Spray with a rust-inhibiting primer and sand lightly, before spraying with lacquer or enamel, either black or the car's color. Hand-held aerosol spray cans are sufficient for this unless you have a compressor and spray outfit on hand.

The replacement engine/transmission unit should be degreased and painted, if necessary, before installation.

Testing the engine

Once you've determined which engine will fit in your car and can be successfully mated with the driveline, you should make some tests to determine the condition of the engine you've chosen.

If the engine hasn't been removed from the car, make sure there is sufficient oil in the sump and coolant in the radiator. The engine doesn't have to be in the car to make the necessary tests, but should be blocked solidly on a skid for safety reasons. If it is out of the car, check the oil dipstick. Pour water into the upper hose opening to protect the engine from serious overheating during the tests. Some mechanics fit a hose between the upper and lower openings for this test. Have a well-charged battery and jumper cables on hand. If the engine is out of the car, run a rubber hose from the carburetor fuel intake into a can of gasoline. Have a fire extinguisher on hand.

Refer to the manufacturer's specifications concerning the compression an engine in good condition should develop. This shouldn't vary by more than five pounds between cylinders on an engine you'd choose. It is easier if you remove the spark plugs for this test, but you can remove them one at a time, if you prefer.

Use either the screw-in type gauge, or the one with the conical rubber end.

You can run the engine on the starter for this test. Mark the compression shown in each cylinder for reference. When you've finished this test, replace the spark plugs.

If the engine is in the car, start it and check the oil pressure. See how quickly pressure shows on the gauge, or how quickly the light goes out. Let the engine run until normal operating temperature and note what pressure is maintained.

If the engine is out of the car, rent an electric oil gauge and attach the wires to the sending unit on the base or oil pump. Start the engine, and note beginning pressure and pressure after the engine is warm. Remember, an engine that is out of the car and running with a minimum amount of coolant will heat up quicker.

Electrical tests will vary, depending on the accessories that are attached to the replacement engine. Using a voltmeter, with one clamp on the alternator or generator, the other to the battery, check the output. It must be above six volts on a six-volt system and above twelve volts on a twelve-volt system to run the engine and the electrically operated accessories.

With the engine running, hold an insulated screwdriver between the top of each spark plug and the engine block, grounding it to the cylinder. If the engine misses, that shows the spark plug is okay. You may want to put in a new set of plugs, once the engine is installed.

Check the wires for worn insulation, signs of future electrical problems. Check electrical connections to all bolt-on accessories, making a note of any that will need attention once the engine is installed.

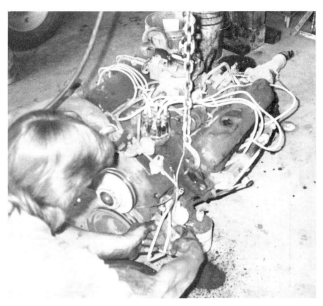

If you buy an untested engine, check the oil pressure by attaching an oil pressure gauge directly to the sending unit. The pressure should surge soon after starting, then drop to the manufacturer's recommended pressure as the motor reaches operating temperature.

When replacing an inline six with a V–8, the engine will sit farther back from the radiator. You may need to install an extension on the fan hub to move it closer to the radiator. If the engine has a different coolant capacity, you may also need a radiator shroud.

If the engine is out of the car and the bellhousing removed, pull the clutch assembly so you can check the condition of the drive plate attached to the flywheel and the facings on the driven plate. Check the condition of the teeth on the flywheel ring gear.

Refer to chapters 5 and 9 for other tests you can make to determine the condition of the engine.

Installing the engine

You may have to bolt some sturdy brackets to the engine, if they aren't already in place. Hook the chains, making sure they don't put excess strain on any part and that they will lift the engine/transmission combination evenly.

With the chains supporting the weight, check that the engine is sitting level. Lift and position it over

Changing engines may mean considerable rewiring to connect all the electrical components and controls. Use new wires and connectors, and follow the wiring guide for your present car, making additions and changes only as necessary.

the refurbished engine cavity. With your helper guiding it away from the firewall, lower it slowly and push it into position.

Slip new cushions in the support brackets and align the holes before releasing the engine's weight from the chains. Install the bolts, washers and nuts, securing it in place.

Fit the universal joint attaching the transmission to the drive shaft. Connect the clutch, manual gearshift and handbrake linkages. Match up and connect wiring for the automatic transmission and oil sending unit. Take care not to cross-thread fittings on the tubing taking the transmission fluid to the cooler or radiator. Connect the speedometer cable, crossover exhaust pipe and any other component you disconnected under the car.

Connect the exhaust pipes to the manifolds, using a new gasket. Connect wiring from the firewall to the engine, matching identification tags. Install and connect the battery. Connect the fuel line, accelerator control linkage and any other wire or cable from the firewall.

If any hoses, wires or vacuum tubes were damaged during the installation, replace them when you connect the automatic choke, spark control, power brake booster and vacuum reservoir. If you removed the spark plugs to avoid damage, install and connect them at this time.

Replace the alternator or generator, air conditioning compressor and power steering pump. Attach the fan and fit new belts, making sure no pulley groove was bent during the operation. Stretch these driving belts tight, before securing the unit in place. Mount the radiator and install new hoses and clamps. Attach the coolant overflow container and connect the tubing to the radiator. Bolt any shroud or baffles to the radiator and attach any front-end sheet metal.

Fill the radiator with a 50:50 permanent antifreeze mixture and add a can of water pump lubricant. Fill the base with oil and install a new filter. Fill the automatic transmission with the correct amount of fluid and install a new filter.

Leave the air cleaner off until you start the engine. However, before you start it, make one final inspection of all wires, hoses, control rods and cables, making sure everything is in place and secured.

If you prime the engine for its first start, have a fire extinguisher on hand to control any backfire flames through the air intake.

Move the car outside, or leave the garage door open, when letting the motor idle for any adjustments. When you're satisfied everything is working properly, fit the air cleaner. You'll need help mounting the hood. Take time to align it properly between the cowl and front-end sheet metal.

Remove any parts that you can sell or trade, or might someday want from the old engine. Use string tags to identify electrical connections on anything you keep. Either take the old engine to a junkyard, or see if some outfit will haul it away for its scrap value.

Chapter 9

Electrical systems

Changes in electrical systems started in the 1950s, when more electrically powered or controlled accessories and newly developed high-compression engines required more power than the long-used six-volt systems could deliver. As increased electrical power demands continued, alternators replaced generators.

The wiring diagram for your car will look like so much spaghetti at first glance. However, with a magnifying glass and reference to the code symbols, you can figure it out.

How it works

You should understand the basic laws of electricity to simplify any troubleshooting and adjustments or repairs you may make.

Current will flow through a wire if it is forced. The force comes from the battery and is measured in volts.

The movement of current is measured in amperes, as shown on the ammeter gauge or light. Resistance to movement of current is measured in ohms. The wires through which the current moves from one connection to another are circuits.

Each circuit must be complete, if the current is to flow. It starts from the battery, leads to a certain component, then returns to the battery. Instead of having every circuit form that loop of wires, the negative terminal of the battery is grounded to the car's frame, and every circuit is grounded at its destination, completing the circuit.

The amount of current needed by the various electrical components differs, since it takes more current to operate the starter than a dome light. Varying thickness wires are used because thicker wire can carry more current. There have to be ways to stop or

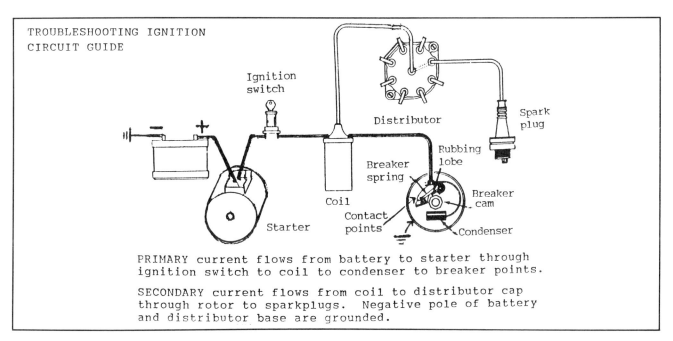

TROUBLESHOOTING IGNITION
CIRCUIT GUIDE

Ignition switch

Distributor

Spark plug

Rubbing lobe

Breaker spring

Breaker cam

Coil

Contact points

Condenser

Starter

PRIMARY current flows from battery to starter through ignition switch to coil to condenser to breaker points.

SECONDARY current flows from coil to distributor cap through rotor to sparkplugs. Negative pole of battery and distributor base are grounded.

control the amount of current flowing through wires. Switches are really circuit breakers and connect or disconnect the current flow on demand. Rheostats lessen the amount of current passing through the wires. Fuses are in the circuits for protection. If current exceeds certain limits, the metal in the glass tube will melt. This is commonly known as a blown fuse.

To understand the electrical system better, and help in troubleshooting electrical problems, you should know the functions of the components and how they operate.

Electrical components
Storage battery

The storage battery is made up of positive and negative plates in an electrolyte solution of sulfuric acid and water. When a load is put on the battery, the sulfuric acid combines with the lead in the plates to make lead sulfate and water, releasing electrical current by this chemical process. When the engine charges the battery, the action is reversed and lead sulfate is released from the plates, forming sulfuric acid.

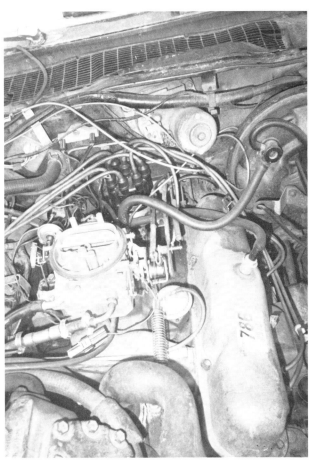

When troubleshooting electrical problems, first be sure the wires from the distributor to the spark plugs and coil are securely in place. The distributor may be at the front or rear on V-type engines, and on the side of the block on inline engines.

Primary and secondary circuits

The primary circuit connects the battery, through the ignition system, to the coil. From the coil, current flows to the condenser and breaker points in the distributor case.

The secondary circuit moves current from the coil to the distributor cap through the rotor to the spark plugs.
Coil

The coil will be mounted on the engine block near the distributor. Current flowing through a wire produces a magnetic field around the wire. When that field breaks down, electricity is generated in wires within the field's lines of force.

The coil contains two long wires wound tightly around a soft iron core. The primary is the low-voltage winding, made up of fairly thick wire. The secondary is the high-voltage winding, made up of fine wire.

With the ignition switch turned on, the low-voltage current flows through the primary winding to the distributor when the breaker points are closed, creating a magnetic field around the iron core. When the breaker points open, the flow of low-voltage current is interrupted and the magnetic field collapses. This generates current in the secondary winding, which flows through the distributor to the spark plugs.
Distributor

The distributor is gear driven at a speed coordinated with the camshaft and is the only moving part in the ignition system. It controls the flow of current to the spark plugs. The metal base contains the primary circuit's breaker points and condenser. One part of the breaker point assembly is grounded to complete the circuit.

The cap, or head, is plastic and contains terminals for the high-voltage wire from the coil. Metal tops embedded in the head pick up current from the passing rotor and send it to the spark plugs.
Condenser

The condenser is the small, cylindrical capacitor attached to the primary circuit which stores surges of current and reduces arcing between the points.
Starter

Located in a round steel housing, the starter is a powerful electric motor that drives against a toothed ring on the flywheel. Needing a lot of current for a short time, a thick, insulated low-resistance wire, or cable, is used. It is activated by a dashboard button, or a contact on the ignition switch. An electromagnetic switch or solenoid engages the drive gear with the flywheel ring gear, turning over the engine.
Generator

The generator consists of an armature and field coil. The armature is a coil of wires that rotates within the field, which is a group of coiled wires forming an electromagnetic coil. As the armature revolves inside the coil, electric current is produced.

Three brushes ride against the armature. One delivers current to the battery. A second is adjustable

Remove the distributor cap to adjust the breaker points in the body of the distributor, as well as to check the contact points in the cap. Check insulation on all the wires. Usually a screwdriver, small pliers or socket wrench is all you'll need for the job.

Note the position of the flattened bottom end of the distributor shaft, if you remove it from the engine block for an overhaul. It must fit in the same position when you install it. Disconnect the hose to the vacuum diaphragm for easier handling.

When rebuilding the distributor, make sure the base plate, which shifts position by vacuum, is secured. Install a new condenser. Check the insulation in the low-voltage wire to the coil. Fit new breaker points and rotor, as well as a new distributor cap.

If the gear on the distributor shaft that rotates the distributor at the same speed as the camshaft is worn, faulty timing will occur. Use a rubber mallet to tap a new gear in place. The distributor shaft usually drives the oil pump as well.

With a replacement gear installed on the distributor shaft, use a punch to drive the pin holding the gear in place. Block the end of the shaft to prevent damage to the shaft and gear during this operation.

If necessary, use a drill to align the holes in the distributor shaft and gear. It will be necessary to use a larger diameter pin if you do this, in order to hold the pin in place and prevent any movement of the gear on the shaft.

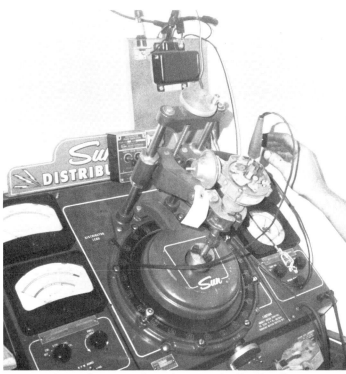

You can have the operation of your rebuilt distributor tested on a machine designed to check every phase of its operation, if you have any doubts about repairs you made. The cost is minimal and any adjustments can be made before installing it in the engine.

to regulate the amount of current and a third is grounded.

A cutout, or reverse current relay, is located in a small housing on the generator and prevents it from drawing current from the battery at slow engine speeds.

Alternator

Adapted from airplane use, alternators correct the two basic deficiencies of the generator and give the added benefit of light weight. An alternator can turn up to 12,000 rpm, stay cooler and deliver up to 50 amps.

In the alternator, the magnetic field rotates inside a wound wire coil. With the generating windings stationary, there is no cooling problem.

Simple in construction, alternating current is changed to direct current by diode rectifiers, which are electrical valves letting current move only one way. Most alternators limit their output, but a few may have a voltage regulator.

Troubleshooting

No matter which car of these years you work on, it will have breaker point ignition; electronic ignition came later. To check the ignition system, you'll need a hydrometer to test the battery, a voltmeter for electrical output, a test light for the circuits and a dwell meter for setting the dwell.

If an electrical component does not work, check the fuse panel first. For the battery, use a hydrometer first to check specific gravity in each cell. If one is weak, perhaps a recharge will suffice. Use your voltmeter to tell what voltage the battery contains. If cells are weak or dead and there is low voltage, the battery must be replaced. Equally important is that both battery cables must be clean and firmly attached at both ends.

Remove the starter from the car. Check for worn or chipped teeth on the drive gear. Replacement gears are readily available. Remove the starter housing to pull the shaft on which the gear rides. Replace the bearings on each end of the shaft if they're worn.

If the battery won't stay charged for more than a few days, check for a loose belt, a faulty regulator, loose cables or a short in one of the circuits, draining the battery.

Starter

If the engine turns over slowly, and the battery is good, check battery posts for corrosion and the wiring connections on the starter circuit.

The starter and drive gear are the larger unit, with the solenoid actuating unit attached. With ignition on and the starter button pressed, current flows through the solenoid, activating the electric motor, engaging the drive gear with the flywheel ring gear.

To work on the starter, clamp the mounting bracket with the solenoid attached in a vise and remove the commutator housing on the end and the main housing containing the field windings. Inspect the bearings supporting the armature and commutator.

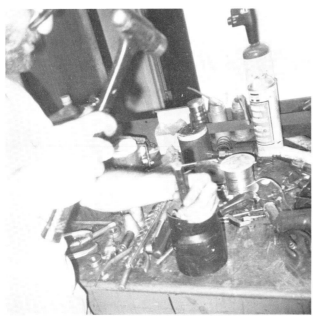

Use a hammer and cold chisel to cut through the rivets attaching the brush holders to the main housing. Use a pop-rivet gun to attach new brush holders. Clean out any metal shavings that may have settled in the field windings before reassembly.

When reassembling the starter, check that the drive flange, which is actuated by a yoke from the solenoid, is not bent. Be sure the machine screws holding the field pole and windings are tight. Check that springs holding the brushes against the commutator are seated.

If the starter doesn't operate when the switch is on, check wiring from ignition switch to solenoid. The solenoid switch may be faulty, not delivering enough voltage to the starter. On cars with an automatic transmission, check for faulty wiring to the park/neutral switch, or a bad switch.

If the starter is noisy, check the alignment of starter to the engine. Make sure it is securely bolted in place.

If the starter just doesn't respond, use a voltmeter set at the Low DC mark to check the solenoid or relay. Touch prongs to each terminal on the solenoid, while the engine is cranked. If the voltage exceeds 0.3, the solenoid is bad.

If the starter runs, but only cranks the engine intermittently, check for chipped or missing teeth on the flywheel ring gear.

If none of these diagnose the situation, the starter should be removed and taken to a shop specializing in electrical repairs. Insist on an estimate before authorizing repairs, as you might save money buying a good used starter from a salvage yard, or a rebuilt unit from an auto supply store.

In some cars the starter may be hard to get at. In these cases, block the rear wheels and put the front of the car on jack stands. Disconnect the negative cable to the battery and wiring to the starter. Notice if any components have to be loosened before removing starter holding bolts.

Coil

Remove the wire from the negative coil terminal. Turn on the ignition, after connecting a jumper wire to the negative terminal. Hold the wire close to some metal part, making it touch intermittently. If there's no spark, check for current between the positive and negative terminal and ground. If the coil is defective, there'll be no spark. Coils can't be repaired, only replaced.

Condenser

If the breaker points are badly burned, a faulty condenser is usually the cause, though pitting can also be caused by a poor ground contact in the distributor. Condensers can only be replaced.

Carbon contact

The short piece of carbon fitted into the center distributor cap terminal is the carbon contact. It touches a small spring on top of the rotor. This must not be damaged.

Contact points

Contact points are small metal contacts embedded in the distributor cap. The rotor doesn't actually touch them, but as it passes, the electrical spark jumps, or arcs, from rotor to contact point. If these are badly pitted, the spark may not arc, or it may be weak. Distributor caps can only be replaced. Tag wires for correct match-up.

Rotor

The rotor is made of plastic and keyed to fit a notch in the distributor shaft and turn with it. A metal insert carries current which arcs to metal contacts in the distributor cap. A spring forces contact with the carbon insert at the wire from the coil. If the end is pitted, replace the rotor.

When troubleshooting electrically operated windows, check fuses first, then the wires attached to the switches. Use your test light on each circuit before removing the door upholstery to get at the electric motor and drive mechanism.

Breaker points

Breaker points are small steel discs that open and close in conjunction with the rotor's movement, passing current to the rotor at the correct time. A thin leaf spring holds them against each other between openings. When these become pitted or worn, they must be replaced. It's a simple job, needing only a screwdriver, small pliers and feeler gauge.

To adjust the breaker points, check the manufacturer's gap specifications. Loosen the holding screw, insert a feeler gauge and tighten the screw. Occasionally smoothing the ends of the small discs with a fine file or emory cloth will keep the points operating efficiently.

Base plate

The base plate fits in the bottom of the distributor housing, to which the condenser and breaker points are attached. Check that it is grounded to the distributor case.

Vacuum diaphragm

The vacuum diaphragm is connected by a hose, or tube, to the intake manifold. It changes the position of the distributor base plate, advancing or retarding

With upholstery and the removable portion of the inner panel out of the way, check that the reduction gear case is tight and that the teeth on both gears are clean and mesh properly. Clean gears with solvent and lubricate with graphite or light oil.

65

Use care not to bend the channel which holds the glass when clamping it in a vise to remove the bolts holding it to the gear case. Detach the gear case from the electric motor for further work. Remove any rust that may have accumulated.

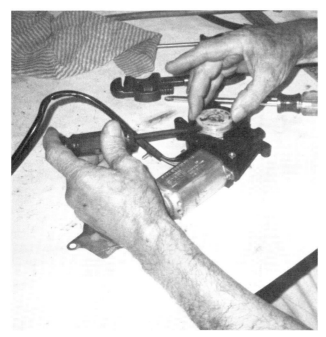

Some cars use a cable to raise or lower the channel in which the window fits. Remove the machine screws holding the cap on the pulley case to either replace a frayed cable, or to thread the cable into the proper groove. Be sure the cable isn't crimped.

Be careful when removing rubber-insulated double-face bolts, as too much pressure can separate the bolts from the rubber insulation. Replacement bolts are available at automotive supply stores or at many hardware stores. Take one with you to match threads.

the spark timing as the load on the engine changes. Disconnect the hose with the engine running. Place your thumb over the hose to determine if there is a suction. If not, check the hose and fittings for leaks.

Make sure the connecting link from the unit to the base breaker plate moves freely. If not, check the connections.

The vacuum units cannot be repaired, but are easily replaced by disconnecting the unit from the attaching bracket, the hose from the unit and the connecting link to the base breaker plate.

Ignition wires

Many times, uneven firing is caused by faulty ignition wires. Remove the wire from the spark plug and hold it close to a ground to see if the spark jumps when that piston should fire. Sparks should be bright, strong and even. If not, plan on replacing the wire(s), as taped repairs are unsatisfactory.

Spark plugs

Spark plugs produce the spark that ignites the air/fuel mixture. With time, as well as internal engine wear, they may malfunction.

Remove one plug at a time. A normal plug will have a light brown or gray deposit on insulator and electrode; black, sooty deposits indicate too rich a fuel mixture. It can also indicate faulty timing, weak spark or low compression. A wet, black insulator and electrode indicate oil bypassing the piston rings or valve guides, brake fluid leaking past the power brake booster, or fluid from the automatic transmission leaking into the vacuum hose on the modulator. These conditions should be corrected before new plugs are installed.

Follow the manufacturer's recommendations on heat ranges and gap settings on new spark plugs.

Dwell

Dwell is the length of time breaker points stay closed when the engine is running. Use a dwell meter. Attach the ground wire to a clean, metal part, and the positive to the terminal on the coil, from which a small wire extends to the base of the distributor.

Set the meter to the number of cylinders. With the engine running, read the dwell in degrees on the meter and compare with the manufacturer's specifications.

If the dwell is incorrect, shut off the engine and adjust the breaker points until the dwell comes within the specified range for your idling engine.

To test alternator or generator output, touch the voltmeter prongs to the battery and the alternator with the engine at fast idle and the headlights and radio or air conditioner turned on. The alternator should deliver over 14 volts or be replaced.

Follow the directions that come with a rebuild kit. Before disassembly, scratch an index mark across the housing parts. Remove the bolts holding the housing together. The shaft with the rotor will come out. Scratch an index mark on the housing and stator coil.

Generator

The generator should produce enough current to keep the headlights, radio and heater operating at average speeds. If it doesn't, first check that the fan belt is tight. Next, remove the circular portion that covers the brushes. The brushes should extend at least ½ in. beyond their holders. Check the wiring to the brushes for breaks. The second brush is adjustable, and can be moved counterclockwise to increase charging. Use air to clean any powdered metal in the area. Spray the opened area with an electrical contact cleaner.

Because of extreme heat in the generator, insulation on wires may have melted, causing shorts.

A beginner shouldn't try to rebuild a generator; it is too complicated. Take it to a shop specializing in this type of work. However, get a cost estimate before having the work done, and compare that with the cost of buying a good operating generator from a wrecking yard, or a rebuilt one from an auto supply store.

Alternator

Because they run cooler and can produce a greater amount of current, alternators are less trou-

Use an Allen wrench to hold the shaft, and an open-end wrench to remove the nut holding the fan to its shaft. The bolt on the shaft may be a left-hand thread, so check the threading before applying any pressure on the nut. Test the rotor coil with an ohmmeter set to the low scale, by touching a probe to each slip ring. Two to 300 ohms are okay. Check for a short to ground it by touching one probe to one slip ring, the other to the rotor shaft. If the needle moves, there's a defective coil.

ble prone than generators. An alternator should produce enough current to start the car quickly and allow all accessories to be in operation at average speed.

Check alternator output with a voltmeter. It should deliver more than twelve volts to keep the battery charged, and more when accessories are in use.

If not, first check that the belt is tight, and that all wires attached to it are tight and in good condition. Adjust the holding bracket to increase tension on the belt. Check that the pulley is tight on the shaft.

There are rebuild kits that allow you to rebuild the alternator, or you can either buy a good used one from a wrecking yard or a rebuilt unit from a parts store. If you buy a rebuilt unit, remove the fan from your present one, as most rebuilds don't come with the fan.

To remove the alternator, first disconnect the negative cable to the battery. Disconnect and tag wires at the unit. Loosen bolts on the holding bracket, easing tension, so the belt can be removed. Remove holding bolts from the alternator and lift it from the engine compartment.

How and where to buy parts

There are several excellent manufacturers of aftermarket electrical components. These are carried in most auto supply stores. Because you want to make repairs and replacements only once, buy top-quality parts. Some dealers still carry factory-made replacements in stock, a source you don't want to overlook.

Many parts stores offer new alternators, generators and starters, as well as rebuilt units, sold with an allowance or core charge for the old one. Before buying a rebuild, ask about the guarantee.

You'll find ads in national car hobby publications an excellent source. Be sure to specify exactly what you need when answering these ads. Often you can find needed parts at car club flea markets as well. You'll even find newspaper ads for cars being parted out.

Know exactly what you need before buying parts. Keep engine identification information with you for reference.

Refer to factory specifications to make adjustments and repairs correctly and easier. Refer to tolerances and specifications suggested by the manufac-

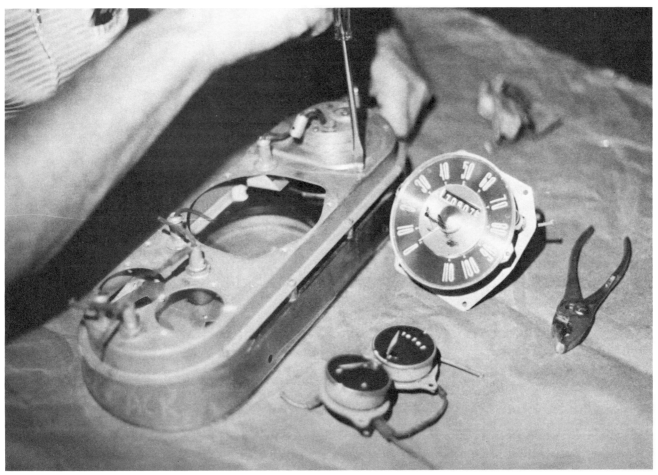

Remove the instrument cluster from the dashboard, after tagging the wires for later match-up. Each dial can be removed separately. Use alcohol and cotton swabs to clean dial faces. Don't use solvent, as it could remove figures and graduations.

When troubleshooting door- or rear-shelf-mounted radio speakers, check fuses and use your test light for a grounded circuit. Look for missing or frayed insulation before removing speaker unit for further testing. Keep speakers clean for better reception.

turer, or as listed in nationally respected car repair manuals.

Changing from a six- to twelve-volt system

With some engine changes, or if you want to install additional electrically operated accessories in your car, you may need or want to change the electrical system from its original six-volt to the more powerful twelve-volt system. This can be done, but you should weigh the cost and the considerable changes the process requires.

First, of course, is the battery. This is the simplest of the changes, providing the battery box, or carrier, will hold what may be a larger unit.

The coil must also be changed to operate on twelve volts. A chalk resistor can be installed on the firewall to handle the increased voltage from the coil to the distributor, so no changes need to be made in the distributor breaker points or the condenser. However, the coil wire must be rerouted to go through the chalk resistor and on to the distributor.

You have some choice as to the generator. You can have it rebuilt to operate on twelve volts at a cost

When removing headlight clusters and other lights, tag wires for later match-up. Clean the metal to which electrical components must ground to complete the circuit. Check and clean the fuse block mountings and the clips holding individual fuses.

Refer to your owners manual and the wiring guide for your car, when testing electric circuits. Look for frayed insulation and spliced wires, as well as for loose connections. Be sure all wires coming through the firewall are protected by rubber grommets.

of about $50 by an automotive electric shop. You can install a twelve-volt same-make generator, new or used, though you may have to make a new holding bracket. A third option is to switch to an alternator, though this, too, will probably require a different bracket.

You can have the starter rebuilt to operate on twelve volts, at a cost of about $75. Your other option is to change to a twelve-volt same-make, new or used starter. Make sure the mounting holes match, and the starter-drive is the same.

You'll have to change all light bulbs to twelve-volt. You can use a resistor on the heater and defroster motors, as well as on the electric windshield wiper, electric windows, seats or other electrically operated accessories.

Many 1950s radios used tubes requiring constant voltage, and you may have some problems using a resistor. Your best bet is to change the radio, though you may have some problem finding one with the same dimensions and dial face.

Gauges and warning lights, such as temperature, fuel and ammeter, use constant voltage and can be

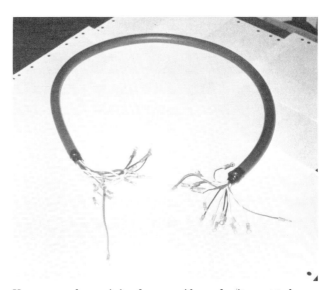

You can make a wiring harness if you don't want to buy a ready-made one. Buy color-coded wire in the correct gauge and pinch-on the connections. Thread the new wires through a piece of rubber or plastic garden hose and tape the ends to hold wires in place.

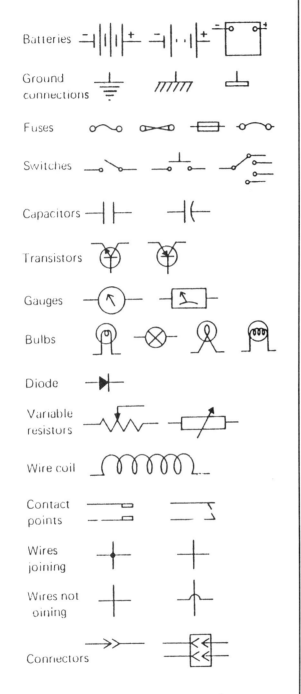

Standard Electrical Symbols

Batteries

Ground connections

Fuses

Switches

Capacitors

Transistors

Gauges

Bulbs

Diode

Variable resistors

Wire coil

Contact points

Wires joining

Wires not oining

Connectors

Check symbols against wiring diagrm for your car.

adapted by installing a resistor to each dial, or to the cluster.

No changes need to be made in the six-volt wires, as a voltage reducer reduces twelve/volts to six/volts, giving 1.5 ohms resistance for four-ampere maximum load, permitting regular six-volt accessories to be used on a twelve-volt system, for under $10. A worst case estimate on a changeover to a twelve-volt system is about $300.

You decide.

USE THE CORRECT GAUGE WIRE FOR EACH JOB	
18-gauge	small bulbs and short leads
16-gauge	taillights, back-up lights, turn signals, gas gauge, stop lights
14-gauge	horn, radio, tape deck, speakers cigarette lighter, heater and defroster and power windows
12-gauge	light switch to fuse block, air conditioning compressor
10-gauge	ammeter to fuse block, alternator generator, battery, headlights and other high power components

Chapter 10

Fuel systems

Gasoline was cheap during the years your project car was manufactured, so minimal attention was given to making the engines stingy with gasoline. On the contrary, these years produced the highest horsepower engines ever fitted to US production cars.

The switch to new high-compression engines gained momentum during the fifties, requiring changes in carburetor design and air induction. A safety-conscious public became aware of gasoline tanks located dangerously near the rear bumper, causing manufacturers to change tank locations or provide safety shields for tank protection.

How it works

The fuel system starts with the tank, mounted toward the rear on all but Corvair, and includes gas lines, fuel pump, carburetor and intake manifold.

The system stores gasoline, sends it to the engine on demand, then supplies it to the cylinders through the intake system, mixed with the correct amount of air.

On all but smaller engines of these years, two-throat carburetors were used. Big, powerful engines were fitted with four-throat carburetors. Throat, or barrel are just other names for the venturi, a tube slightly constricted in the middle, through which air is mixed with gasoline and fed into the intake manifold passages. To equalize distribution of the air/fuel mixture on multi-cylinder engines, two- or four-barrel carburetors were fitted.

Two-barrel carburetors are essentially a pair of single-barrel carburetors incorporated into one casting and working together. A common choke plate covers both venturis. The throttle plates operate on a single shaft, and a common float bowl feeds both barrels.

Four-barrel carburetors are basically two, double-barrel compound or progressive carburetors joined in one casting. At low engine speeds the engine operates on the primary two barrels. Under heavy loads, or on demand, the progressive linkage causes the secondary throttle plates to spring open. The choke plate may cover the primary venturis only, or there may be two choke plates covering all four barrels, with choke linkage that operates them together.

Troubleshooting

If the engine turns over and has a strong spark, but won't start, first check the fuel supply. If the tank contains gasoline, remove the air filter and look into the carburetor while pumping the throttle linkage; you should see a steady stream of gasoline. Remember that gasoline weakens the longer it remains unused, so you might want to add fresh gasoline to the tank.

When the engine is cold, the choke plate, which looks like a damper, should be nearly closed. At normal operating temperature, the choke plate should be open.

If the choke is working and gasoline enters the throat, the engine may be flooded. Hold the gas pedal to the floor for a few minutes, then use the starter while the pedal is down. Don't pump the pedal.

If you didn't see gasoline in the carburetor when you pumped the throttle, remove the fuel line at the carburetor, and aim it into a can or bottle. Have someone operate the starter. The engine should pump a steady flow. If not, the problem may be a clogged filter or faulty fuel pump.

With the fuel line disconnected from the carburetor, crank the engine. If no gasoline spurts from the line, remove the inline filter. If gasoline now flows, the problem is a dirty filter.

If no gasoline pumped through the line with the filter removed, disconnect the line at the inlet side of the pump. Blow through the fuel line. You should be able to blow air through the line, and air bubbles should be heard at the gas tank filler neck. If bubbles are heard when blowing through the line, the line was probably not clogged, so the fuel pump is faulty and must be replaced or repaired. If no bubbles are heard,

73

Disconnect the gas lines and electrical connections from the sending unit when removing the tank for repairs. Because fumes remain in an empty tank, it's safer to have repairs made by a professional. Sealers for pinpoint leaks must be used cautiously, as directed.

either the fuel pickup is clogged, or there's an air leak in the fuel line.

Tests for individual fuel system components are needed to determine which part is at fault, and if adjustment or repairs can be made. If not, replacement is necessary.

Gas tank

For the gauge to read correctly, gas tanks must be free of large dents. For safety reasons they must be free of even small leaks. The cap must fit snugly and the vent must allow air to fill the space used by the fuel consumed.

Gasoline may have evaporated or lost much of its power if the car has sat unused for a long period. If the cover is missing, dirt and water may have entered the tank, causing sludge and tiny rust holes.

There are cleaners for removing scale and sediment. Use sealants to plug pinpoint holes, but follow directions carefully. Serious leaks must be repaired by welding, with the tank removed from the car.

To remove the tank, block the front wheels and put jack stands under the rear frame. Disconnect the gas line. Tag and disconnect wires to the gas gauge. Remove the bolts in the holding straps, or from the flanges around the edges of the tank.

Caution: Explosive vapors remain in empty tanks. Have repairs made at a qualified repair shop.

Fuel lines

Make a careful inspection of the fuel lines. If there are any abrasions or crimps, the line should be

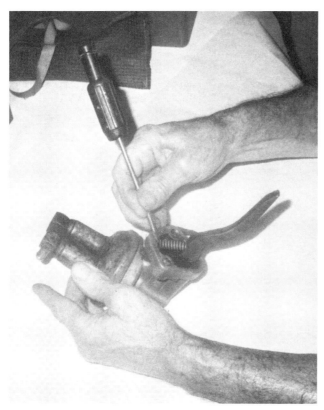

Disconnect the gas line from the tank and the line from the pump to the carburetor before removing bolts holding the pump to the engine. Use a screwdriver to pry out the spring between the actuating arm and casting of a mechanical fuel pump for disassembly.

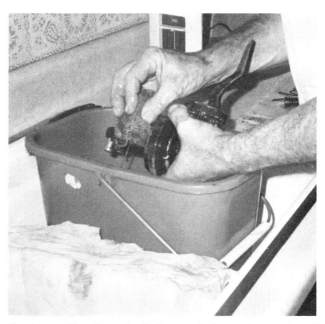

Drain gasoline from the fuel pump before using steel wool in a strong solution of household detergent and water to clean oily accumulations from the fuel pump. Rinse with clear water and wipe it dry before disassembly. Check for wear at the engine end of the actuating arm.

replaced. Check the fittings; they must be tight and leak-free. Grommets must protect any line passing through holes in the frame. Small clips, holding the line in place, must be tight to prevent leaks in fittings from vibrations.

Fuel pump

Your car will have either an electric or mechanical fuel pump. Electric pumps may be mounted along the gas line, or near the tank or engine. Mechanical pumps are bolted to the engine and operated by an arm or rod from a lobe on the camshaft.

Mechanical pumps are simple devices made up of a spring-loaded diaphragm and two one-way valves. When the actuating arm raises the diaphragm, gasoline is drawn into the chamber. When the diaphragm is lowered, fuel is sent to the carburetor.

New and rebuilt pumps are available from auto supply stores, or you can buy a good used one at a salvage yard. Rebuild kits are available for both electric and mechanical pumps.

When installing a fuel pump, be sure to prime it after it is in place, or it may not have anything to pump.

Cleaning the carburetor

The carburetor may need only a thorough cleaning, instead of an overhaul. Remove the air cleaner, and disconnect and plug the gas line with a golf tee or self-tapping screw. Attach a hose from the cleaning kit to the carburetor and run the engine until the cleaner is gone. (This works better than pouring a can of carburetor cleaner into the gas tank.)

If this treatment allows you to adjust the carburetor for smooth performance and steady idle, it should be all that is necessary. However, if the cleaner doesn't give these results, because of a leaky or faulty accelerator pump, worn gaskets, deteriorated float or clogged metering needles, a carburetor overhaul is necessary.

Rebuilding the carburetor

To meet the demands for the higher speeds and sudden bursts of power that the new engines of these years offered, multi-barrel carburetors were developed and fitted to many cars.

Carburetor rebuilding is a complicated and delicate job. There are many small parts that interact with other small parts, making disassembly risky. Fragile springs and gaskets have to be handled carefully. However, if you have patience and average mechanical skills, and are willing to work slowly and carefully, you should be able to rebuild a carburetor from these years, saving a lot of money.

To remove it from the car, first disconnect the gas line from the fuel pump, then the vacuum line from

Use solvent to clean the inside parts of the pump when disassembling it at your workbench. Buy the correct rebuild kit and follow repair directions carefully. The diaphragm, gaskets, springs and other parts are fragile. Be sure the filter screen is clean also.

Disconnect gas lines, vacuum tube to the automatic choke and throttle controls when removing the carburetor from the intake manifold for repair. Be careful not to damage threads on the mounting bolts. Plan on using a new gasket between the carburetor and intake manifold.

Clean the carburetor with solvent and disassemble it at your workbench. Many carburetor castings are made of pot metal, and threads will strip easily and parts may break if too much pressure is applied. Note the order in which you remove the many small parts.

the manifold to the automatic choke. If the car has a manual choke, disconnect that at the carburetor. Disconnect the throttle control linkage, so nothing is connected to the carburetor. Remove the four nuts holding the carburetor to the intake manifold, and lift it straight up.

Cover the openings in the intake manifold to keep dirt out of the intake system. Use a golf tee or a self-tapping screw to keep the fuel line clean.

After degreasing, move it to a clean, well-lighted workbench. Usually, small open-end wrenches, screwdrivers and pliers will handle the job.

Stampings on the carburetor or a small, attached metal tag indicate the make and model number. Because many cars used carburetors made by the same manufacturer, you should have no trouble locating the correct rebuild kit. Refer to the appendix for interchange information.

Cut some blocks of wood and drill holes matching the venturi holes in the carburetor flange. These blocks should be high enough to allow the throttle plate to be in the open position and allow control rods to operate freely.

Note the order in which you start disassembling the unit. Some beginners find it helpful to take some snapshots from each of the four sides of the carburetor before they take it apart. They use these as visual reminders of where and how outside parts and controls fit.

Clean small parts with solvent, using a strainer in a large can. Store cleaned parts in a compartmented container to keep them separated. Use string tags to identify certain parts for later match-up.

Use solvent and pipe cleaners on small passages and tubes. A compressed air canister helps force out sediment loosened by the solvent.

Disconnect and remove the bi-metallic choke plate spring. Remove connecting rods to the vacuum diaphragm. Look for small clips and pins in connecting links from the top part of the carburetor to the accelerator pump and choke plate.

Remove machine screws to separate the sections. Many carburetors are made of pot metal and won't stand much force. Use solvent on the threads. If parts stick, tap them lightly with a rubber mallet.

As you remove the float, shake it lightly. If it has leaked, you'll hear gasoline sloshing inside. If the carburetor is dry when you disassemble it, submerge the float in water and look for air bubbles. Leaking floats must be replaced.

With the float out of the chamber, unscrew the needle valve and threaded seat. Remove the accelerator pump, as you'll be replacing the rubber cap on the plunger.

With the main metering jets, valve assembly and venturi cluster exposed, clean the inside thoroughly.

When removing the idle mixture and idle speed needles, remember the number of turns it takes to

Use solvent to loosen stubborn machine screws and fittings. You can't put a carburetor in a vise, so hold it firmly when removing small parts. Because of intricate design and interconnected parts and controls, disassembly must be logical and deliberate.

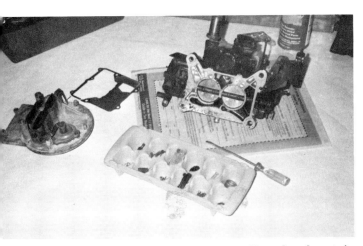

Even two-throat carburetors are complicated and contain many parts. Usually only screwdrivers, small open-end or socket wrenches and pliers are all that are necessary for disassembly. Store small parts in a plastic ice cube tray to keep them separate.

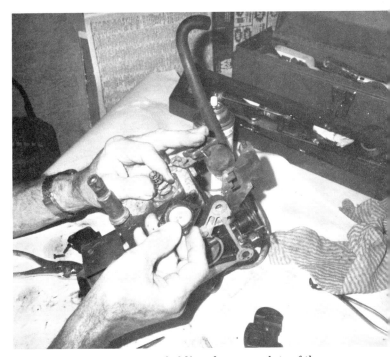

Remove the machine screws holding the cover plate of the power valve. The diaphragm is spring loaded, so expect it to pop up when pressure is released. The carburetor castings contain many built-in fuel lines and passages, which must be cleaned for efficiency.

77

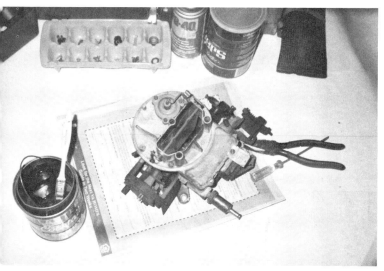

Many inner parts can be cleaned by soaking in solvent and brushing with a small paintbrush. Handle all gaskets carefully. Use solvent and air pressure to clean screened filters before replacing them. Use light oil to lubricate linkages.

When installing small parts, it often helps to dip them in solvent to match threads. Hand turn machine screws and bolts before using a screwdriver or wrench to tighten them. Don't apply too much pressure, or you may strip the threads in the casting.

unscrew them from the housing. You'll need to use the same number of turns to put the carburetor in essentially the same adjustment as it was before disassembly. Plan on fine-tuning it later.

Follow the instructions and illustrations in the rebuild kit closely. Work slowly, as you fit new and newly cleaned parts. Be careful tightening the machine screws that hold the sections together, as too much pressure can strip threads in the pot metal castings. Handle all gaskets lightly.

To test the float for leakage, remove the cover on the float chamber. Remove the needle valve which is activated by the float to control gasoline flow into the float chamber. Remove the pivot pin and immerse the float in water to check for air leaks.

Use a screwdriver to hold the throttle plates to their pivot shafts, when assembling the carburetor. Be sure the accelerator linkage allows the plate to leave both the vacuum passage and idle air bleeds open when the throttle plate is closed.

When installing the newly rebuilt carburetor, use a new gasket where it sits on the manifold. Fit the carburetor in place and finger tighten the nuts before securing them. Connect the gas line from the fuel pump, and the hose from the manifold to the automatic choke. Attach all control rods and cables. Make sure all connections are tight.

Before attaching the air cleaner, and with the engine idling, adjust the needle valves for smooth running and idling. Refer to the manufacturer's recommendations, when making fine-tuning adjustments. Later you can have the exhaust gases analyzed at a tune-up shop to check on your work. Sources for specific information on carburetors and carburetor rebuilding are included in the appendix.

Automatic choke

Automatic chokes replaced hand-operated chokes in the 1950s. A bi-metallic spring is attached to one end of the choke plate; the other end of the choke plate is connected by rods to a vacuum-operated diaphragm and throttle plate linkage.

When the engine is cold, the spring is tightly coiled, closing the choke. When the engine warms, the spring uncoils, forcing a vacuum-operated piston to turn the shaft, opening the choke plate. Other linkage

After rebuilding and adjusting the carburetor, check all gas line fittings and controls. Make sure the inline filter is clean. Install a new filter in the air cleaner, and connect any air hose to front-end sheet metal to complete the job.

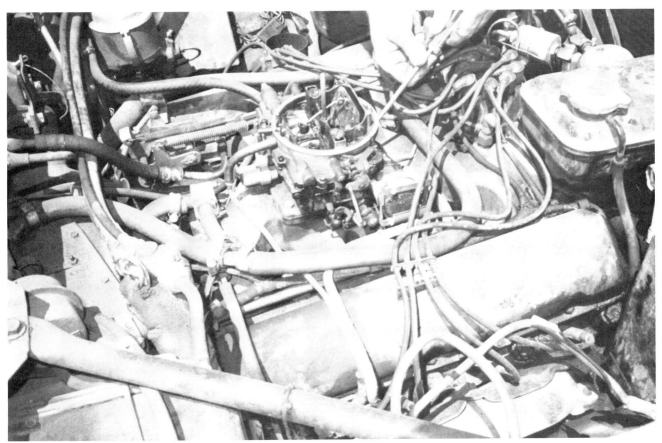

With the engine at fast idle, use a screwdriver to adjust the idling air/fuel mixture jet for smooth running. When you *have this adjustment right, set the linkage to get the correct idle speed, which should be about 800 rpm.*

Some manufacturers installed glass filter cups on carburetors in the early 1950s. Loosen the thumb screw to release the bail holding the cup in place. Clean the screened filter at the top. If the line to the tank is clogged, disconnect it at the fitting and blow through it.

on the choke shaft is connected to throttle plate controls.

If the automatic choke malfunctions, first check the vacuum from the manifold. Refer to your engine's specs. If there isn't sufficient vacuum, the piston moving the shaft can't work. Check the tubing from the manifold to the vacuum diaphragm. Connections must be tight at both ends, and the tubing should not be damaged.

Remove the screws holding the choke housing in place. Check to see in which slot the spring is fitted. Spray both spring and housing with solvent. Check the choke plate shaft to be sure the piston can move freely in the vacuum chamber. Parts must not bind.

Fit the spring end into whichever slot makes the choke plate close tightly. Set the pointer to the correct index mark on the housing and tighten the screws.

If the choke plate still won't close, replace the unit, as no repairs can be made to the vacuum diaphragm.

Switching to a four-barrel

To get extra speed and performance from your engine, you may want to replace the original two-barrel carburetor with a four-barrel. In most cases this can be done, but it requires more than just swapping the carburetor itself. You must change the intake manifold to accommodate the four venturis. If a four-barrel was originally offered on your engine as an option, there'll be no problem changing intake manifolds. Even if the four-barrel wasn't offered on your particular engine, you may find an intake manifold from another engine manufactured by the same parent company, that will fit your engine block.

On certain valve-in-block straight sixes and eights, two carburetors were used; each carburetor fed half of the cylinders. In these instances, you may be able to locate the manifold used with the twin carburetors and make a change to the more powerful combination.

Only on low-production, long-orphaned makes should you have any trouble locating a replacement manifold to hold the larger carburetor. There may be minor problems you'll have to solve, though. The throttle linkage may have to be changed or modified, and some control cables rerouted. The vacuum line from the manifold to the carburetor will have to be fitted. The gas line from the fuel pump to the carburetor may have to be changed. There should be no problem, however, with the fuel pump supplying enough fuel for the new carburetor.

Study factory specifications to learn if a four-barrel will fit your engine block. Talk to owners of similar cars equipped with four-barrels. Refer to exchange manuals. Learn if the manufacturer changed the bore or stroke, or used a different camshaft and changed the timing in the four-barrel option.

Armed with the information you need, browse the want ads for high-performance parts, and cars and engines being parted out. Read ads in car hobby publications. Attend any car club flea markets that are nearby. Look in salvage yards; you may be able to pick up a four-barrel and intake manifold from the same model car.

Make sure the vacuum ports are clear when you use a rebuild kit, so the vacuum-operated automatic choke diaphragm can operate properly. Two-barrel units cover both venturis with a common choke plate, and a common float bowl serves both barrels.

Fuel-injection systems

In the late 1960s, some manufacturers offered a fuel-injection system as an extra-cost option for those who wanted extra performance.

Fuel injection provides more power and uses less fuel than a carburetor. It squirts a precisely measured amount of fuel, either directly into the combustion chamber, or against an intake valve. The components are an electric fuel pump, filters, fuel metering unit, fuel lines and injector nozzles, and a vacuum tube between the manifold and the metering unit.

It is a simple system, but there's little you can do to repair it yourself. Take the car to a qualified mechanic for this work.

Removing the intake manifold

Because of differences in engine construction, directions may vary somewhat. This is how I approach the task. Prop the hood wide open. Remove the air cleaner. If the heater hoses are in the way, they must be disconnected. This may mean draining the radiator. Disconnect the gas line and the vacuum tube to the automatic choke. Disconnect the throttle linkage and the wires to any instrument sending unit. Remove the nuts holding the carburetor to the manifold and lift it, along with any gasket or spacer, off the engine.

Use a socket wrench to remove the nuts or bolts holding the manifold to the block. In some cars you'll need to remove the valve covers. If the distributor shaft protrudes through the manifold, it must be removed. If so, note the position of the blade end of the shaft, as it must go back in the same position to fire correctly.

With everything attaching the manifold to the block removed, grasp the carburetor-holding studs and lift the manifold straight up. In some cases, you may need to use a pry bar to separate the two. The manifold is a heavy casting, so handle it carefully.

Directions on cleaning and rebuilding carburetors have been covered on previous pages. The carburetor you're going to use should have had this treatment already.

Installing the manifold

Have a new set of gaskets on hand. Use a blade and solvent to clean off any remnants of the old gaskets, either on your engine or on the replacement manifold. Both must be cleaned for an airtight mating.

Degrease the replacement manifold and paint it the correct color, if needed. Coat mating edges lightly with gasket cement.

Fit the large gasket in place, and position the intake gaskets. Place the manifold and finger tighten the nuts or bolts, before securing them tightly. If you had to remove the distributor shaft, be sure to position it correctly and tighten in place. Connect any instrument sending wires; then connect the heater hoses and controls.

Fit any gasket or spacer on the manifold holding studs and fit the replacement carburetor. Make all the necessary connections, as outlined, so the carburetor can function.

You may need to prime the carburetor for its first start. Have a fire extinguisher handy in case of a backfire through the venturis.

Install the air cleaner, check the radiator coolant and all connections, and the job should be done.

Chapter 11

Cooling system

Styling changes in front-end design on cars of these years often resulted in lower hood lines and less direct air movement to radiators, causing engineers to rethink their past solutions to cooling problems.

The high-compression, high-revving engines developed during these years, many with air conditioning compressors and other engine-driven accessories, put added demands on the cooling system.

How it works

Your car's cooling system is designed to keep the engine at its most efficient temperature. Liquid is pumped to the top of the radiator and is cooled, as it flows to the bottom, before being returned to the engine.

A pulley-driven pump keeps the coolant moving. Also, a pulley-driven fan draws air through the radia-

tor, helping the cooling process at slow speeds. A thermostat holds the coolant in the engine block, until it reaches a preset temperature, before sending it to the radiator.

Often, a thermostatically controlled clutch on the fan releases the fan from its pulley and lets it free-wheel, when air temperature flowing through the radiator is 150 degrees F or 65 degrees C.

Starting in the late fifties, most cars changed to a pressure system, in which the radiator cap allows the coolant's temperature to rise until it reaches 14 psi, before opening a valve sending the coolant into an overflow tank. When the temperature drops, a small inlet valve allows air into the holding tank, letting the coolant reenter the radiator's expansion tank.

Because of lower front-end designs and more powerful engines, cooling systems have become more complex. Thermostatically controlled fans, some with flexible blades, are hidden behind shrouds that are fitted to direct and concentrate airflow through the radiator.

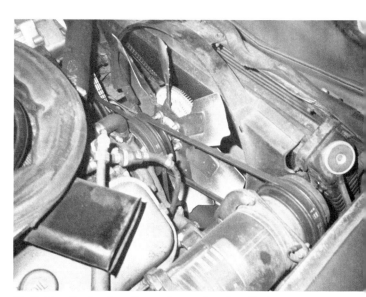

To lighten the load on the engine and reduce fuel consumption, a thermostatically controlled fan clutch releases the fan from its pulley and lets it freewheel when radiator air is less than 150 degrees F. If the silicone clutch coupling leaks, the unit must be replaced.

On many automatic transmission cars, part of the radiator core cools transmission fluid sent to and from that section of the radiator by small tubes.

Radiator

Your car may have a crossflow or a downflow radiator, the former being designed to conform with lower hood lines, yet still handle the increased cooling needs of high-displacement engines. The downflow type was used on small-engine cars that hadn't switched to low front-end designs.

Water pump

The water pump is the heart of the cooling system. Mounted in the block or cylinder head, it is driven by the fan belt and circulates water from the engine block to the top of the radiator's expansion tank. As the coolant flows to the bottom of the radiator, it is drawn back to the engine block by the water pump's action.

Fan

Mounted close to the radiator, the fan's function is to draw air through the radiator at slow speeds. The same belt that operates the water pump usually operates the fan.

Thermostat

Mounted between the water pump outlet and the upper radiator hose, the thermostat holds coolant in

With the radiator removed from the car, you can make a thorough inspection to determine the location of leaks. Many cars use a crossflow radiator in which the coolant enters at the top and flows across, rather than down, to the collecting tank for reuse.

Disconnect the fan shroud and remove the bolts holding the radiator core to the front-end sheet metal to lift it from the car. It usually isn't necessary to remove the air conditioner condenser. Be careful not to damage either the radiator or condenser cooling fins.

Leaking radiators, or radiators that can't be cleaned by a readily available commerecial flush, should be repaired and cleaned in a caustic solution at a radiator repair shop. You can save money by removing and later installing the repaired radiator yourself.

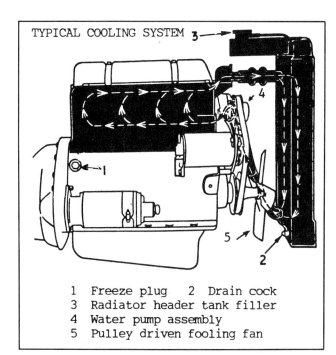

TYPICAL COOLING SYSTEM

1 Freeze plug   2 Drain cock
3 Radiator header tank filler
4 Water pump assembly
5 Pulley driven fooling fan

the engine block until it reaches a preset temperature, before opening and allowing the water pump to send it to the radiator.

Hoses

On most cars there are two radiator hoses, one at the top of the radiator and the other at the bottom. Their function is to allow the hot coolant to be pumped from the engine block to the radiator and carry the cooled liquid back to the engine block.

Fan belt

The fan belt transmits the engine's power, taken from a pulley on the front of the crankshaft, and drives the water pump and fan. The same belt, or other belts, may drive other power-operated engine components.

Troubleshooting

There are three reasons for the cooling system to malfunction. The first is a mechanical problem caused by failure of a component. The second is that the engine is putting out more heat than the system can handle. The third is damage to one of the components.

First, check the coolant level when the radiator is cool. If the level is low, fill it to the recommended level and look for obvious leaks in the radiator, hoses and around the water pump. Also, look for leaks around the cylinder head. Though you'd notice if the engine has been misfiring, caused by coolant bypassing the cylinder head gasket and leaking into the engine base, check the oil dipstick, looking for drops of water. If there are no leaks at these checkpoints, fill the radiator to the recommended level and drive the car for a reasonable time, keeping close check on the heat gauge or light.

If the coolant is low when you check it next time, the cooling system may be clogged, causing coolant to spill out of the overflow tube. Check by squeezing the upper hose while the engine is running. It should become hot and pressurized in a few minutes. If you don't feel coolant moving, check for a bad thermostat or faulty water pump.

Check to see if the fan belt is tight and not worn or frayed. Look for spots on the radiator core indicating high-temperature or high-pressure leaks. If you see these, the radiator needs repair.

Check if coolant is circulating to the heater by pinching the heater hoses. If you can't feel flow, one of the hoses may be clogged. If the temperature of each

You can buy already reconditioned and guaranteed radiators for many cars at radiator repair shops on a trade-in basis and install them yourself. Always use new upper and lower hoses and pressure release cap for best results.

Radiator repair shops carry a large supply of upper and lower collecting tanks, filler necks and side and bottom brackets, so any car's radiator can be repaired. Compare repair cost estimates with the cost of buying a tested replacement from a salvage yard.

When installing a replacement radiator, spray it with a thin coat of black paint, taking care not to clog the air passages between the cooling fins. Bolt it securely in place before attaching any shroud or air ducting. Replace a frayed or worn fan belt.

hose is much different, the heater core may be clogged.

If the engine overheats after these tests, you should first flush the system. Choose a recommended flush and follow the directions. This should clear the radiator core. Check the coolant recovery system for worn hoses and for a malfunctioning air inlet valve. Also check the radiator pressure cap. *Do not remove it when the radiator is hot.*

Check the freeze core plugs, located in the engine block. If one of these leaks, it must be replaced.

Bugs lodged in the radiator core can collect dirt and, in time, keep air from coming through. This problem differs from a clogged core, in that flushing won't help. Remove the fan shroud and using your garden hose, adjusted to a fine spray, turn up the pressure and force the bugs and dirt out of the core. Spray only from the engine compartment toward the front of the car.

Check the thermostat by removing it and suspending it in a pan of cold water. Use a candy thermometer to show the temperature as the water heats. The thermostat should open within five to ten degrees

After draining the radiator, loosen the clamp and remove the upper radiator hose. In some cars, you can remove the thermostat at this point in the first stage in repairing the radiator or water pump. Have replacement parts on hand before starting the job.

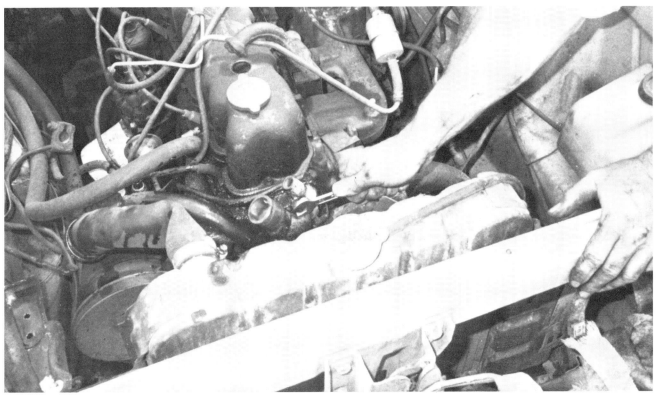

Loosen the alternator or generator bracket so you can remove the fan from its pulley. Use an open-end or socket wrench to remove the bolts holding the pump casting to the engine block. Take the pump to your workbench for disassembly.

Have the correct rebuild kit on hand when you take the pump apart. Follow directions with the kit and clean the parts you'll be reusing in the rebuild. Tap against a piece of wood when fitting replacement bearings. Use gasket cement sparingly.

of the temperature marked on the unit. If it doesn't, it must be replaced.

If you noticed a leaking gasket around the water pump, remove the old gasket and clean the mating surfaces on the water pump and engine. Install a new washer. If you use gasket cement, use it sparingly to avoid getting any in the system.

A simple test to see if the water pump is moving the coolant is to remove the radiator cap and start the cold engine. Within a few minutes you should see water flowing into the expansion tank at the top of the radiator.

You can buy new or rebuilt water pumps at auto supply stores, or a good one from a wrecking yard. You can also rebuild the present one by using a rebuild kit and following directions and illustrations for installing it.

Don't overlook the dashboard-mounted heat control valve. If the engine continually overheats, or

gets to the operating temperature slowly, this may be the problem. A faulty valve or control cable must be repaired or replaced.

Dragging brakes can put an extra load on the engine, causing it to overheat. Test by getting the car to about 30 mph, then put it in neutral. If it slows quickly, instead of coasting normally, the brakes may be dragging. When the car has stopped, feel each wheel. If they're hot, or one is hotter than the others, the brake system must be checked.

Another often overlooked cause of engine overheating is excess backpressure in the exhaust system. If an exhaust pipe is crimped, or the muffler jammed, these can impede the flow of exhaust gases, making the engine work harder and overheat. Trace the exhaust system, looking for dents and crimps. Any damaged component must be replaced.

Review the results of your troubleshooting tests to determine which of the problems can be repaired

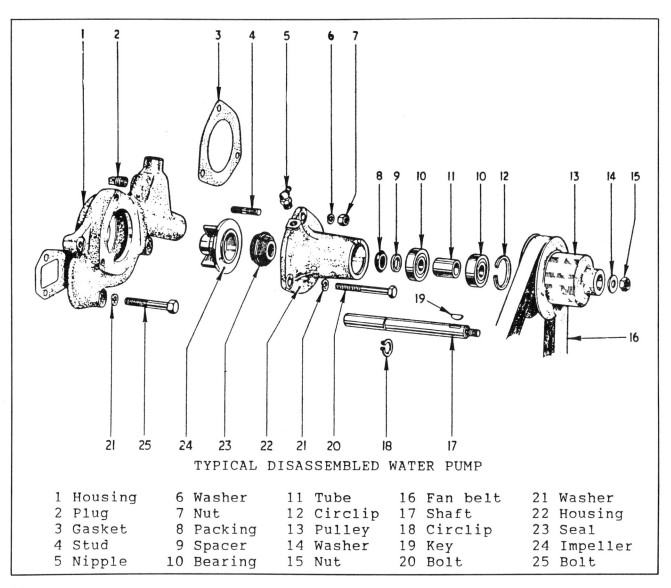

TYPICAL DISASSEMBLED WATER PUMP

1 Housing	6 Washer	11 Tube	16 Fan belt	21 Washer
2 Plug	7 Nut	12 Circlip	17 Shaft	22 Housing
3 Gasket	8 Packing	13 Pulley	18 Circlip	23 Seal
4 Stud	9 Spacer	14 Washer	19 Key	24 Impeller
5 Nipple	10 Bearing	15 Nut	20 Bolt	25 Bolt

Here is an important part of the cooling system you won't see unless you're making engine repairs. Water passages in the cylinder heads and block often become clogged with scale and rust. Many times a good flush will loosen scale, postponing scraping water passages clean.

Corvair's air cooling system requires little attention. Remove the air duct and use compressed air to clean the cooling fins on the cylinders. Be sure the long drive belt is in good condition, and adjust the alternator bracket to keep the belt tight.

and which can only be corrected by replacing the component.

Removing the radiator

To remove the radiator for repair or replacement, first drain the system. Remove the hoses, cutting them if necessary. You may need to remove any bolted-on sheet metal in front of the radiator. You may also need to remove the fan shroud on some cars. You should then be able to lift the radiator up and out of the engine compartment.

Repairing the water pump

Have a replacement pump or a rebuild kit on hand. Drain the system and remove the belt from its pulley. Remove the holding bolts and pull the housing, including the pulley, from the engine.

Follow directions in the rebuild kit. Remove the pulley and clean the entire unit with a degreaser. Pry out existing seals and packings. Clean and lubricate the shaft with water pump grease. Fit the new seals and packings. Tap the old bearing out of place and the new one in. Clean mating parts of the pump and engine and install a new gasket. If you use gasket cement, use it sparingly to keep it out of the system.

Slip the fan belt over the pulley and tighten the bolts on the housing. Pour a can of water pump lubricant into the radiator before you fill the system.

If the thermostat needs replacement, remove the old one, while working on the water pump. Clean the rim on which the thermostat sits and insert the replacement.

Air-cooled engines

If you chose a small, gutsy Corvair as your project car, it has a powerful, air-cooled engine. Fins cast into the base and cylinder head provide extra cooling surfaces, without the need for liquid coolant and the necessary components of a liquid-cooled engine.

A belt-driven fan draws in outside air and forces it through ducts past the fins, drawing away heated air.

In order to do their job, the fins must be kept clean. Periodic high-pressure air hosing will remove dirt and grime accumulated on the fins.

It is imperative that the long belt that drives the cooling system be in good condition and tight. Have a helper operate the starter intermittently, so you can examine the belt carefully. Look for any splits or cracks, frayed edges and ply separation. Also, look for any bent pulleys. The pulleys must operate easily on their shafts.

The fins on the cylinder blocks must be clean. Use compressed air to blow away accumulated dirt. The air ducts and baffles must be clean and securely in place to do their jobs properly.

The finned oil cooler and transmission fluid cooler on automatics are within the air duct housing. Use a degreaser to remove any oily deposits, which can hold dirt, causing a loss in their cooling ability.

The Corvair's cooling system is efficient and simple. It takes but a little time to keep it at maximum efficiency.

Chapter 12

Exhaust system

Exhaust systems had to change as cars became lower, some with unit body/frame construction. Larger capacity engines produced more exhaust. As V-8s replaced inline eights, crossover pipes had to be accommodated, either under the hood or beneath the car. Resonators were added to help tune out engine noise. Some tail pipes were even vented through the bumper, giving more ground clearance, though this was more of a styling gimmick than an engineering advance.

How it works

The last upward stroke in the four-cycle engine is the exhaust stroke. This forces the burned air/fuel mixture out of the exhaust valve into the exhaust manifold, where it travels through a lead-in pipe to the muffler and farther on into the resonator and out the tail pipe.

The system has three main functions. It must carry the noxious fumes away from the passengers. It

Though the exhaust system starts at the exhaust manifold, the first part you'll be concerned with is the junction of the lead-in pipe with the manifold. Because of extreme heat, the nuts may seem welded on the manifold studs. Let solvent soak into the threads.

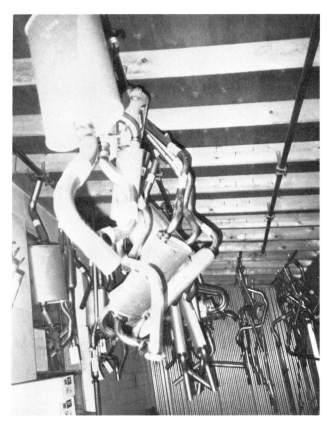

Save money by buying a ready-made exhaust system for your car. If you can't find one, you can buy the components you'll need. Factory specifications furnish information on the recommended backpressure. You can buy the sections you'll need.

also must cool the gases to acceptable levels. The third is to quiet exhaust shock wave noises. To accomplish these, a pipe carries the gases from the manifold to the muffler, where they pass through a series of baffles and perforated plates to cool and quiet the exhaust.

Many cars have a second, smaller muffler called a resonator, to tune out additional noises and cool the mixture further.

The tailpipe carries the exhaust to the rear of the car, where the car's motion helps carry it away. Flexible hangers along the system compensate for engine vibrations and hold the system securely.

Troubleshooting

Some problems with the exhaust system can be determined by sight and sound from outside the car. A lot of exhaust noise means a leak in the system. This could come from a faulty gasket where the exhaust manifold mates with the engine block, as well as rusted-through pipes and muffler. You may see fumes coming from under the car, a further indication of leaks along the system.

The next step is to get under the car and inspect the system from front to back. Any crimped or damaged pipe, rusted-through muffler or a broken weld where the crossover pipe joins means exhaust leaks.

If there are exhaust stains at pipe joints, there are leaks. A damaged muffler, resonator or tail pipe can allow fumes into the car and must be replaced.

Check the clamps, flexible hangers and straps along the line. These must be securely attached to the system and the car's frame to keep engine vibrations from causing leaks. Any that are broken can be replaced easily.

The only safe and permanent repair to the exhaust system is to replace any damaged part. Don't have patches welded on the muffler, or use wrap-on repairs. Stay away from flexible tubing as a replacement for rusted curved pipes, as this won't pass many states' inspection codes.

Sources for parts

You should always use new parts when working on the exhaust system. Muffler specialty shops will furnish the parts you need and often have already assembled systems for many cars. They can fabricate an entire system for orphaned cars, though some of these used exhaust components used on other makes. Many auto supply stores carry mufflers, clamps and attaching hangers. They'll have reference books, so you can get an exact replacement. Stay away from salvage yards for these parts.

Replacing components

Since all but unclamping the manifold or lead-in pipe joint must be done under the car, put the car

When replacing sections of the exhaust system, check the hangers and gaskets to be sure the repaired system will be airtight and yet allow for engine vibrations. Muffler repair shops carry a complete assortment of the parts you'll need.

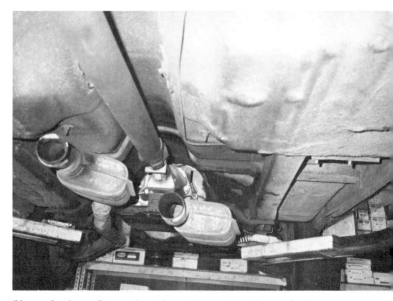

If you don't need to replace the entire system, buy only the parts you'll need. If you feel the system may have been modified over the years, measure the pipe diameter to be sure to get matching components. Use new clamps, and follow inlet/outlet pipe markings.

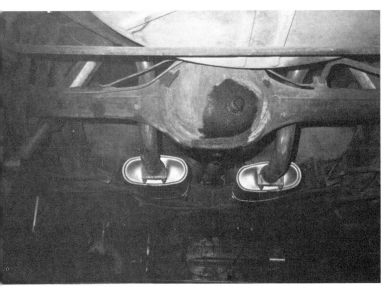

Unless one pipe or muffler has been damaged, if your car has a dual exhaust system, it's better to replace both pipes and mufflers at the same time to equalize backpressure. Place jack stands under the frame high enough so you'll have working room. Wear goggles.

solidly on jack stands, allowing you room to move around.

Caution: To avoid cuts from rusted, jagged metal, use gloves when removing old exhaust pipes. Wear goggles to keep rust particles out of your eyes.

Douse the bolts and nuts with solvent and use a wire-bristled brush to clean threads. Many times, old bolts will have to be cut away, as heat and rust can ruin threads. You may have to use a bolt-cutter or hacksaw, even a small pry bar to remove some of the components.

Lead-in pipes

There may be one or two lead-in pipes, depending upon the manufacturer's design. These clamp to the exhaust manifolds, and run from the engine to the front of the muffler. On many V-type engines, one of these pipes crosses over to join the other pipe just ahead of the muffler.

These pipes are often dented by stones thrown up by the front wheels. In time they may rust out and need replacement. When buying replacement pipes and clamps, be sure to get the gasket that fits between the pipe and manifold.

On some cars, separating and later rejoining the crossover lead-in pipes can be done from top side. The connection where the pipe meets the muffler must be made underneath.

After cleaning the threads, fit a deep socket to the nuts. Use a long drive to loosen the nuts. If they won't budge, you may have to cut the bolts or clamp with a hacksaw. There may not be much room here; work slowly so you don't damage any nearby part.

With the pipes disconnected at the front, remove the hanger and clamp where the pipe enters the muffler. You may need a sling to support the muffler while you do this, as these will not be easy to remove. Once this joint is disconnected, you can pull the pipes from under the car.

When installing the replacement, couple the pipes to the manifold first, then to the muffler. It may

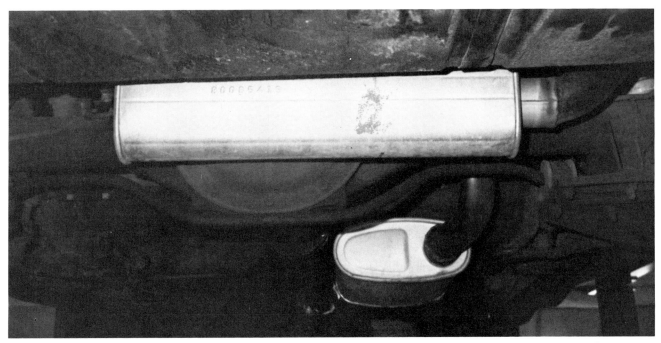

You'll usually need to replace muffler and resonator at the same time. Use solvent and a wire-bristled brush to remove rust on the clamp and hanger threads. You may need to slip a piece of pipe on your socket drive for extra leverage.

help making the muffler connection easier, if you loosen the hangers behind the muffler to provide some back-to-front movement.

Muffler

If you're replacing the muffler, remove the clamps at the front and back. One, or both of these, may be combined with a flexible strap connecting it to the frame. If you can remove the bolts from the clamps on the inlet and outlet, the pipes can be spread and the muffler removed. In many cases these bolts will have to be cut. You may find it easier to remove the bolts holding the hangers to the frame, letting the hangers come off with the muffler, and remove them at your workbench if you plan to reuse them.

Occasionally, you'll have to cut through the inlet and outlet pipes, or even pry the old muffler free. Since you won't be reusing it, it doesn't matter how you get it out.

The muffler has to handle extremely hot and poisonous gases, which are forced out of the combustion chambers several thousand times per minute. These shock waves have to be silenced and cooled before they're passed to the rest of the system. For these reasons, be sure to get the correct muffler for your car's engine displacement. Inlet and outlet ends are marked clearly.

The muffler may be long and heavy. Fashion a sling to support it while you work. When installing the new muffler, you may find it easier to loosen the hangers along the system, so you'll have some back-to-front movement. These should be tightened, once the pipes have been fitted to the muffler.

After muffler pipe

This may also be the tailpipe on some cars, or it may simply run from the muffler to the resonator. Because of the placement of the resonator, this pipe may be irregularly shaped, with the hangers difficult to reach. After cleaning the threads, fit a socket to the nut and, using the longest drive that space will permit, remove the nuts from the hangers or clamps.

If there is a resonator along the line, treat it as another muffler, with inlet and outlet clamps and hangers bolted securely to avoid exhaust leaks and keep it in place. Note inlet and outlet markings, as the resonator must fit only one way. Finger tighten the clamps and hangers to help in positioning the unit. Once it's in position, secure the nuts.

There should be a hanger from a brace under the luggage area, near the end of the car's frame. Some cars mounted the gas tank as the floor of the luggage area, so don't drill any holes to reposition a hanger.

If you're replacing the tailpipe, which is often bent or damaged when backing the car, remove the nuts on the present hanger, or disconnect the hanger from the car's frame and remove it with the old pipe.

You may need only a replacement for the pipe that fits over the rear axle. If muffler shops don't have one on hand, they can form the bends you'll need for a perfect fit. Slide the replacement over the old pipe and clamp it securely to prevent leakage.

When fitting a new resonator and tailpipe, make sure the flexible hangers are in good condition. Extend the tailpipe beyond the end of the car's body to keep fumes out of the car. Use an open-end or socket wrench to tighten all nuts and bolts.

Fit the new hanger over the replacement pipe and finger tighten the nuts, until you have the pipe positioned correctly before securing them.

To carry the exhaust fumes down and away from the car and to protect the rear bumper from exhaust stains, many owners attach a plated extension to the tailpipe.

Changes in the system

If you changed your engine for one with greater displacement, or made significant changes in carburetion and the valvetrain, you may need a different size muffler to handle these changes. Refer to factory specs to determine this.

You may want to change a single exhaust system on a V-type engine for twin exhausts. This can often be done without having to change exhaust manifolds, by discarding the original lead-in pipe that included a crossover joint and replacing it with two lead-in pipes that feed directly into separate mufflers.

Make sure there is room under the car for two lead-in pipes, two mufflers and two resonator/tailpipes. If the current system passes through openings in frame cross-members or other braces, there must be corresponding openings on the other side. Make sure there is room for a pipe on each side of the luggage compartment.

You must also be sure the additional pipe doesn't run so close to a gas line or fuel pump that its heat could cause fuel to evaporate before it reaches the engine.

Once you're sure there are no obstacles to adding a second muffler and pipes, determine the capacity of the mufflers you'll need. The original was designed to handle twice the volume of exhaust gases. The new ones will need to handle only half that amount, so can be smaller and with less backpressure. Knowledgeable people at muffler shops can advise you on the correct muffler. You should also check with your motor vehicle bureau, so you won't get stopped for having an exhaust system that exceeds legal decibel limits.

When installing the second system, try to follow pipe lengths and curves, making it as close to the original as possible. This is easier on separate body/chassis cars, than on unit body/frame construction.

If you've disconnected any part of the exhaust system to work on the transmission, universal joint or drive shaft, be sure all clamps and brackets are firmly reattached to prevent vibration from cracking a pipe and causing exhaust leaks.

Drill and mount the same number of hangers, placing them correctly and securely. Tighten all clamps so the second system is as safe and rattle-free as the original.

Tailpipe as a stethoscope

The tailpipe also acts as a stethoscope, through which you can gauge some aspects of the engine's performance. Missing or irregular exhaust notes can be caused by poor carburetor adjustments or ignition problems. Blue smoke indicates oil consumption, either through worn piston rings or faulty oil seals on valve guides. A sooty residue can indicate automatic transmission fluid sucked through the modulator, or brake fluid drawn through vacuum hoses into the combustion chamber from a defective power brake booster.

For safety's sake, as well as for efficient, quiet performance, make sure the exhaust system is in perfect condition. The cost is small, and though the work may be tiring and at times frustrating, it's worth it.

If hangers or brackets become loose, close-fitting parts can rub against each other causing wear, as well as annoying noises. Check the clearance between the muffler and spare tire well, gasoline tank or other undercar components.

Many V-type engines have a crossover pipe just ahead of the clutch assembly. Check these for leaks, and that vibration, because of loose hangers and clamps, hasn't caused the Y-shaped joint to leak. You can spot exhaust leaks by a sooty deposit on the pipes.

Chapter 13

Transmission and clutch

The clutch on manual transmission cars and the torque converter on automatics, connect and disconnect the engine's power on demand. These mechanical combinations also make various gear ratios available, as well as a change in directions.

At first, automatic transmissions were offered only as an extra-cost option. Buyer demand in the 1950s and 1960s caused automatics to be offered as standard equipment on many cars, replacing the dependable and efficient syncromesh transmission.

With every manufacturer offering at least one model with brute power, blinding speed and rubber-burning acceleration in the late 1960s, there was a return to manual transmissions. Tying in with the macho speed image, some were featured as "Four on the Floor" and were an extra-cost option.

Automatic transmission and torque converter

Your project car may have a torque converter and automatic transmission.

Automatics employ a fluid coupling between the engine and transmission. These are called torque converters and replace the clutch on manual shift cars. Torque converters are a sealed unit with little to go wrong. They can only be replaced when they wear out.

There were over forty types, including variations, of automatic transmissions during the fifties, sixties and early seventies. This tremendous difference in specifications makes it impossible to cover everything pertaining to every type and model. General information on their function, as well as repair, should be helpful, and sources for this are included in the appendix.

Many automatics, especially those fitted on cars manufactured by the same parent company, will fit their other makes, though specifications may differ.

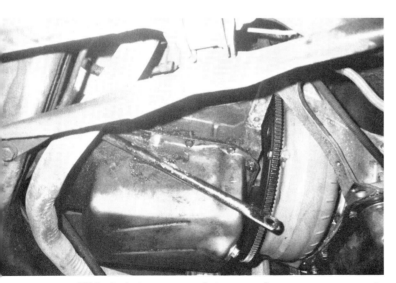

With the bottom cover plate exposed, you can remove nuts from the bolts holding the torque converter to the flywheel. Torque converters cannot be repaired, but you can replace a faulty one after disconnecting the bellhousing/transmission unit from the car.

Since you may not have the use of a lift when removing the automatic transmission, place the car solidly on jack stands, allowing yourself plenty of space. Rent a transmission jack to support its weight, when removing holding bolts. Disconnect the front universal.

How they work

Automatic transmissions start just behind the flywheel, where two saucer-shaped, vaned discs face each other in a sealed, oil-filled container (the torque converter). As the engine-attached disc, or input rotor, turns, its vanes force fluid to move with it. This forces the vanes on the transmission-attached disc, or turbine, to move too. There is no mechanical linkage between these discs, relying on hydrokinetic force to transmit the power.

Fluid under pressure moves through passages in the gearbox, where epicyclic, or planetary gear trains in constant mesh are controlled by friction clutches (bands) acting on the outside of internally toothed gears that carry the planetary pinions.

A selector lever (or buttons) allows the driver to keep the transmission from changing up, or force it down to change the action (direction) of the high-pressure fluid that controls clutches and brakes, which hold or release certain parts of the epicyclic gear train.

Troubleshooting

If there is grabbing or rough shifting; if it doesn't shift at correct speeds, grabbing on first shift to drive or reverse; if there is no movement in one or more speeds; if the transmission overheats; or if there is slipping or grabbing in gears when accelerating or slowing, first check the fluid level, following the manufacturer's tips.

These conditions could also be caused by contaminated or scorched fluid, a leaking vacuum hose or a defective vacuum modulator or governor. These are all problems you can fix yourself.

If these aren't corrected by the aforementioned remedies, or the engine starts with the transmission in gear, you need the services of a transmission repair shop.

Rebuild kits

There are rebuild kits for most popular automatics. If you follow directions carefully, have a clean workbench available and have average mechanical ability, an automatic transmission can be rebuilt. The kits are not suggested for beginners, however, because of their complexity.

You can, of course, install a rebuilt automatic, or one in good condition that can be purchased from a salvage yard.

Swapping automatics

You may want to update or change your present automatic for a later, improved one. Many times, automatics manufactured by a parent company can be used on more than one of their makes. However, an adapter, which is readily available, may be needed to mate a later-model unit to your engine.

Transmission options often were offered originally. Information on interchangeability of automatic transmissions is available at transmission repair shops, and source information is included in the appendix.

Removing automatics

The torque converter and automatic transmission can be removed as a unit, leaving the engine in the car.

Place the car solidly on jack stands, high enough so you can slide under easily. Disconnect the shifting

Disconnect the front universal, any supports, shift linkage and tubing to the cooler. Remove the starter and bolts holding the housing to the engine block to pull the torque converter and automatic transmission. Remove bolts holding the flywheel to the converter.

If you have above-average mechanical experience and skill, you should be able to rebuild your automatic. Buy the correct rebuild kit and follow the directions that come with it. Remember the order in which you take it apart. Keep your work area spotless.

97

When removing the pan from the automatic, examine any sludge or residue in the fluid—sure signs of wear in the clutches. If the fluid is brown, it indicates the transmission has been low on fluid or running too hot. The normal color is pink.

Though this automatic has been removed from the car, note the filter in the bottom. The filter should be replaced with every fluid change, usually about every 15,000 miles. Check the fluid level every few thousand miles for trouble-free driving.

Repairing automatics is beyond the capability of the beginner, because of their complexity. You can save money, though, by removing it for rebuilding or replacement.

linkages, wires and cables, which should be tagged for later match-up. Drain the fluid. A crossover exhaust pipe may have to be removed for working room. Rent a transmission jack to support the unit's weight. Use a piece of wood on top of a jack to support the engine's weight, before you remove the bolts in the transmission mounting brackets. Remove the bolts holding the bellhousing attaching the torque converter/transmission case to the engine block. Disconnect the universal joint at the front of the drive shaft. Disconnect the tubing from the transmission to the cooling portion of the radiator.

If the car has a floorshift, you may have to remove the shift gate and lever, possibly some portion of a center console. Disconnect the speedometer cable.

With everything disconnected, and the weight on the jacks, pull the unit back from the flywheel and move it from under the car.

If you're going to rebuild the unit, use the degreasing procedures previously outlined. Your workbench must be absolutely clean, so not even lint can get into the parts.

Installing automatics

With the car solidly placed on jack stands, cradle the unit on the transmission jack and push it into

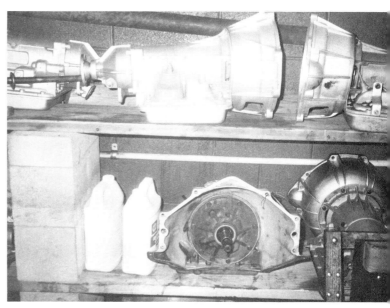

Transmission shops keep rebuilt units on hand, or will rebuild yours. Salvage yards sell tested units. Save money by buying a rebuilt or used unit and installing it yourself. Rent a transmission jack to make the job easier, quicker and safer.

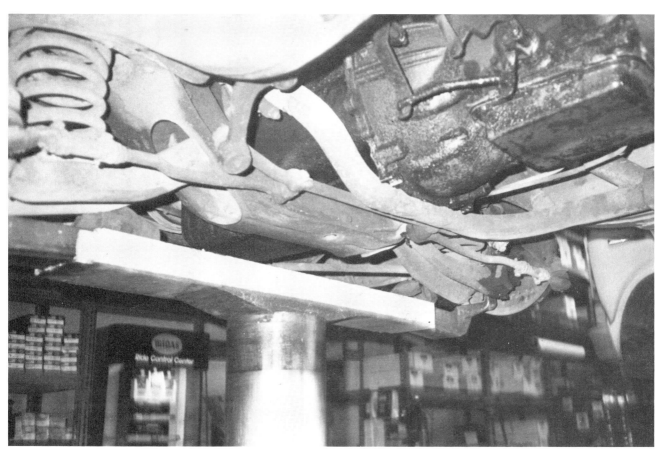

Clean the shift lever linkage which is externally mounted on all but electrically controlled automatics. Adjust the rods and shafts to take up excess play. Check that all pivots, *pins and cotterpins are secure and that all springs are in place.*

place, mating the torque converter to the flywheel. Bolt the bellhousing to the engine and insert the cushions and bolts in the transmission mounting brackets. Connect the universal joint at the front of the drive shaft.

With the unit solidly in place, connect the shift linkages. Match up all wires. Connect the speedometer cable. Attach any above-floor components to complete the job.

Manual transmission and clutch

Because of the close interaction of the clutch and manual transmission, much of the troubleshooting exercise can be done at the same time. However, clutch and transmission problems can be adjusted or repaired separately.

If the clutch slips or grabs, its linkage and driven plate needs cleaning, adjusting or replacing. If gears grind or clash when shifting, the shift lever is hard to use or the transmission is noisy, first check the lubricant level. Remove the plug on the side of the unit. Lubricant should be above the plug.

If there's a grinding noise as you shift through the gears, a whining noise at speed or when slowing that wasn't corrected by lubrication, the problem is in the gears, which you may be able to repair.

Difficulty shifting, or gears that grind while shifting, can be caused by incorrect or loose gearshift linkage, a warped or worn clutch plate or worn or weak clutch springs. You can repair or replace all of these. Read the following pages.

If the transmission is locked in gear, can't be shifted into gear or pops out of gear while driving, the trouble can be either in the linkage or an internal problem.

Clutch repair

You'll save time by having a replacement clutch plate and throw-out bearing on hand. Specify engine size when buying these. The clutch assembly is in the bellhousing on the engine side of the transmission.

Place jack stands at the front and rear. Put blocking under the transmission and engine for support. Disconnect or remove the following: transmission mounting bolts and cushions, drive shaft at the front universal joint; handbrake and clutch pedal linkage; all wiring connected to the transmission; and the speedometer cable. On some cars you'll have to remove the crossover pipe and any parts of the shift lever that extend through the floor.

Remove the bolts holding the bellhousing to the engine and slide the housing and transmission unit toward the rear, so it is out of your way. This exposes the flywheel with the clutch assembly attached. Remove the bolts holding the clutch cover to the flywheel assembly, exposing the pressure plate, which may contain a diaphragm spring, or coil springs around its circumference. With these removed, you'll see the clutch-driven plate, which has lining on both sides. Slide this from the splined shaft, leaving the clutch drive plate attached to the flywheel.

If the drive plate has been scored by exposed rivets on the worn clutch plate, it must either be replaced or turned down on a lathe to remove the scoring.

Check the throw-out bearing (this is behind the clutch plate) that is moved by pedal action against

Remove the transmission and bellhousing as a unit to expose the clutch assembly. Remove the six bolts holding the clutch assembly to the flywheel, exposing the clutch drive plate. The scored drive plate needs to be turned down on a lathe at a machine shop.

Remove the six bolts holding the clutch-driven plate to the flywheel. A scored plate, or one worn down to the rivets, must be replaced. The three prongs are activated by the puller yoke attached to the clutch pedal. The throw-out bearing cushions clutch action.

the puller yoke. This forces the strong, main coil spring to compress and release the clutch. If the bearing is scorched or worn, it should be replaced at this time. Lubricate the replacement bearing lightly when installing it.

Check the coil springs fitted between the pressure plate which clamps the clutch plate against the flywheel. If any of these appear smaller than the others, they should be replaced.

When reassembling clutch components, clean and grease the splined shaft lightly, so everything slides in place easily. With the new parts installed, align the splines so the bellhousing can mate with the engine and bolt it securely. Attach the coupling on the front drive shaft universal joint. Attach the clutch pedal and gearshift linkages. Connect the wiring, speedometer cable and any other components you had to disconnect.

Transmission repairs

All transmission repairs must be made with the unit removed from the car. Even if you don't plan on repairing it yourself, you can save money by removing it and later installing it yourself.

On a few cars, the transmission may be a separate unit bolted to the rear of the bellhousing. If this is the case, you won't need to remove the bellhousing. Once the clutch linkage, gearshift controls, wiring and the speedometer cable are disconnected, the transmission can be removed. Use a jack to support the splined input shaft, as you remove the bolts holding the unit to the bellhousing. Slide the transmission back and from under the car.

There are no repair kits for manual transmissions. Though one with average mechanical skills can repair a manual transmission successfully, it is not

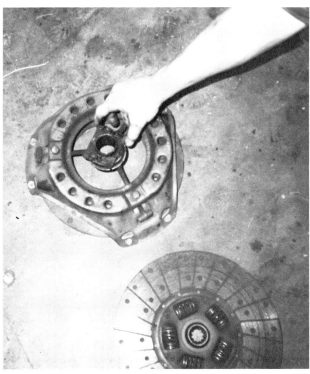

With the clutch assembly separated, inspect the throw-out bearing for wear. It fits over the splined shaft. When activated by clutch pedal linkage, it pulls the fabric-lined driven plate away from the drive plate, disconnecting power to the rear wheels.

Have the clutch drive plate turned down at a machine shop to remove all ridges and scoring. Though there's a good bit of work necessary to get at the flywheel and remove it from the car, the machine shop work is inexpensive.

Disregard the crankshaft pulley piled on top of the replacement clutch driven plate and the newly fitted flywheel ring gear. If you found any missing or chipped teeth on the flywheel ring gear, you'll need to install a new ring gear.

recommended for the beginner. Either have it repaired at a transmission shop, buy a rebuilt unit or get a replacement in good condition from a salvage yard.

Many transmissions were manufactured by the same supplier for various car companies. There is also wide use of the same, or slightly modified units, among cars of the same parent company, making finding a replacement easier.

You may want to change a three-speed to a four-speed or to one with an overdrive for increased performance and economy.

When installing the transmission, use blocking to support its weight, as you match the splines and install the bolts holding the transmission to the bell-housing. All parts should fit easily and must not be forced. Connect the shift linkage, cables and any wiring.

Be sure the transmission is filled with the recommended lubricant, and that the drain plug is tight.

Overdrives

An overdrive transmission is usually controlled by a dash-mounted switch. It is designed so the final

Disconnect the drive shaft at the front universal joint, remove any mounting bolts, and disconnect the speedometer cable before removing bolts holding the bellhousing to the engine. On certain cars you may have to remove the starter to pull the unit out.

gear drive is through a free-wheeling clutch anytime car speed exceeds engine speed. However, when car speed is greater than the preset speed, approximately 30 mph, a solenoid locks the sun gear in the transmission so free-wheeling can't occur. A cutout governor downshifts into direct drive at about 20 mph, taking the car out of overdrive.

The locked sun gear makes the overdrive planetary pinions rotate the internal ring gear at a speed

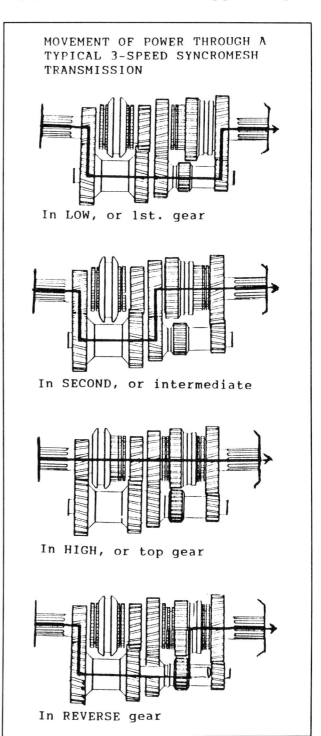

MOVEMENT OF POWER THROUGH A TYPICAL 3-SPEED SYNCROMESH TRANSMISSION

In LOW, or 1st. gear

In SECOND, or intermediate

In HIGH, or top gear

In REVERSE gear

If the transmission needs repairs, disassemble it at your workbench. Note the order in which you removed each part. Clean all parts in solvent. Any worn parts should be replaced before reassembling the unit. Work carefully and slowly for best results.

Remove the bolts holding the transmission case to the bellhousing. Disconnect the shift lever. With the cover plate removed, inspect gear teeth and sliding shafts for chipped teeth or splines and for scorching from lack of lubrication. Clean the inside of the case.

greater than that of the input shaft. This, in effect, gives the car an extra forward speed, with lower rpm. A solenoid controlled kick-down switch on the accelerator linkage downshifts from overdrive to direct drive on command.

Troubleshooting the overdrive

If the overdrive won't work, first check the operation of the solenoid directly to the battery. Check the fuse on the relay. Check movement of the control lever in each direction. It shouldn't have more than ¼ in. free travel before the lever moves. Use a test lamp, with ignition on, between the kick-down switch terminal and ground. You should hear the sound. Ground the kick-down switch terminal on the relay. If the lamp won't light, the relay is bad. Operate the kick-down switch several times to make sure it isn't sticking. Ground each accelerator terminal on the switch, one at a time. If you can't hear the solenoid, replace the kick-down switch.

If the overdrive won't release, make an electrical check. With the control switch in the on position, turn on the ignition switch. If you hear a click in the relay switch, the trouble is electrical. If there is no sound, the trouble is mechanical and the unit must be repaired.

Disconnect the wire at the governor; if this releases the overdrive, the governor is faulty. Disconnect the wire between the kick-down switch and the governor; if this releases the overdrive, there's a short in the wire. Disconnect the wires from the relay and from the governor at the kick-down switch; if the overdrive releases, the kick-down switch is faulty. Disconnect the wire from the solenoid at the relay; if the overdrive releases, the relay is faulty. If none of these release the overdrive, the trouble is mechanical and the unit must be repaired.

The overdrive assembly and the transmission must be removed from the car if an overhaul is required. Because an overdrive transmission is complex, it is advisable to have the overhaul done professionally, unless you have above-average mechanical ability.

Overdrive maintenance

The overdrive is supplied with oil from the transmission. Cars with overdrive require one extra pint of oil at refills. Overdrive units often have separate fill and drain plugs. Terminals on wires should be tight and kept clean. Wires should be inspected periodically for chafing or deteriorating insulation.

Sources for additional information on overdrives are included in the appendix.

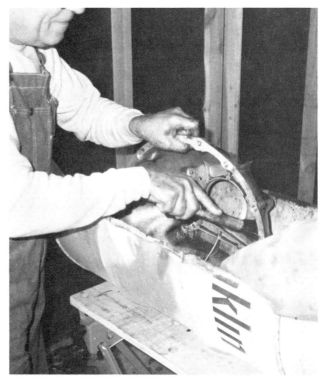

You can remove floor-mounted shift levers from the top by driving the pin from the base of the lever. If there is a center-mounted console, you'll need to remove the screws holding it to the floor, before you can get to the shift lever.

Clean the inside and outside of the bellhousing in solvent with a paintbrush. One half of a 55 gallon drum makes a great cleaning tub for large, irregular castings. Use a wire-bristled brush and putty knife on hard accumulations around ridges and in crevices.

Drain the fluid from the pan before removing the bolts holding it to the case. Tighten any loose bolts before fitting a new gasket and attaching the pan. Fill with recommended fluid and run the transmission through the gears and check the fluid level again.

It is not difficult to update the automatic as long as it is from the same car family. Transmission shops have interchangeability lists. You can also change from a manual to an automatic, if that was a factory option. Salvage yards are a good source.

From manual to automatic

You may decide to replace your manual transmission with an automatic. In most cases this can be done. It is easier if the manufacturer offered an automatic as an option with the same engine. It is also easier to make the switch if the transmission you choose is fitted to other makes from the same parent company. The changeover to an automatic includes the clutch assembly, which will be replaced by the torque converter. Also included will be a change in shift control linkage, and possibly some wiring and trim changes.

There are adapters that will allow almost any engine to be mated with almost any automatic. These are available from auto supply stores and firms advertising in car publications. The major automatic transmission shops have interchangeability information. Sources for specific information on engines and automatics are also included in the appendix.

To make a wise choice, weigh what you expect to gain from the change against the modifications you'll have to make.

Measure the length and width of the new unit and compare it with the space available. The frame crosspiece may have to be moved. Mounting brackets may have to be changed. Floor pans and transmission hump may have to be reworked. New mechanical linkage may have to be fitted to accommodate the transmission. Because the drive shaft must be carefully balanced, any change in its length must be done professionally. These and other problems must be considered before deciding on which automatic you want to install, if you decide to make the change.

You'll have no difficulty locating a wide variety of transmissions. Classified ads in newspapers offer rebuilt transmissions and units from cars being parted out. Salvage yards test and store automatics from wrecked cars. The big national transmission shops offer rebuilt and guaranteed units, on a take-out or installed basis. Shop around, making comparisons as to condition and price before purchasing.

Installing the automatic

If you bought a used unit, drain the old fluid, clean the pan and fit a new filter before you start installation. Follow the previous directions given for installation, but only after you've made the necessary changes to the body and frame. Any changes to the drive shaft will have to be made once the unit is in place.

Before removing the jack stands, make a final check that everything is in place and properly tightened.

Fill the transmission with the correct amount of high-quality fluid. Start the engine and move the quadrant through the shift points a couple of times to circulate the fluid. Let the engine reach operating temperature, and refill the fluid to the correct mark on the dipstick.

Sources for information on automatic transmissions are included in the appendix.

Chapter 14

Drive shaft and differential

To get the engine's power from the transmission to the driving wheels, several components which include the universal joints, drive shaft, differential and rear axle shafts make up what is called the drivetrain. Each component plays a very important role in the process.

The universal joints act as double-jointed hinges to allow the up-and-down movement of the rear axle over varying road conditions and compensate for added weight in the car. There is usually one on each end of the drive shaft, but some cars have a third universal joint in the middle of the drive shaft.

The drive shaft is a hollow tube with one section of the front and rear universal joints attached to it.

Some cars use a two-section drive shaft with a universal joint fitted in the middle.

The differential, mounted in the center of the rear axle, changes the engine's rotation of the drive shaft at right angles to the rear axles. It contains gears that balance power to both wheels, yet allow one wheel to turn faster than the other when cornering. The rear axles transmit the power to the driving wheels.

These components must be in good condition to perform their functions because of their interaction.

The introduction of high-performance personal luxury cars, such as Chrysler's 300 Series and Chev-

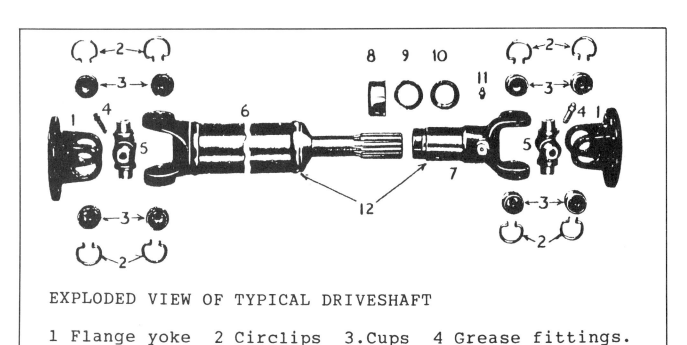

EXPLODED VIEW OF TYPICAL DRIVESHAFT

1 Flange yoke   2 Circlips   3.Cups   4 Grease fittings.
5 Spider   6.Driveshaft   7 Sliding yoke   8 Dust cap
9 and 10 Washers   11 Grease fitting.

rolet's Corvette in the mid-fifties, and vigorous promotion of the pony and muscle cars of the sixties, caused design changes in many drivetrain components. Development of the limited-slip differential and constant velocity joints were but two of these developments.

Troubleshooting

If you noticed vibration that was hard to locate and a clunking noise at low speed during your test drive, it can be the universal joints. Block the front wheels and put jack stands under the rear frame, so there's no weight on the wheels or back axle. Grip the drive shaft near each U-joint and twist each section in opposite directions. If you find motion at the rear of the joint, there is play you should try to eliminate by tightening the flange bolts. Make the test again. If there is still play, the universal joint is most likely worn out. There are rebuild kits for many universal joints.

If, during your test drive, you noticed uninterrupted humming and recurring staccato, or shaking sounds from under the mid-section of the car, these indicate the drive shaft is out of balance. You may be able to correct minor imbalance by installing one or more proper circumference worm-drive clamps, trying different positions of the tightening screw until the problem is solved. Drive shaft repair shops can balance the shaft for you by heating, welding on weights and checking the balance electronically. You'll save money by removing the shaft, taking it to the shop and later installing the balanced shaft.

Several problems can develop in the differential, and most can be determined by sounds during your test drive. If you heard a low-pitched growling sound during turns, more pronounced in left turns than right, the differential gears are probably worn. The noise may be more pronounced during acceleration

The front end of the drive shaft, as you'll see it when you've removed it from your car. The splined slip yoke fits over the splined transmission output shaft. Remove the circlips holding the spider in its sockets to free the universal joint for repair.

and/or deceleration. First check the lubrication level in the differential case. If this doesn't correct or substantially reduce the noise, the gears inside the case must be examined for wear.

Worn ball or roller bearings supporting the rear axle shafts can produce a growling sound that in-

The rear end of the drive shaft, as you'll see it when you've removed the four bolts holding the flange to the pinion gear housing at the front of the differential. Remove the lock rings holding the spider in place to work on the double universals.

When working on the drive shaft and differential, place jack stands to support the rear axle. When checking differential bearings and gears, remove the back plate on the differential case. Be careful not to damage hydraulic brake lines that are attached.

Attaching worm-drive hose clamps to balance the drive shaft is one way of balancing it. A more scientific method is to take the shaft to a shop specializing in this work. A machine can measure the run-out in thousandths of an inch.

creases with speed. The bearings can be packed with the recommended grease and reinstalled to the correct tension. If the noise continues, the bearings may need replacing.

If you see oil marks on the inner side of the rear wheels and tires, this indicates that differential oil is leaking past the felt or neoprene washers on the differential side of the rear wheel bearings. New seals and washers must be installed to correct this.

Removing the drive shaft

Whether removing the drive shaft for balancing, or to get at the universal joints, you should put the car solidly on jack stands. Put the shift in neutral. Use a file to make a mark across the shaft's yoke and cross-flanges so the shaft can be reinstalled to its original position. Start removing the shaft from the rear.

If you're going to work on only one universal joint, make a sling to support the shaft's weight while working on the universal joint at your workbench.

If the drive shaft is the two-piece type, remove the bolts holding the support bracket to the frame cross-member. If there are shims, make note of their number and position for later installation.

Remove the bolts or clamps that attach the shaft to the differential flange. Lower the flange and pull it toward the rear to slide out the splined yoke at the transmission end.

Plug clean rags into the open end of the transmission slip yoke to stop fluid leakage.

Clean and degrease the shaft; this often means scraping off small, tarred stones that have stuck to it. Have the shaft balanced professionally, with the universal joint matched to your file markings. Spray a coat of rust preventing paint on the balanced shaft before installing it on the car. Remove rags and clean the splined end of the transmission. Clean the splines in the front slip yoke and slide it into place. Support the shaft with a sling. Align holes and bolt the rear flanges together. Position and bolt any center support bracket in place, adding shims as needed.

Repairing drive shaft and universal joints

To repair or replace these flexible joints at each end and possibly the center of the drive shaft, start at the rear. With the drive shaft removed, as previously detailed, separate the sections of the joints. A cross-member, shaped like a plus sign, is fitted into the front yoke and a flange on the rear yoke. Thin roller bearings in bearing caps fit over each end of the crosspiece and are held in place by snap rings.

Essentially, the same type of joint is at each end of the drive shaft. On some cars, the yoke is bolted to the pinion shaft, and the cross-member is held by

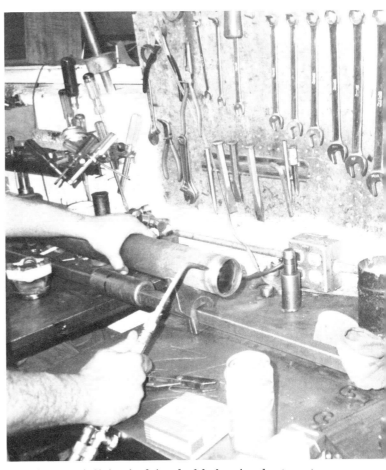

At a shop specializing in drive shaft balancing, heat must be used to expand the end of the drive shaft to accept the yoke end of the universal joint. Care must be taken to be sure the drive shaft isn't overheated and warped out of shape.

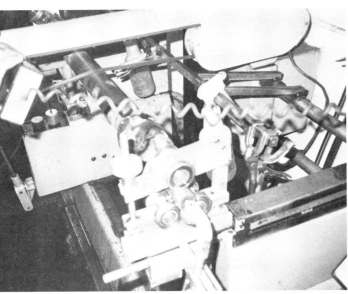

With the drive shaft turning, a strobe light is used to determine where weights need to be put to bring the shaft into perfect balance. The machine also indicates the amount of weight necessary. This takes the guesswork out of the balancing job.

Clean the collar on the yoke end of the universal joint, and use a hammer to tap it into the expanded open end of the drive shaft. As the heated metal cools and shrinks, it holds the universal yoke in place, without bolts being necessary.

With the repaired universal mounted in the balanced drive shaft, the unit can be tested to prove that the work was done *correctly. With the balanced drive shaft installed in the car, the annoying vibration and rumble will disappear.*

On some universals, the cross-member is held either by steel C-straps that are bolted to the yoke, or by U-bolts that pass through the yoke. The cross-member must be unbolted from the yoke before the drive shaft can be removed.

U-bolts that pass through the yoke, or by steel C-clamps bolted to threaded holes in the yoke. Free the cross-member from the yoke on each end of the drive shaft by removing the snap rings that hold the crosspiece. Work on the universals at your workbench.

Buy a rebuild kit and follow the enclosed directions. With the crosspiece removed, degrease the parts. If you have access to an arbor press, force the bearings out of their holders. Otherwise, tap against a wooden block on top of the bearing in one direction to force it out of its sleeve. Tap in the other direction to remove the remaining bearing.

Use an arbor press, or tap the new bearing into place. Coat lightly with oil to make fitting the crosspiece easier. Fit the snap rings into their grooves to hold the crosspiece in place. Assemble the crosspiece and yoke. Install the C-clamps or U-bolts that join the components to complete universal joint repairs. If there is a grease fitting, make sure it is clean and grease the unit.

Working on the differential

The differential reduces drive shaft speed to practical wheel speeds. The pinion, or input gear at the drive shaft end of the unit, mates with the ring gear, turning the engine's rotations to the axle shafts by ninety degrees.

When cornering, the inner wheel offers more resistance to the engine's power than the outside wheel, because it has the same amount of work to do in a shorter distance. As the gear's tooth load becomes different, the cluster of planetary gears turns, forcing the bevel gear attached to the axle shaft to speed up until conditions become normal again. In time, often because of lack of lubrication, these gears will wear to the point where they have to be replaced.

Replacement cluster gears, final-drive crown-wheel gear bearings and other parts are readily available. Many cars used differentials supplied by the same manufacturer, making parts interchangeable. Automotive supply stores have interchange manuals and specification sheets to help you. Additional sources of information are listed in the appendix.

Some repairs to differentials can be made by persons with average mechanical skills. Other more complex repairs should be made at a repair shop.

Rather than spending a lot of time and money rebuilding a differential, it's usually easier and less expensive to locate a rear-end assembly in good condition from a salvage yard and install it yourself.

Removing the rear axle assembly

When removing the rear axle assembly, place jack stands solidly under the frame, high enough to allow easy working room.

Details will vary, depending upon the suspension system. Disconnect the universal joint at the differential, releasing the drive shaft. Make a sling to support its weight. Remove the rear wheels and rear brake backing plates which hold brake components. Dis-

Usually, the needle bearings in the crosspiece wear out from lack of lubrication. If the yoke isn't worn, clean it with solvent. Remove the bearing caps and push the crosspiece into the yoke. Replace the bearing caps and secure the lock rings.

connect the fittings holding the brake line to the axle housing. On leaf spring suspensions, put jacks near the outer ends of the housing to support its weight. Release pressure on the shock absorbers at the axle. Disconnect the antisway bar at the axle. Remove the U-bolts holding the springs in place, freeing the axle and differential housing.

You may find a short-splined jack shaft fitted into the end of the drive shaft, which is hollow. If the splines are worn or chipped, heat the drive shaft to remove the damaged section. Heat it again, when you tap the new section in place.

Remove the rear universal joint and the bolts attaching the pinion casting to the other half of the differential housing. Examine the bearings that support the pinion shaft and axle shafts. Examine the teeth on the ring gear, cluster gears and pinion.

Remove the bolts holding the rear universal flange to the pinion shaft of the differential and pull it free. Pull the drive shaft toward the rear of the car to pull the slip yoke from the splines on the transmission. Repair universals at your workbench.

On rear-coil-spring cars, follow the same procedures in positioning, supporting the axle housing, disconnecting the universal joint, removing the brake backing plates and drums and brake line fittings to the axle. Disconnect the shock absorbers and the antisway bar at the axle.

Use a punch to drive out the bolt through the control arm bushings at the axle housing. If the bushings are worn, replace them when you install the replacement axle. Detailed directions are in chapter 15.

If there's a clamp attaching the bottom of each coil spring to the axle housing, remove the holding bolt. Some systems relied only on the car's weight to hold coil springs in their sockets. With everything attaching the housing to the frame disconnected, pull the unit from under the car.

Directions for removing the bolts holding the brake backing drums to the axle housing assume these will have been removed at the salvage yard, when the unit was taken from the car. If this isn't the case, you have a choice of using the original or replacement brake assemblies.

Caution: Be careful when removing the lower shock absorber bolts because of pressure in the unit.

Installing the rear axle assembly

Clean and degrease the replacement unit. Mask the universal joint flange and any open hydraulic lines. Spray with rust-inhibiting paint for protection.

If you removed the rear axle for rebuilding the differential, axles and hubs, clean and degrease the unit. Spray it with a rust-inhibiting primer and a final coat of black enamel.

Be careful not to damage handbrake cables, if they're attached.

Get help moving the unit in place and blocking it on the jacks. Connect the universal joint flange. Adjust the jacks to lift the housing to the level necessary to fit the U-bolts attaching the leaf spring to the housing. Finger tighten all four nuts before tightening them securely. Attach the antisway bar to the axle housing.

You may need to remove the jacks from under the housing and place them between the housing and the car's frame to push the axle down to align the shock absorbers.

On coil-spring cars, ask a helper to block the housing and help position it, while you align the bolts on the universal joint flange at the differential. Align the holes on the control arm and axle housing. Put a few drops of oil on the bolt before tapping it through the bushing in the control arm. Finger tighten the nuts on one side of the car before starting on the other. When both sides are in place, tighten the nuts securely.

Be sure the upper insulator is in place on top of the spring before fitting the top of the coil into its cup. With the car's weight supported by jack stands, you shouldn't need a spring compressor to get the bottom of the coil into the bottom spring cup. The raised side of the retaining cap fits over the spring's contours. Tighten the bolt holding the cap in place. Be sure to fill the differential with the recommended lubricant.

When connecting the original or replacement brake assemblies, you'll have to fill the hydraulic system and purge it of air. Connect and adjust the handbrake cables.

Rear axles

Axle shafts transmit the power from the differential to the wheels. Splines on the inner ends fit into matching splines on differential gears. These sometimes wear. A sudden burst of power may break a worn axle shaft. Usually, replacement isn't difficult.

Because of their interchangeability, you should have no problem finding a replacement, either at an auto supply store, or from a salvage yard.

Directions differ because of differences in car design. On most cars, the job can be done entirely at the wheel end. Occasionally, work will be required at the differential end, too, depending upon where the axle shaft broke.

With the front wheels blocked and the rear axle on jack stands, remove the wheel exposing the brake drum. The rear drum is attached to the outer end of the wheel hub assembly, which is attached to the outer end of the axle shaft. Remove the bolts or lugs holding the brake backing plate to a flange on the axle.

You should be able to pull the axle shaft out of the axle housing. If the break is at the differential end of the shaft, you may have to remove the plate at the rear of the differential housing to get at it.

Use a new gasket if you removed the cover plate. Fit a new oil seal if you had to remove the side gear to

Remove the nuts holding the axle flange to the wheel hub, and pull the axle shaft out of the hub. Because some differential oil may spill out on the axle, have a pan ready to catch it. With the shaft removed, you can remove the tapered roller bearing in the hub.

get at the broken shaft. Make sure the drain plug is tight, and refill the case with the recommended differential lubricant.

After removing the axle shaft, inspect the bearings in the hub assembly. Examine the inner cone,

To remove the tapered roller bearing from the hub, pry out the circlip holding the bearing into its race. Examine the bearing for wear or pitting and replace it if necessary. There'll be no problem getting the replacement. Use solvent to clean inside the hub.

If you want to change the wheels on your car, you may find they won't fit your hubs. Buy adapters at automotive stores, which will fit the hub studs on your car and the stud holes in the wheels you've chosen. Always change both wheels on an axle.

roller cage and outer race on roller bearings in the hub, or the sealed ball bearings at the outer edge of the axle housing. If these are scorched or show wear, replace the bearings at this time.

Fit a new grease seal and lubricate the inner bearing assembly. Bolt the hub assembly and brake backing plate to the axle flange. Wipe some light oil on the replacement shaft and push it into place through the wheel bearing and through a bearing at the differential end of the housing and into the differential side gear. You may need to rotate the shaft until the splines line up. Do not try to force the shaft into place.

On tapered axle shafts, fit the outer roller bearing, washer and lock nut. On the sealed ball-bearing type, fit the retaining washer and the lock nut. Fit the drum and mount the wheel to complete the job.

Rear hubs

Rear hub designs may differ on some cars. The free-turning hub is mounted on two tapered roller bearings. A locking, adjusting nut changes bearing tension. When the nut is adjusted correctly, the wheel can spin freely without any end play. A cotterpin holds the lock nut in place.

Tapered roller bearings are fitted onto the axle shaft inside the axle housing. The brake backing plate is bolted to the flange on the axle shaft. A second, smaller roller bearing fits on the outer edge of the axle shaft and is held in place by a washer and lock nut with a cotterpin.

On some cars you may find a slot machined into the outer end of the tapered axle shaft, with a key made to fit the slot. An oil seal, bearing and a washer with a key made to fit into the slot, and a lock nut with a cotterpin complete the assembly.

Because of differences in design and engineering processes, there are variations in repairing each component in this chapter that cannot be covered in this book. You'll find sources for detailed, specific information listed in the appendix.

Chapter 15

Rear suspension system

Great changes took place in rear suspension systems during the fifties, sixties and early seventies. Wider tires and smaller wheels are obvious exterior changes. Underneath the car, tubular shock absorbers replaced the former arm and lever type.

Coil springs with trailing arms replaced leaf springs on some cars. Longer, softer leaf springs with newly designed shackles and mountings were fitted to cars not switching to coils.

The center of gravity was lowered, giving much better roadability to handle the increased power of the newly developed engines. Sway and antiroll bars were designed to accommodate the extra stresses of high-speed cornering.

Unit body/frame construction used on many cars required changes in mounting rear suspension components. Introduction of compacts, subcompacts and midsize cars called for lighter weight and space-saving rear suspension systems, which could be used on other models within the same car family.

Rear suspension systems aren't complicated, nor are they overly difficult to repair. Most repairs can be made by the beginner. These are mostly weekend jobs, allowing the car to be in use during the week.

The components
Leaf springs

Leaf springs are long, semi-elliptic springs, mounted well out toward the ends of the axle, have a stationary attachment on the front end and a movable shackle at the rear. Varying length leaves are held in place by a center bolt and in alignment by clips equidistant from the center. The number of leaves varies with the car's weight.

Coil springs

Coil springs are made of tempered steel and vary in height, diameter, number of coils and thickness of the steel used. They fit into sockets at the top and bottom, with rubber bumpers to absorb shocks when bottoming.

Trailing arms

Trailing arms are strong steel forgings or stampings attached to the frame to prevent back-to-front axle movement. Up-and-down movement is allowed by pivots.

Antisway bars

Often called a track bar, the antisway bar, a tubular component designed to keep the car level on curves, is usually fitted to the left end of the axle or trailing arm and attached to the frame on the right.

Shock absorbers

Your car will probably have telescopic shock absorbers. Some will be adjustable for soft or firm ride. A piston attached to the frame moves inside a cylinder attached to the axle. As the wheels move up or down, fluid in the cylinder cushions the movement. These cannot be repaired, only replaced.

Troubleshooting

Your test drive should have given you a good idea of the rear suspension system's condition. If the car continues to move up and down after a bump, the shock absorbers are worn, and if the car has rear coils, they may have lost their tension. Excessive lean on corners, if the tires are at normal pressure, indicates worn shock absorbers, a weak spring, worn spring shackles or worn bushings in the antisway bar. If the car bottoms easily when going over ordinary dips in the road, check the rear springs, as well as the shock absorbers.

If the car has a trailer hitch, or has been used to pull a trailer, expect to find extra wear in the suspension system, as well as wear in the drivetrain.

Sloppy cornering, in which the rear end seems to have trouble tracking, normally means worn bushings in spring shackles and bushings. Worn bushings in trailing arm mountings will also contribute to this problem.

On cars with independently sprung rear suspensions, first look at the tires. Excessive wear on the outside indicates positive camber; more wear inside means negative camber. Zero camber means the tires' treads contact the road evenly. Camber is the inward or outward tilt of the wheels from perpendicular.

Put the rear frame on jack stands to check for spacers turned in between the coils in an effort to reduce rear-end sag, or make the car sit level. With the weight off the wheels, examine the bushings attaching the trailing arms to the car's frame, as well as those to the axle housing. On solid axle cars, with leaf or coil springs, examine bushings on the track, or antisway bar. Looseness can contribute to excessive leaning on corners.

When scheduling repairs, always make those first that affect the safety of the car. Others can be made when it is convenient. Some jobs, like shock absorber replacement, can be combined with other jobs, such as spring bushings or brake repairs.

Tools and supplies

You may need to rent a small arbor press to force out old bushings and push new ones into place. You

Shock absorber placement varies between makes of cars. You may find one mounted ahead of the axle on one side and in back of the axle on the other to resist twisting. Most sit farther apart at the bottom than at the top for stability. Heavy straps limit downward travel of the axle.

should rent a spring compressor for the rear coils. You will need a jack and a set of jack stands. Your socket set, open-end wrenches, set of punches and a ball peen hammer and everyday hand tools should be all you'll need.

Buy replacement coil springs, bushings and shock absorbers at auto supply stores, where specification sheets should be available. Refer to the manufacturer's specs when buying parts.

If you buy leaf or coil springs at an auto supply store, or used ones from a salvage yard, be sure the springs bought in pairs are the same height.

Leaf springs

To remove rear leaf springs, block the front wheels and put jack stands under the frame, taking weight off the suspension system. Use a jack under the rear axle to relieve tension on the springs and bushings. Remove the nuts from the front mounting and use a punch, or tap against a piece of hardwood to drive the bolt out of the spring eye. On some cars this bolt will be encased in a rubber bushing. Other cars will have a steel or brass bushing, through which the bolt fits. You'll have to drive the bushing out of the spring eye. Do the same at the shackle end to release the spring from the car's frame.

If installing new shocks, remove the bottom bolt first and remove the units. If not, disconnect only the bottom.

Remove nuts from the U-bolts holding the spring to the axle housing. The spring is heavy, so be prepared. Use a putty knife and wire-bristled brush to remove dirt, and solvent to remove grease and oil. Use emery cloth to clean the spring eyes, removing any

Tap the replacement bushing through the frame-mounted bracket and spring eye, being careful not to damage the threads on the bolt. Fit the washers and nut. On some cars there may be a castellated nut with a corresponding hole in the bolt for a cotterpin.

bits of the old bushing. If you paint the spring, use a rust-inhibiting paint for protection, and do it before installing it.

Put the spring back on the axle, and finger tighten the nuts on the U-bolts at this time. Align the front spring eye with the mounting bracket. Use a punch or block of hardwood against the bushing and tap it in place. A thin coat of oil or graphite usually makes this easier. Use the same procedure at the shackle end of the spring.

Once the spring is in position, tighten the nuts on the bolts through the spring eyes, then the nuts on the U-bolts to finish the job. It's easier to complete one side at a time, rather than removing both springs to work on the spring eyes. Be sure to check the rubber bumpers on the frame or axle that protect against bottoming. If these are worn, they should be replaced at this time.

Coil springs

To remove rear coil springs that have spring expanders turned in between the coils, or springs that have become weakened from loss of tension or constant overloading, block the front wheels and put jack stands under the rear frame. The weight of the axle will stretch the coil, making removal easier.

On live axle suspension systems, coil springs fit into cups that are either bolted to the axle housing or made a part of the housing casting. On some cars, a cap fits the contours of the lower coil end and is bolted in place; others depend on the weight of the car to hold the springs in place. There is an insulating pad in the top cup to prevent squeaks.

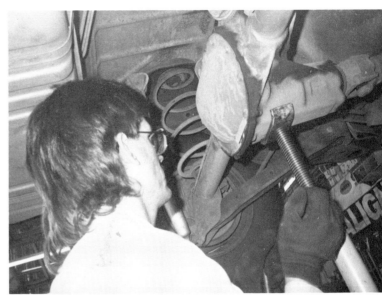

To replace the rear coil springs on cars with a live rear axle, place jack stands solidly under the frame. This takes the weight off the suspension system. Put a jack, which will act as a pivot, under the center of the differential case.

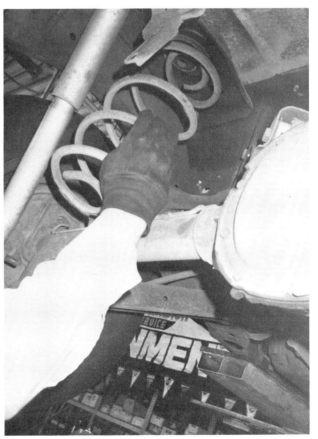

With one hand, pull the axle housing down, freeing the spring from the lower cup. Pull the coil out of its socket at the top. You may need to remove a section of the exhaust pipe for working room. Coils often taper, getting tighter toward the top.

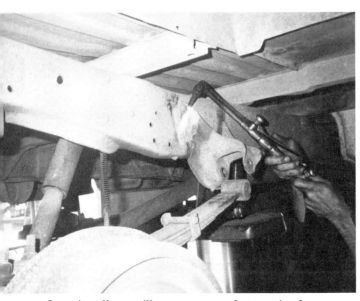

Occasionally, you'll come across a bent spring hanger, as on this 1960s van. You may have to use a cutting torch to remove the old rivets or bolts. You can bolt or rivet the replacement hanger in place, making sure it is properly aligned.

On a few cars, you may find the rear shock absorber is positioned within the coil spring. If this is the case, remove the bolt at the bottom of the shock and leave it in place, unless you intend to replace the shock absorber, too. If the shock absorber isn't within the coil, disconnect it at the bottom and leave it in place.

Remove the bolt holding the cap and pull it out of the spring. You'll need to rent a clamp to compress the spring for removal and later installation. Be careful when spacing the threaded hooks to the coils. Tighten evenly, compressing the spring. Remove it from the cups and out of the car. Release the clamp tension evenly.

Clean and degrease the spring cups, and spray with rust-inhibiting paint. Replacement springs should be clean and painted, too. Check the rubber stops in the top and bottom cups. If they're worn, replace them. They're molded over a threaded shaft for easy removal.

Compress the replacement spring. If the shock absorber fits inside the coil, slip it in before placing the spring in its cups and insert the top bolt. Place any top insulating pad on the spring and release the tension on the clamp slowly, making sure the coil fits into the indentations in the cups. Remove the clamp and insert the bolt holding the bottom cap in place. You may need to use a jack under the axle to align the shock absorber with its bracket.

Trailing arms

Since coil springs can handle only up-and-down axle movement, positioning and stabilizing is done by pivoting trailing arms between the car's frame and the live axle housing. There are bushings at each end of the arm, which may need replacing.

With the front wheels blocked and the rear frame on jack stands, remove the wheels. Use a jack to relieve tension on the bushings. Work the front bushing first. Remove the nuts and tap the bolt out of its bushing. Next, remove the nuts and tap out the bolt at the axle end.

You may need to use an arbor press to push the bushing from the trailing arm, if you can't tap it out

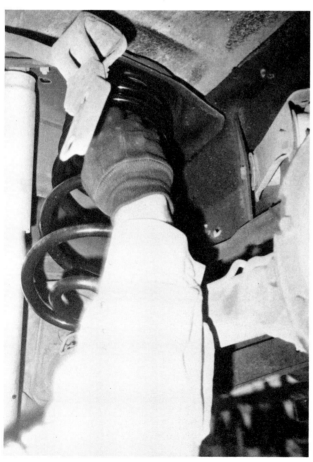

Insert the top of the replacement coil spring into the socket at the top, making sure it is seated. Pull the axle housing down and push the lower end of the coil into the lower cup. Some cars fit a bolt-on cap at the top and bottom of the coil spring.

You won't view your car's rear suspension system from this angle. Semi-trailing arms pivot at an oblique angle to the wheels. The coil spring sits ahead of the axle and the shock absorber behind. Rear body mounts are ahead of the trailing arm bushing.

118

with a punch and ball peen hammer. On some cars, the bushing may be rubber molded around the bolt. Use emery cloth to clean any remnants of the old bushing. Clean and degrease the trailing arm and spray it with rust-inhibiting paint.

Match the forward end of the control arm to the frame and slide the bolt in place. Turn the nuts only a thread or two, to allow movement when fitting the arm to the axle. Adjust the jack against the axle to help align the holes for connecting the lower arm. With both ends of the arm in place, tighten the nuts and fit cotterpins to complete the job.

Trailing arms with independent rear suspension

Cars with independent rear suspension bolt the differential housing to the car's frame. Universal joints at each end of the rear axles allow the wheels to handle road shocks independently. The Y-shaped trailing arms pivot at right angles to the wheels, with two bushings at the front end of the arm and the rear of the arm attached to the hub housing.

Some cars mounted the control arms to pivot at an oblique angle to the wheels, allowing a minimum amount of camber change with changing road conditions.

Block the front wheels and place jack stands under the car's frame. Remove the wheels. Use a jack

When replacing tubular shock absorbers, remove the bolt holding the bottom (cylinder) end to the axle or spring hanger. Support the car's frame on jack stands, so only the pressure of the axle's weight can force the shock absorber down when the bolt is removed.

The differential may be bolted to a bracket on the rear cross-member, preventing side-to-side movement, but allowing some up-and-down movement on swing axle cars.

This permits a minimum of camber change to be engineered into the rear suspension system.

119

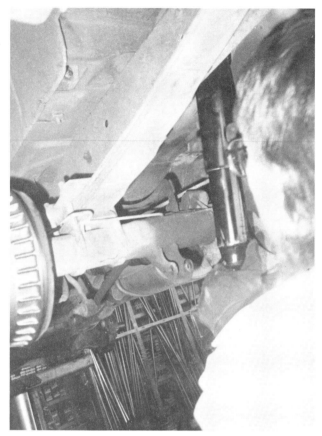

Slip the bolt on the piston end of the unit through the eyes in the bracket and finger tighten the bolt. This makes it easier to align the hole in the shock absorber with the holes in the bracket. In some cases you may need to lift the axle slightly with a jack.

to position the hub housing to relieve tension on the control arm pivots. Remove nuts and tap the bolts, which usually include rubber molded bushings. Use emery cloth to clean the bolt/bushing holes. Clean and degrease the arms and spray with rust-inhibiting paint.

When installing the refurbished arms, align the holes in the body/frame mount first, tapping the bushings into place, but not attaching the nuts. Use the jack to adjust axle height so the control arm can be connected at that end. With all bolts in place, tighten the nuts and install cotterpins to secure the arms.

There is no way the beginner can change the camber of independently sprung rear wheels, other than installing new, correct tension springs.

Installing shock absorbers

Placement of shock absorbers may differ according to the car's design. On most cars, the shock absorber sits at an angle attached to the outer end of the axle or trailing arm and the car's frame. This bracing stance gives additional protection against body lean on curves.

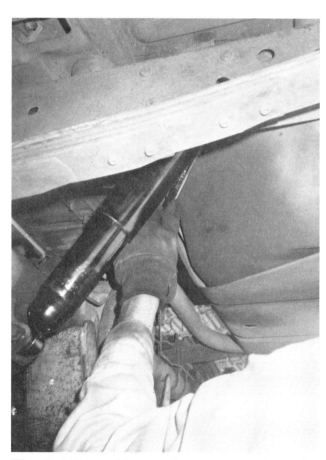

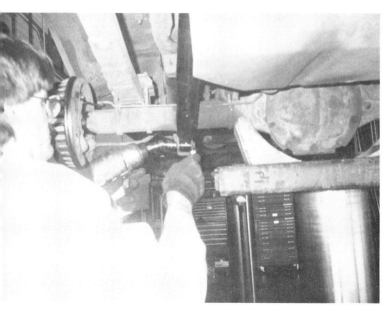

Tighten the nut on the bolt, holding the lower part of the shock absorber in place. The rubber bushing in the attaching end of the unit allows the bolt to pivot slightly as the axle moves up and down, or as weight inside the car varies.

When the bottom end is secured, use an open-end wrench to tighten the nut, holding the top shock absorber bolt in place. Placement of the gas tank or exhaust pipes often makes tightening these nuts a slow process in the limited space.

Tubular shock absorbers can only be replaced, as there is no way to repair them. You can buy new shocks to fit your car at auto supply stores. It's not worth trying to locate good ones at a salvage yard.

Block the front wheels and put jack stands under the rear frame. Use a jack to adjust tension on the shock. Remove the bolt holding the sealed bottom cylinder to the axle, before removing the top bolt, which controls piston movement. On some cars the upper bolt can be reached only from the inside of the luggage area.

Note: For safety reasons, you must not remove any shock absorber holding bolt until the piston arm is fully extended.

Position and fit the bolt through the top part of the new units and use a jack under the axle to align the holes so the lower bolt can be slipped into place. Tighten all bolts.

You may find a setting pointer on the new shocks. Be sure both sides are set to the same degree of firmness.

Antisway/track bars

The antisway or track bar helps cornering by reducing body sway. It is bolted to the axle housing on the left side and to the car's frame on the right. If the bushings are worn, they must be replaced.

To replace the bushings on the antisway/track bar, block the front wheels and put the rear frame on jack stands. Use solvent and clean the nuts. Fit a socket wrench and remove the nuts. Tap the rubber-encased bushings from the rod. Use a wire-bristled brush to scrub away rust and grime before coating the

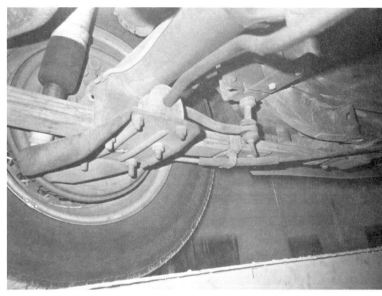

Check the rubber bushings in the antiroll bar attached to the spring hanger or axle and frame on one side, running across to the same type of mounting on the opposite side. Replace them if worn. The twisting action of the rod helps minimize body roll.

rod with an antirust paint and tapping the new rubber bushings in place. A light film of oil or graphite can make the job easier. Fit the washers and tighten the nuts to finish the job.

Reference material on rear suspension systems and the interchangeability of components is listed in the appendix.

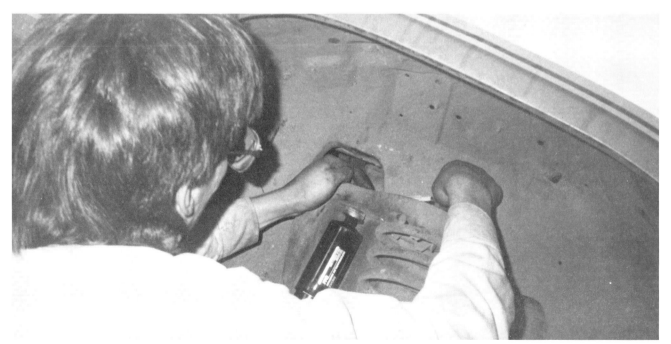

On some cars with rear coils, the top of the shock absorber will have a threaded end on the piston rod to which a washer, spring washer and nut must be fitted. This is often a part of the stamping that holds the top of the coil spring.

Chapter 16

Front suspension system

Front suspension systems evolved slowly for the first few years after World War II. Some hint of things to come started with Studebaker's short-lived Planar system, Kaiser's promised torsion bars (aborted before production) and Ford's overdue abandonment of transverse springs.

In the 1950s, front suspension systems had to keep pace with the development of high-performance

Some GM cars in the early 1950s attached a lever-type double-acting hydraulic shock absorber mounted on the front frame cross-member. The frame end of the upper A- arm is attached to the actuating shafts of the shock absorber, cushioning the movement.

engines. The accepted A-arm configurations were refined. Torsion bars, mounted parallel or transversely to the chassis, came into use.

Coil springs moved from between A-arms to a position above, giving better cornering in the 1960s. As the decade ended, some manufacturers discarded the upper A-arm for a coil spring mounted on a strut high in front-end sheet metal.

Ball joint studs replaced spindle bolts, as knuckle joints were attached to the ends of the upper and lower suspension arms, simplifying the system.

Antiroll bars, which help to transfer and balance cornering forces, were added to give better stability and steering control.

Troubleshooting

You can make visual, hands-on road tests to determine the condition of your car's front suspension system.

If the front end sags to one side, and it isn't because of a soft, or mismatched tire size, you can expect to find a weak coil spring and worn shock absorber. If from a side view the car is noticeably lower in front than the rear, this is another indication that the front coils are weak.

The wheels should be nearly perpendicular to the ground. If one, or both are at an angle, either slanted out at the top or bottom, it is worn ball joints, kingpins or spindle bolts. If an examination of the front tires shows uneven tire wear, or there are wavy cups on the outside of the tread, these also point to kingpin, spindle bolt or ball joint wear, a potentially dangerous condition.

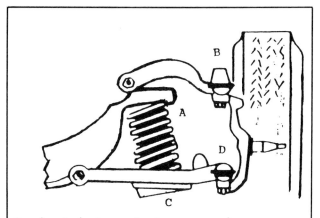

Typical independent suspension system with spring mounted between arms. (A) Coil spring. (B) Load bearing ball joint. (C) Spring hanger or support. (D) Steering ball joint.

With the rear wheels blocked and the front frame on jack stands, examine the coil springs. If you see any turned-in spacers, plan on replacing the springs. These should usually be replaced in pairs, for better balance.

On a road test, if the front end dips when you apply the brakes moderately, it's a sign of weak coils or shocks. If it keeps bobbing after the stop, that's further proof. If the car lurches around corners and wanders as you drive straight ahead, the ball joints must be replaced.

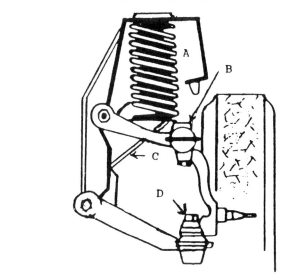

Typical independent suspension system with spring mounted above arms. (A) Coil spring with upper and lower supports. (B) Load bearing ball joint. (C) Tie brace to frame. (D) Steering ball joint.

If your car has suffered front-end damage, it may be easier to replace the front-end assembly containing the cross-member, springs, lower A-arms and antisway bar than make individual repairs to these components. The salvage yard's low price may help you decide.

123

There is close interaction between the front suspension and steering systems. Often, wear in one causes wear in the other, making final diagnosis of the problem more difficult. It is wise to plan front suspension and steering repairs at the same time, if possible, to reduce duplication of effort and for best results.

Sources for parts

You'll have no trouble finding replacement parts for front suspension systems of cars of these years. There is tremendous interchangeability of parts between cars by the same parent company. Also, some suppliers furnished certain components to several car manufacturers. Auto supply stores have interchange manuals on front suspension system parts and can furnish identical replacement parts.

Salvage yards are a good source for replacement springs, A-arms, torsion bars and other components for older cars. Check each item carefully before you buy. Coil springs must be the same height and have the same number of coils. Cars with air conditioning often had heavier coils than cars without air. Torsion bars must have solid, undamaged splines. Spring seating cups in A-arms must not be rusted. However, while you're at it, install new bushings and ball joints, if the ones in the used parts appear to be the least bit worn. It's easier to make these repairs with the components out of the car and install the repaired replacement.

To keep the front suspension system in proper alignment you should always follow factory specifications for your particular car. Sources for this information are listed in the appendix.

Clean rust and grime from the upper and lower pivot bolts on the upper and lower A-arms widely used on cars of the fifties, to install new bushings. It is not necessary to remove front-end sheet metal when replacing a spring or shock absorber.

Replacing bushings

There is no adjustment for worn bushings on A-arms, or any joint in the suspension system. Bushings must be replaced if your test drive indicated excess play or movement in the front end. Because of differences in design and construction, details may differ between makes. The procedures are the same for systems with one or two A-arms. Have replacement parts on hand when you start.

Block the back wheels. Remove weight on the suspension system by placing the front frame on jack stands. Remove the wheels and work one side at a time. Normally, the hub and brake assembly won't have to be disassembled for this work. Remove the bolts holding the brake backing plate to the hub flange, taking care not to damage the flexible brake line. Make a sling to hold this out of your way. There may be a strut from the lower A-arm forward to the frame to protect the A-arm from braking stresses. If this is in your way, it should be removed. There may also be an antiroll bar running from one A-arm forward to the frame, across the car, and to the corresponding A-arm on the other side. This may need to be disconnected at each A-arm.

A long shaft, threaded on both ends, fits through bushings in the front and back of the upper A-arm, holding it to the frame. On some cars, there may be a short, threaded shaft for each bushing. Remove the cotterpins, nuts and washers and tap the shafts out of their bushings. Use a ball peen hammer to tap against a cold chisel or piece of hardwood to force the bushings out of the A-arm. Do not hit directly against the A-arm, as you can cause a burr, making the fitting of replacement bushings difficult.

Support the lower A-arm with a jack, and follow the same procedures used to remove the shafts and bushings from the upper A-arm.

Tap the bushings out of the brackets attached to the frame, through which the shafts also fit. Use solvent and emery cloth to clean these holes.

If the bushings are badly worn, the shafts on which the A-arms pivot may have to be replaced. If not, clean them with solvent and fine emery cloth and coat with oil or graphite.

Press the new bushings into place, in the A-arms, as well as those in the brackets attached to the frame. If you can't tap the new bushings into the A-arms, you may need to use an arbor press to do the job.

With the bushings in place, align the upper A-arm with the bracket on the frame. Tap the shaft into place, securing the upper A-arm to the frame.

Use a jack to position the lower A-arm, and follow the same procedures to fit the pivoting shaft into the new bushings on the lower A-arm and frame.

On some cars, you'll need to remove the coil spring and shock absorber before removing the bushings in the A-arms. Directions for these jobs are covered later in this chapter.

With new bushings and shafts in place, the A-arm unit can be attached to the hub flange. Bolt the strut

You may need to remove the bracket holding the brake tubing to install new bushings in the upper and lower A-arms. Remove the ball joints at the top and bottom, which hold the steering knuckle and stub axle.

Install new bushings on the pivot shafts holding the upper A-arm to the front frame as on this 1957 Cadillac. The coil spring, with shock absorber inside, fits through a hole in the frame, lowering the car considerably.

Attaching brackets, bolted to the front frame cross-member, hold the shafts to which the lower A-arms are attached. Tap in new bushings and install new grease fittings to give them *longer life. Clean and repaint suspension components with black enamel.*

to the lower A-arm, as well as the A-arm end of the antiroll bar. Attach the brake backing plate and drum and wheel to complete the job.

Torsion bars

Torsion bars are tempered steel rods used in place of front coil springs to absorb road shocks and help position the wheels in A-arm systems. Spring steel is treated with heat or pressure to make it supple enough to return to its original shape after being twisted, without becoming brittle after repeated twisting. The bars are usually mounted longitudinally, but may also be mounted transversely. One end of the longitudinally mounted bar is connected securely to a bracket on the firewall or frame, the other to a pivot-

On cars with torsion bar front suspension, remove the front brake caliper, front rotor and hub assembly. Install new ball joints on the steering knuckle and A-arm. Be sure the torsion bar is solidly attached to the car's frame.

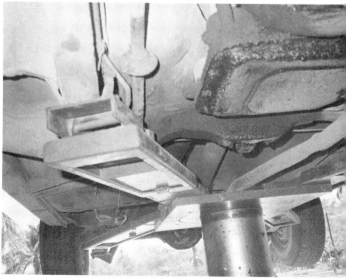

Check that the rubber bumper, which keeps the torsion bar from bottoming out against the car's floor in severe bumps, is in good condition. To replace it, remove the nut holding the bar to the car's frame and slide the old one off and the new one in place.

ing suspension shaft to an A-arm. If the rods are transversely mounted, one end will be attached to the front frame on the opposite side of the car, with the other end attached through a trailing arm to an A-arm.

Torsion bars are adjustable usually at the mounting end to vary the car's ride height, as well as control the firmness or softness of the ride.

To replace bushings in the torsion bar system, follow directions previously described on positioning the car. On longitudinally mounted bars, there'll be one A-arm, either upper or lower, with a rod attached to the torsion bar acting as the other A-arm. On transversely mounted torsion bars, there are usually two A-arms, with one end of each bar attached to the upper or lower A-arm.

Replacing bushings in A-arms is as described previously. Both ends of the bars are square, hexagonal or splined, so the twisting motion of the bar controls up-and-down movement in place of the spring.

There will be a supporting bushing mounted toward the A-arm end of the bar. Release the clamping tension at both ends of the bar, so it can be tapped

from the bushing. Use a blunt, cold chisel or arbor press to force the old bushing out. Clean the hole with solvent and emery cloth and press the new bearing into place. A light coat of oil or graphite will help ease the rod through the new bushing.

Check the attachment where the torsion bar clamps to the frame. This must be tight. Check both ends of the bar, making sure the sharpness of the splines or edges have not eroded. To do their job correctly, the ends cannot move in their housings as the bar twists.

Normally, both torsion bars should be rebushed at the same time, so plan the job accordingly.

When reassembling the system, adjust each bar to the factory-recommended figure for an even ride and best control.

Antiroll bar

Sometimes called a stabilizer, the antiroll bar is attached to the lower A-arm on one side, extends forward, is attached to each side of the front frame rail and extends back to the lower A-arm on the opposite side. Its function is to transfer some of the

When working on suspension systems with the car on jack stands, make sure no fuel or brake tubing is damaged. Examine the car's floor, an important structural part of *unit body/frame cars. Look for early rust-throughs, as on this 1967 Mustang.*

Remove the coil spring from upper A-arm if you find a turn-in spacer in the spring. Remove the bolts holding the upper shock absorber and spring flange in place, before working on the lower end. You may need a spring clamp to compress the spring.

When using a spring clamp to compress a coil spring, be sure to space the clamps evenly around the spring. Tighten each of the three clamps a little at a time so they can't slip out of place. Remove the encased shock absorber before compressing the spring.

braking force from the wheels to the car's frame and to cut down body roll on turns.

Rebushing anti-roll bars

Remove the bolts holding the bushing caps to the front frame member and disconnect the arms attached to each lower A-arm. This will allow you to remove the unit from the car and take it to your workbench for removing the old bushings. Clean and degrease the bar and use rust-inhibiting paint for protection, before inserting the new bushings in their caps. Slide the new bushings on the bar and finger tighten the bolts holding the caps to the frame. You may need a jack under the A-arms to align it with the bar. Finger tighten the ends of the bar to the A-arms, before tightening each nut securely.

Replacing front coil springs

To replace the front coils, position the car as previously described to allow yourself plenty of working room. Some cars fit the front shock absorber inside the coil spring, with the lower eye attached to the lower A-arm and the upper eye attached to a bracket on the frame. Usually, you only have to disconnect the lower A-arm to start work on the spring and shock absorber. Remove the bolts holding the strut between the A-arm and the frame. Remove the cap holding the bottom of the spring in its socket. Remove any turned-in spring expanders. Attach a rented spring compressor, with the threaded hooks evenly spaced. Compress the spring until it is tight enough to be free of the retaining cups and can be lifted out.

If the shock absorber is encased by the coil, remove the bolt through the bottom eye holding the cylinder to the A-arm, then the bolt through the top eye. This will allow the shock absorber to come out when you remove the spring.

With the spring out of the car, release pressure on the hooks slowly to remove the clamps from the spring.

Worn or weak springs usually mean worn rubber stops at both top and bottom of the A-arm or spring cage. Remove the stops, clean the surface and install new stops.

Clean and degrease the upper and lower spring holding cups before coating them with rust-inhibiting paint, and before fitting the insulating pad at the top.

Attach the clamp to the replacement spring and tighten it evenly, compressing the spring. Set the spring in place, with the shock absorber inside it, and release pressure slowly and evenly, making sure the top and bottom of the coil fit into indentations in their cups.

Fit and attach any cap at the bottom of the coil. Slip and secure the bolt through the top eye of the shock. Use a jack, if necessary, to position the lower A-arm so the ball joint can be attached, as well as the lower end of the shock absorber. Bolt the strut to the lower arm. If you had to disconnect an antisway bar to remove the spring, connect it to the A-arm to complete the job.

Replacing front struts

The front coil spring is combined with a telescopic strut on some cars. The lower end of this strut is attached to the upper end of the spindle. A domed metal cap is held in place by bolts. At the center of the cap is a nut and washer which is fitted to a piston end of a hydraulic shock absorber encased in the tubular strut. The flexible rubber bushing between the domed cap cushions the strut.

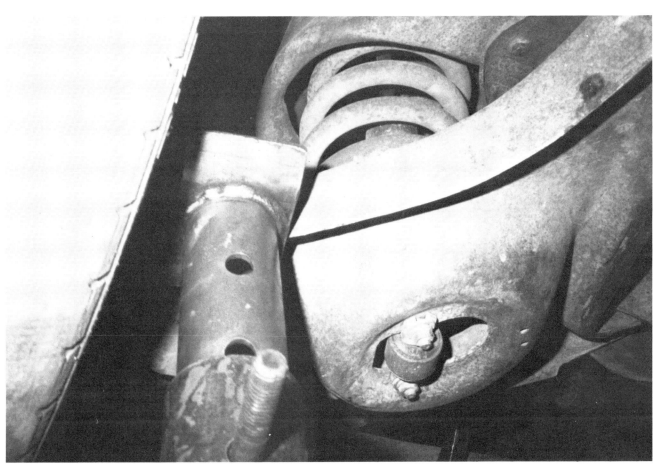

With the front frame solidly on jack stands, put a jack solidly under the lower A-arm so all pressure is released on the nuts holding the bottom of the tubular shock absorber in place. When the jack is removed, you can remove the nut and bushing at the top.

To remove coil springs mounted above upper A-arms, remove the retaining plate at the bottom. Rent the specially engineered clamp that will compress the spring while holding the coils in alignment. Lift the spring, with clamp attached, from the car.

Since the entire strut turns with the steering knuckle, the bushing at the top doubles as part of both the steering and suspension systems.

If the spring must be replaced, remove the upper flange, which is just below the flexible rubber mount,

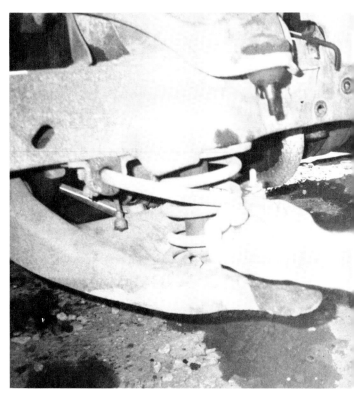

Remove nuts from the upper and lower ball joints and the ends of the stabilizer bar, and tap the threaded end of the ball joints to free them from the upper and lower A-arms. Clean the sockets into which they fit, before fitting replacement joints.

and the spring can be lifted out of the lower flange. Install the new spring, replace the upper flange and install a new rubber bushing in the domed cap. Fit the washer and tighten the cap in place.

Lubrication

Suspension systems will last longer and function better, if parts are well lubricated. Install grease fittings and follow factory lubrication suggestions.

Sources for specific information on front suspension systems are listed in the appendix.

Chapter 17

Steering system

As engineers moved engines forward, putting more weight on the front end, they also added demands on the steering system. Wider tires, common in these years, required more steering effort when parking. What's more, the added speed and power the new engines delivered demanded a more precise and responsive steering system.

Power steering was introduced by Chrysler, as an option in 1951, and quickly became an option on other heavy cars, finally becoming standard on large cars. Power steering was soon offered as an option on smaller cars as well.

Types of systems

Whether manually operated, or power assisted, you'll find one of these three types of steering systems on your car. The manufacturer's specifications will tell you which type.

Worm and roller

The worm and roller is the most commonly used type. The gearbox contains a spiral threaded gear at the end of the steering shaft. This meshes at right angles with a roller gear attached to the drag link.

Recirculating ball

The gearbox of the recirculating ball system contains a spiral gear on the shaft, which fits into threads on a grooved track. This becomes the driven gear and is attached to the drag link. As the worm gear turns, small steel balls circulate through the grooved threads. As they reach the end of the threads, a tube allows them to return to the beginning of the thread track, completing the loop.

Rack and pinion

Simple and direct, the rack and pinion gearbox is attached to the bottom of the shaft. As the steering wheel is turned, the shaft meshes with teeth cut into one section of the tie-rod, and moves the wheels to the left or right.

Proper operation of each system depends on solid gearbox mounting, thorough lubrication, resilient bushings and bearings in good condition in all joints. Adjustments, repairs and parts replacement are within the average beginner's capabilities. Front-end alignment is the exception; it must be done professionally.

Troubleshooting

Because of the close interaction of steering and suspension system components, many of the trouble-shooting suggestions have been covered in the previous chapter. Make the visual checks already described.

If during your road test the car pulled to one side, check for uneven tire pressure and unbalanced wheels.

The recirculating ball steering system utilizes small steel balls that roll in grooves on the steering shaft as the worm gear turns. As the balls reach the end of the threads, a tube allows their return to the beginning of the track, completing the loop.

With the front end on jack stands so the weight is off the wheels, grasp the wheel at front and back and at top and bottom. Movement in either direction indicates wear in the ball joint linkage or bearings, spindle bolts or steering knuckle joints.

Remove the bolts holding the hub assembly portion of the steering knuckle. Remove the nuts on top and bottom of the spindle bolt. Drive the bolt out to install new bushings between the steering knuckle and the end of the lower A-arm. Install new grease fittings.

This could also mean the front end is out of alignment, loose front wheel bearings or steering linkage. If the front wheels shimmy, this can indicate worn tie-rod ends, loose or worn steering linkage or worn front wheel bearings.

The steering wheel shouldn't turn more than an inch in either direction before the front wheels turn. Excess play in the steering wheel can be caused by a worn gearbox, worn bushings in the drag line and worn ball joints in the tie-rods.

Poor steering wheel return can mean gearbox wear, front-end misalignment, lack of lubrication in the steering linkage or worn ball joints.

If the car has power steering and you find it hard to steer, first check the fluid level, then make sure the drive belt is tight. Check for leaks in the fittings at the ends of the power steering hoses. The trouble could be caused by worn bearings or vanes in the pump. If there's a loud squeal on sharp turns, it indicates a slipping or worn belt. A grinding noise can indicate low fluid level.

Based on your troubleshooting discoveries, schedule any necessary repairs or replacements, combining them with front suspension repairs to avoid duplicated effort.

Replacing spindle bolts

Spindle bolts, also known as kingpins, are really the pin in the steering hinge at each wheel. They can't be repaired, only replaced. If worn, the bushings through which they fit will probably be worn, too. Plan on replacing both kingpin and bushings at the same time.

Block the rear wheels, put jack stands under the front frame and remove the wheel. Remove the brake drum and the backing plate from the hub flange as a unit, and tie them out of your way.

The spindle bolt runs through the wheel end of the upper and lower A-arms and the steering knuckle. Remove the bolts holding the bushing journals to the upper and lower ends of the A-arms. Take the knuckle joint, with the stub axle attached, to your workbench for spindle bolt removal.

There may be threads on one or both ends of the spindle bolt. Remove the nuts and washers. Tap against wood to drive the spindle bolt out. Be careful not to damage the knuckle joint when driving out the bushings. An arbor press can make this job easier.

Clean the holes in the upper and lower A-arm bushing journals and the hole in the steering knuckle with solvent and fine steel wool. Coat the new bushings with light oil or graphite. Tap against a piece of wood to protect the bushings as you seat them.

Align the A-arm bushing journals with the knuckle joint and insert the spindle bolt. Tap against a piece of wood to avoid damaging the threads.

Fit washers, tighten nuts and install cotterpins holding the spindle bolt in place. Bolt the top bushing journal housing to the upper A-arm. Use a jack under the lower A-arm to help you position the lower bushing journal which has to be bolted to the lower A-arm. Tighten all nuts securely, attach the brake backing plate to the flange on the knuckle joint and mount the wheel to complete the job.

Spindle bolts are also used on cars with torsion bars in place of coil springs. Removal and replacement procedures are essentially the same.

Remember any problems you encountered while working on one side, so you can avoid them on the other side.

Replacing ball joints

Spindle bolts, or kingpins, gave way to upper and lower ball joints in many cars in the late fifties. These ball studs, protected by a strong rubber cushion, fit snugly into a lubricated socket. Though the ball can circulate freely in the socket, it can't slip out of it. Since they allow movement on more than one plane, they permit the wheels to move up and down with the suspension system, while being steered at the same time.

The knuckle joint with hub flange fits between the upper and lower A-arms and is connected to them at the top and bottom by ball joint studs.

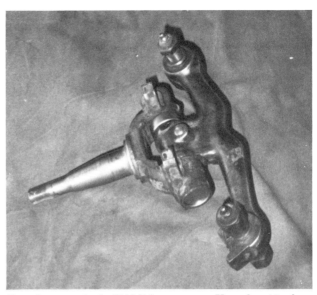

Buy the correct rebuild kit for your car. Use solvent to clean the steering knuckle assembly before taking it apart. Inspect the stub axle for wear. Remove the spindle bolt and bushings. Install the new bushings and tap the replacement spindle bolt in place.

Put the front end on jack stands. Use a jack to relieve pressure so the top and bottom bolts that separate and position the upper and lower A-arms can be removed. Take the steering knuckle with stub axle to a workbench for installing new bushings.

Fit the top pivot of the repaired knuckle joint into the upper A-arm. Jack the lower A-arm in place to align the bottom holes. Fit the top of the shock absorber and slide the spring over it. Compress the spring and attach the bottom of the shock absorber.

133

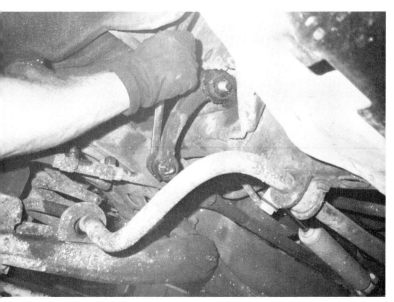

With the front end on jack stands and the wheel removed, replace worn bushings, which are an integral part of the steering system idler arm. Remove the top and bottom nuts and pry the arm loose. The nut is at the top of one end, and at the bottom of the other.

Block the rear wheels and position the front frame on jack stands. Use a jack under the lower arm to relieve tension, as you remove the machine screws holding the stud to the arms. With these removed, tap

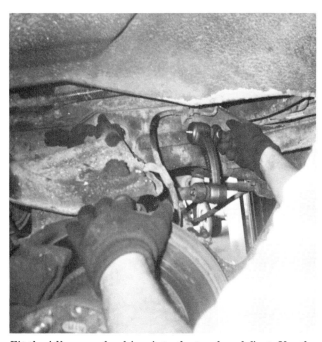

Fit the idler arm bushing into the track rod first. Use the leverage the rod provides to align the top bushing with the hole in the idler arm frame bracket. Tap the bushing into place and tighten the upper and lower nuts securely.

the ball joints out of the A-arms and steering knuckle; tap up to remove the upper stud, and down to remove the lower one. This frees the knuckle joint, which is attached to the stub axle.

Clean the holes through which the ball joints fit with solvent. Clean and degrease the steering knuckle. Position and align the steering knuckle and tap the upper ball joint stud in place. Finger tighten the machine screws at the top and the nut at the bottom.

Use a jack to help align the lower arm and steering knuckle. Tap the ball joint stud in place and finger tighten the nut. Using a socket wrench, tighten all machine screws and nuts and install cotterpins.

Ball joints will last much longer if you install grease fittings and lubricate the joints.

Replacing bushings

All joints in the steering system are protected by bushings. As these wear, sloppy control results. If your troubleshooting indicated this condition, bushing replacement is necessary.

As with other steering system repairs, put jack stands under the frame, releasing all tension on the joints. Use solvent and a wire-bristled brush to clean rust and grime from the threads.

Work one joint at a time, removing the cotterpin, nut, washer and any spacer. Tap out the old bushing. Clean the holes in both parts with solvent and insert the replacement bushing. Use your jack to help align the holes, and tap against a wooden block to protect threads.

All replacement bushings should fit snugly, but shouldn't be forced into place. Tighten each nut securely, after making sure all spacers and washers

Install new grease fittings with all bushings you replace in the steering or front suspension system for longer life. The idler arm attaches to the track rod connecting the two tie-rods, turning both front wheels in the same direction.

134

are in place. Fit cotterpins. Install a grease fitting if possible to give longer bushing life.

Whether the bushings are on the tie-rod, drag link or steering arms, they are all removed and installed in the same manner. You'll have no trouble locating new replacement parts at auto supply stores. Many steering systems were made by one supplier and furnished to more than one manufacturer. Parts interchange manuals give this information.

Power steering repairs

If your troubleshooting indicated any problem with the power steering system, you should make repairs, many of which you can do yourself.

Driven by a V-belt from a crankshaft pulley, a pump forces fluid to both sides of a piston in the hydraulic cylinder. This is attached to the gearbox in worm and roller systems, and to both sides of the gearbox in recirculating ball types. The pump housing will be where the pinion meets the rack in rack and pinion systems.

A valve controls fluid flow. In straight-ahead steering, pressure is equal. When the steering wheel is turned, fluid is forced to one side of the piston through the high-pressure hose, pushing the driven gear in one direction. Fluid on the other side of the piston is returned through the low-pressure hose to the reservoir.

Have the necessary parts on hand before starting work. Block the rear wheels and put the front frame

Thread the bushing end of the track rod in place. Fit the bushing into the pitman arm attached to the steering gearbox. Use a box- or open-end wrench to tighten all connections. Fit cotterpins into the castellated nuts to secure the system.

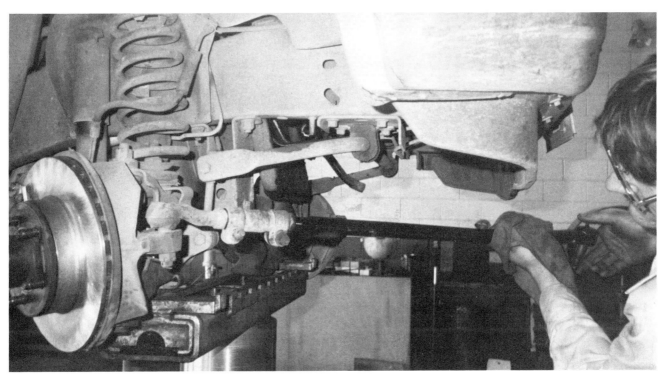

Screw the threaded end of the replacement track rod into the end of the tie-rod. You may have to adjust the length of the track rod in order to align the front wheels. After installing *any component in the steering/suspension system, have the front end aligned.*

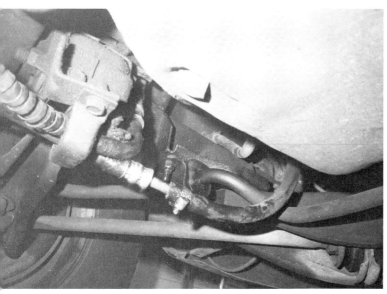

Examine the high- and low-pressure hoses from the reservoir to the pump mechanism. If you find wet or crimped hoses, they must be replaced. If there are leaks around the steel fittings, replace them, taking care to prevent cross-threading.

Though there are rebuild kits for certain power steering pumps, some are complicated and difficult for the beginner to handle. Rebuilt replacements are readily available at reasonable prices. You can usually locate a used pump at a salvage yard.

Check the belt driving the pulley on the power steering pump, which may be part of the reservoir. If the belt is loose,

back off the holding nut and pry the unit so the belt is taut before tightening the nut, keeping the unit in position.

on jack stands. Drain the system. Loosen tension on the drive belt. Remove the bolts holding the pump in place. Disconnect the hoses from the pump, later from the cylinder case. On some earlier systems the pump and reservoir were separate, but since the late fifties they have been combined.

There are rebuild kits for some pumps. The work is tricky, but can be handled by persons with average mechanical skill. Follow directions carefully, if you decide to use a rebuild kit, and keep the work area clean and free of lint.

There are rebuilt power steering units available from auto supply stores, and good used ones from salvage yards. When buying a used pump, check the pulley shaft bearing to be sure it isn't worn. Because of parts interchangeability, you should have no trouble finding a replacement power steering pump.

Check the hoses carefully. If there are any abrasions or indications of leaking around the fittings, the hoses should be replaced. Ready-made replacements are available for most cars, or certain shops will make hoses to fit.

Remove and degrease the outside of the unit. Disassemble and clean the piston assembly, replacing any packings that are brittle or worn. Check the fittings on the unit, making sure they are tight and not cross-threaded. Make sure the rod from the piston to the tie-rod, or other mounting on the steering system is free of rust and not bent. Bolt the repaired unit in place securely.

Attach the pump/reservoir unit, making sure hose fittings are tight. Fit the unit on the mounting bracket and slip the belt over the crankshaft and

After your repairs, have the front end professionally aligned. Rods and gauges are necessary to set the correct caster, camber and toe-in, which are necessary for easy handling and safe driving. The cost is low.

Replacement gearboxes with built-in power steering pumps in good condition are available at salvage yards. Because many within the same family of cars are interchangeable, you won't necessarily have to buy from the same make, model or year.

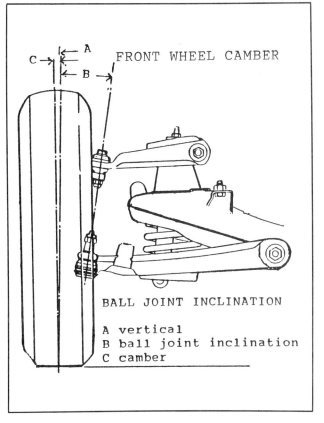

FRONT WHEEL CAMBER

BALL JOINT INCLINATION

A vertical
B ball joint inclination
C camber

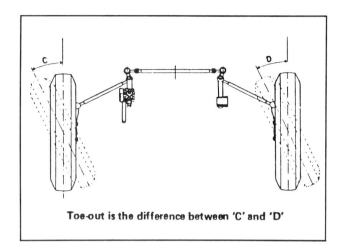

Toe-out is the difference between 'C' and 'D'

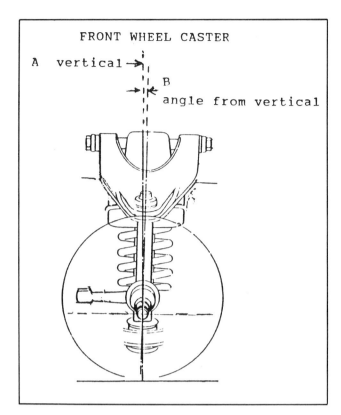

FRONT WHEEL CASTER

A vertical →

B
angle from vertical

drive pulleys. Use a pry bar to stretch the belt tight, and tighten the holding bolt. Fill the reservoir with the recommended fluid. Run the engine and turn the steering wheel from lock to lock a few times. Check and refill the reservoir.

Leave a clean newspaper under the repaired unit the first night to check for leaks. Only periodic checking of the fluid level and belt tension is required.

When you've finished with steering system repairs, take the car to an alignment shop for a professional checkup.

Follow the manufacturer's specifications when making all repairs and adjustments to the steering system.

Sources for additional and specific information on steering systems are included in the appendix.

Chapter 18

Brakes

As traffic increased and cars became faster and more powerful during these years, brake systems had to be improved. Twin-chamber master cylinders provided extra safety by dividing the flow of hydraulic fluid. Larger drums allowed faster heat dissipation, and power assists gave quicker stops with less pedal pressure. Disc brakes were introduced in the mid-sixties as an option on some cars.

Your car's brakes change motion energy into heat energy. How quickly they accomplish this, and the dissipation of that heat, indicates their efficiency.

Troubleshooting

If your test drive indicated other than dependable, quick stops, the brake system needs an overhaul.

If the pedal is low, check the fluid level; check for air in the system; inspect brake adjustment at wheels; look for a weak flexible hose; check for a warped rotor or drum; notice if there is a faulty wheel or master cylinder; and check for brake drum or pad wear.

If you found that a hard push on the pedal resulted in little braking, the problem could be caused by the following: fading due to overheating; grease or brake fluid on the linings or pads; glaze on the pads or linings; a faulty power booster; or low or no vacuum at the power booster.

A spongy or creeping brake pedal is usually caused by a leak in the hydraulic system, low fluid level, air in the brake lines or a weak flexible hose.

If the brakes grab, check for air in the line, a leaking brake cylinder, grease on the linings or pads or front-end misalignment.

Cars that pull to one side, when the brakes are applied, usually have worn linings, grease on the linings or pads or scored rotors or drums.

If the brakes are noisy, check for linings or pads that are too thick. The pads or linings may be glazed, or there may be dirt in the brake assembly at the wheels.

To check on some of the aforementioned problems, the brake drums will have to be removed and brake components taken apart. Directions on how to do these jobs are covered in following pages.

Parts availability

Because of standardization of brake parts within cars manufactured by the same parent company, parts are readily available. Many manufacturers bought components from the same supplier, making parts interchangeability easy. Auto supply stores can get you just about any brake part you'll need. If you buy drums or rotors from a salvage yard, plan on having them turned down on a lathe before use.

To replace brake shoes, or rebuild the wheel cylinder, use a jack to support the axle. Remove the wheel. Insert a punch in a hole in the drum and tap against it to jar the drum from the hub. Lay the drum open side down and tap against it to loosen asbestos dust.

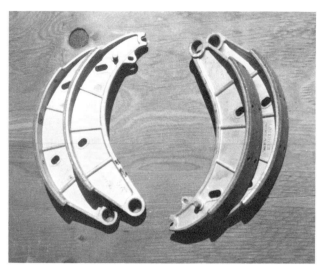

Brake lining should be the same thickness on all parts of the shoe. Lining thickness should be at least $\frac{1}{32}$ in. above the rivets, bonded shoes no less than $\frac{1}{8}$ in. thickness. Lining thinner on one end indicates a broken or stretched spring, or seized parts.

There are rebuild kits for master cylinders and drum brake wheel cylinders, as well as for disc brake cylinders and certain power brake units. Badly pitted master and wheel cylinders can be rebored and sleeved by machine shops if necessary.

New or relined brake shoes are available on a trade-in basis. You must buy new pads for disc brakes, as worn pads can't be relined, so there is no trade-in. If there is a quality choice, buy the ones with the longest guarantee to postpone doing the job again.

For safety reasons, don't put off making needed brake repairs.

Inspecting brake linings

Some inspections require removing the wheel and brake drum, others can be made visually with the wheel and drum or rotor in place.

Put the axle solidly on jack stands so the wheels can be turned. Look for a rubber-plugged inspection hole near the outer edge of the backing plate. Use pliers to remove the plug. With a bright light, you can see the amount of lining on the shoes. New linings on brake shoes are about $\frac{3}{16}$ in. thick, so you can gauge the wear on the shoes. Be sure to replace the rubber plug to keep out dirt.

With the wheel removed, look for the inspection hole near the outer edge of the drum, through which you can see the lining. Turn the wheel to see the thickness of the entire lining on both shoes.

If the lining appears worn to $\frac{1}{16}$ in. thickness, there's the risk of scored drums from rivets, so the brake drums must be removed for a closer inspection. If the linings are bonded to the drums, thickness can be as low as $\frac{1}{32}$ in. before replacing.

There is usually an inspection hole in the caliper and piston assembly on disc brakes, which allows you

Measure the drum. If it is bell-mouthed, that is, wider against the backing plate than at the wheel, or if the drum has been scored by rivets, it can usually be turned down on a lathe at a machine shop or a shop specializing in brake repairs.

Brake rotors that have been scored can often be given additional life by turning them down on a lathe. This work is done at a machine shop, or brake repair shop. The machine measures the metal removed in thousandths of an inch.

140

to see the thickness of the lining on the inner pad. Look along the edge of the outer pad to gauge its thickness.

Inspecting drums and rotors

If the brake shoes or pads are worn, you need to inspect the drums and discs. Discs can be inspected visually, once the wheel is removed. If they are scored, and have deep concentric marks, they should be turned down on a lathe, or replaced.

Brake drums must be examined for scoring by rivets from worn shoes. Directions for inspecting brake drums differ because of construction and assembly methods. Some drums are made integral with the hub and can only be inspected if the hub is removed from the axle. On other cars, the brake drum and hub are separate, with wheel mounting studs holding the drum in place, making inspection easier.

Hub removal

Remove the wheel to get at the hub. Use slip joint pliers to remove the dust cap. Withdraw the cotterpin from the castellated bearing adjustment nut and remove the nut. Back off the brake shoe adjustment star wheel so there is no pressure against the drum. Rock the drum, and the bearing and thrust washer should slide far enough on the shaft so you can remove them. Pull the brake drum containing the inner bearing and grease seal from the axle.

Stuff clean rags in the hub to keep brake dust and dirt out of the bearing, while you inspect it. If you find scoring, grooves or discoloration, the drums can usually be turned down on a lathe. If the drum appears to be bell-mouthed, that is, the diameter is wider at the open end, it usually must be replaced. This is usually caused by worn or warped shoes, broken or weak springs or parts that may bind.

Caution: Do not inhale brake dust, as many brake linings contain asbestos. Do not use compressed air to clean brake components.

Spread newspapers on your workbench. Drop the drum face down from a couple of inches, jarring dust loose. Remove the bearing. Sponge with a detergent and water solution to remove the rest. Rinse with clear water and dispose of the papers. Slosh the brake assembly with the solution, let it stand about ten minutes; then scrub with a stiff-bristled brush and rinse with clear water.

Linings

Replace bonded linings worn to a $1/16$ in. thickness, and riveted linings worn to $1/32$ in. of the rivet heads.

Use solvent to clean grease and grime from brake drums before working on them. If you don't want to take them to a coin-operated car wash for cleaning, use kerosene mixed with a strong household detergent and a soft-bristled brush to do the job.

Because of the danger of inhaling asbestos fibers when working on drum brakes, use a hot detergent solution and a soft-bristled brush to scrub the parts. Rinse with clear water. Never use compressed air to blow out the dust.

When making replacement brake lines, it is usually necessary to flare the ends after the fittings have been slipped on the tubing. Rent or borrow a handy tool made for this use. You may want to wrap the lines with plastic tape to avoid vibration noises.

Linings worn thinner at one end indicate weak or broken springs, binding parts or defective brake shoes. Linings worn on the outer edge indicate bell-mouthed drums.

Inspecting hydraulic systems

Look for signs of leaking fluid where the brake lines join the master cylinder and the wheel cylinders. Check the fittings where flexible hoses screw into cylinders or brake calipers. Also check the seal where the operating rod goes through the power unit or into the master cylinder. Examine all fittings along the line, and look for spots where dirt has stuck to tiny leaks, to make sure there are no external leaks.

Most leaking fittings can be cured by tightening them. Leaks in fittings to caliper cylinders and flexible hoses usually require replacing the parts. Damaged lines must be replaced.

To check for internal leaks you can't see, such as fluid bypassing one of the pistons, seals or valves, start the engine and press the brake pedal for at least thirty seconds. If the pedal creeps slowly toward the floor, without any loss of fluid in the reservoir, there's a leak

Clip hydraulic brake lines along the frame to keep them from chafing. Fit rubber grommets anyplace a brake line fits through a hole in the chassis. Be sure fittings on flexible tubing are tight and that the tubing can't be pinched by moving parts.

within the master cylinder, which will have to be repaired.

If the pedal creeps, and there is a loss of fluid in the reservoir, there's a leak around one of the bleeder valves, or one of the brake cylinders is leaking. You can usually spot which one, by looking for fluid on the brake backing plate, or caliper. That cylinder assembly will have to be rebuilt or replaced.

Rebuilding wheel cylinders

If leaks indicate the wheel cylinders need rebuilding, buy the appropriate rebuild kit. This is a job you should be able to do in one day.

With the parts on hand, put the car on jack stands and remove one wheel at a time. Remove the hub and drum assembly, exposing the brake mechanism. From under the car, use a screwdriver to adjust the star wheel so the shoes are in the full-out position. Disconnect the brake line and remove the bolts holding the wheel cylinder to the backing plate.

Disconnect the brake shoe return springs. You may have to remove the springs from the shoe hold-down pins. Spread the shoes and pull the cylinder from the backing plate.

Clean and degrease the cylinder before disassembling it at your workbench. Remove the bleeder valve. Pull the actuating links from the cylinder and remove the dust caps. Tap out the pistons and plungers, and remove the inner spring. Clean the inside with solvent, and soak pistons, spring and actuating links in solvent.

If the cylinder bore is pitted, it costs less to replace it than to have it resleeved at a machine shop.

After having the brake shoes relined and the wheel cylinders rebuilt, clean and paint the backing plate before mounting any components. Adjust the shoes to the full-in position when mounting the drum and wheel. Fill the reservoir and purge air from the lines.

Assemble the cleaned and replacement parts, following directions on the rebuild kit. A little brake fluid helps slide the pistons and plungers in place. Fit the dust caps and install the bleeder valve. Bolt the

Before and after. Disconnect and remove the hydraulic wheel cylinders from the backing plate. Dismantle and clean with solvent. Pitted cylinders can be resleeved, or replaced.

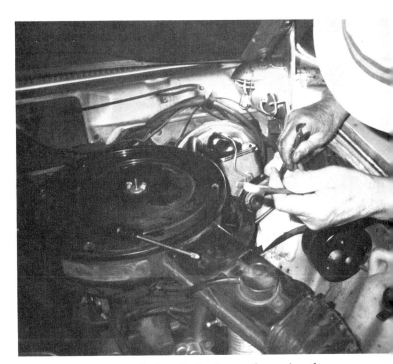

After repairing or replacing the brakes and purging the lines of air, refill the master cylinder and check the line fittings. Adjust brakes by turning the star wheel to the full-out position, and back it off until the wheel turns without binding.

repaired cylinder to the backing plate and connect the brake line. Attach the shoe return springs and fit hold-down springs to their rods. Replace the hub/drum assembly and wheel to complete the job. When all wheel cylinders have been repaired, fill the reservoir and purge the system of air.

Spin the wheel, and from under the car, turn the star wheel, or adjusting nut to force the shoes against the drum. When you can no longer turn the wheel by hand, back the shoes away from the drum until the wheel turns without dragging.

Rebuilding master cylinders

The master cylinder, combined with the reservoir and bolted to the firewall or frame, also can be rebuilt in one day if you have the appropriate rebuild kit on hand.

Disconnect the fittings attaching the lines. Disconnect the operating rod from the pedal. Remove the nuts holding it to the frame or power unit at the firewall and lift it from the car. Brake fluid can damage the car's paint, so keep it tipped to prevent spilling any on the fender panel.

Clamp the power brake diaphragm solidly in your vise to take it apart. Use pliers to straighten the crimps holding the two parts together. Make some notes on the order in which the inside components are fitted, to make reassembly easier.

Empty the fluid and use solvent to degrease the outside, before taking it apart. Remove the plunger dust cap. Note the progression in which you disassemble it. Remove the seals, plunger, springs and pistons. You'll be fitting new seals and plungers, but soak the other parts in solvent.

Clean the inside of the unit thoroughly, making sure the tiny orifices in the cylinder are clear to allow the fluid to pass through.

You may notice rust spots inside the reservoir or cylinder. If scrubbing with solvent and emery cloth doesn't remove the spots, the unit isn't worth repairing. You can buy a rebuilt unit from an auto supply store, or a rebuildable one from a salvage yard.

Fit replacement parts into the cylinder, following directions on the rebuild kit. A few drops of brake fluid will help slide washers, cups and packings in place. Fit the fragile gasket carefully and attach the dust cup to the operating rod. Be sure the tiny vents on the cover plate are open and that the bail-type fastener holds it tight.

Attach the repaired cylinder to the frame or firewall and tighten the nuts securely. Finger tighten the fittings to all hydraulic lines before a final tightening. Fill the reservoir with the recommended fluid. The brake lines will have to be purged of air, and the reservoir filled to the full mark or to ½ in. from the top.

Power brake booster repairs

It helps to understand how the power booster works, before replacing the unit or making repairs. It is attached to the firewall and the master cylinder attaches to it. As the pedal is pressed, hydraulic fluid opens a valve admitting air into one side of a diaphragm, which is inside the vacuum chamber. This

Once the vacuum-operated diaphragm is disassembled, clean each part with solvent. Assemble replacement parts according to directions with the kit. Check the hose to the intake manifold, and if it leaks replace the hose and clamps.

causes a pressure differential. As vacuum is maintained, atmospheric pressure on the other side of the diaphragm pushes the piston in the master cylinder, applying the brakes.

Upon release of pedal pressure, a coil spring releases the diaphragm to its original position.

On some 1950s cars, the booster can be disassembled for repair. On later models, the diaphragm cover was crimped and sealed and thus cannot be repaired by the beginner.

Make some tests before buying a replacement or rebuilt unit. Before starting the engine, pump the brake pedal a few times to use any vacuum reserve. Press the pedal firmly and start the engine. You should feel the pedal move down a bit, as vacuum adds to your foot pressure.

Since the booster unit works on the engine's vacuum, disconnect the vacuum hose or tube to the booster. With the engine running, put your finger over the tube's end. You should feel the vacuum. If you don't, trace the tubing looking for leaks. Remove the tube and either blow or run a wire through it. It must not be blocked. Check the vacuum connections on the booster and manifold.

Use a vacuum gauge to determine what vacuum the engine is pulling. It should test to at least 15 psi. Some cars fitted a mechanical pump to furnish vacuum for the brakes. This should also pull at least 15 psi.

Remove the vacuum inlet valve from the booster unit. After cleaning it, test by sucking air through it. It should open in one direction only.

Some cars added a reserve vacuum tank near the firewall, which provided vacuum for the brake booster in case the engine stalled. Check this tank, tubing and connections for leaks. Any defective power booster component should be repaired or replaced.

Rebuilt units are available at moderate cost and can be attached easily. You may not have to disconnect the hydraulic lines. Disconnect the vacuum line and the brake pedal plunger rod. Remove the bolts holding the master cylinder to the booster, and the bolts holding the booster to the firewall.

Install the replacement booster by bolting the unit to the master cylinder. Bolt the booster to the firewall. Connect the pushrod to the brake pedal. Then connect the vacuum line to complete the job.

Replacing brake shoes

Most brake problems can be corrected by installing new brake shoes. This is an easy and relatively quick job.

You can buy replacement brake shoes on a trade-in basis from most automotive supply stores. Their specification sheets will furnish the necessary information.

With the car solidly on jack stands, remove the wheel and hub, as previously directed, to expose the backing plate holding the brake assembly.

Use pliers to remove the shoe return springs. Remove the hold-down springs from the brake shoe hold-down rods. Remove the clips and washers holding the shoes to the pivot shafts. Push the shoes from

To be sure the power brake diaphragm is getting the correct amount of vacuum from the engine, use a vacuum gauge connected to the outlet in the intake manifold. Refer to factory specifications for the recommended vacuum figure.

To remove the brake shoes, use a screwdriver or prong to release each spring from the shoes. Because they will be under tension, use gloves to protect your hands as they spring loose. Remember the progression in which each is removed for easy assembly.

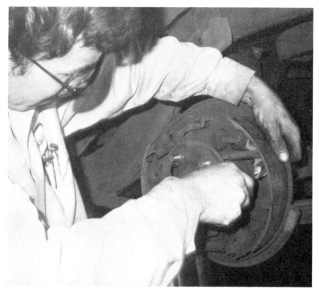

Use pliers to remove the small hold-down spring, which fits over the positioning pin on each shoe and holds the shoe to the backing plate. The bottom of the shoes may fit over positioning pins, or be notched to fit over the end of the adjusting mechanism.

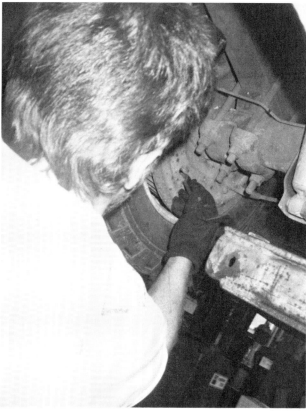

Remove the rubber cap on the access hole on the backing plate. A lug hole may also act as an access hole to aadjust drum brakes. The hole acts as a fulcrum for a heavy screwdriver or brake spoon for brake adjustments. Fit plug after adjustments.

the actuating links and remove them from the backing plate.

Clean any brake lining dust from the backing plate, as directed earlier. Put a little graphite on pivot shafts and brake shoe positioning rods, before fitting the new brake shoes. Attach the clips and washers on the pivot shafts and the springs over the shoe positioning rods. Use pliers and a screwdriver to stretch and attach the shoe return springs.

Match the actuating links from the wheel cylinder into the notches in the brake shoes. Turn the adjusting nut or star wheel to the full-in position to accommodate the new, thicker linings.

Replace the cleaned brake drum, and on combined drum and hubs, fit the oil seal, bearing, positioning washer, nut and cotterpin. Fit the dust cap before mounting the wheel.

Before you remove the jack stand, spin the wheel and turn the star wheel to force the shoes against the drum. When you can no longer turn the wheel by hand, back the shoes just far enough from the drum so the wheel turns without any drag.

Replacing disc brake pads

Disc brakes were adapted from airplane use to solve brake cooling problems. A flat disc, rotating with the wheel, takes the place of a brake drum. Hydraulically operated calipers force brake pads against the disc by clamping action. The disc or rotor isn't distorted by heat generated, so no braking area is lost. Some cars used double discs, separating the braking area by air passages to hasten cooling.

All components at the wheels are exposed to air, which helps dissipate heat.

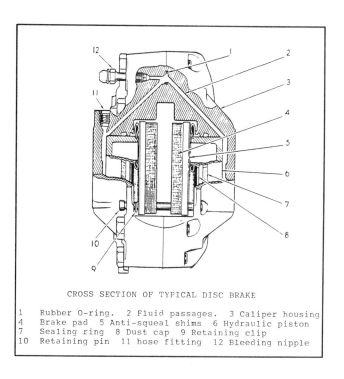

CROSS SECTION OF TYPICAL DISC BRAKE

```
1    Rubber O-ring.  2 Fluid passages.  3 Caliper housing
4    Brake pad  5 Anti-squeal shims  6 Hydraulic piston
7    Sealing ring  8 Dust cap  9 Retaining clip
10   Retaining pin  11 hose fitting  12 Bleeding nipple
```

With the wheel removed, use a socket wrench to remove the bolts joining the two parts of the caliper housing. Buy the correct rebuild kit and follow the directions. All parts must be spotless. A little brake fluid helps parts slip into place.

Use water-pump pliers to hold the hydraulic pistons in place when mounting the caliper housing to the small backing plate. To help cool the brake pads, a large portion of both sides of the revolving disc is open to the air.

Remove the pads and insert a piece of fine, abrasive paper in its place and spin the disc to clean and deglaze it before installing the new pads. Glaze that has formed on the rotors must be removed so replacement pads will work properly.

With new pads in place, the wheel cylinder rebuilt and the caliper housings bolted together, drive the positioning pins in place. Install the bleeder nipple. Attach the brake fluid line. Fill the reservoir and purge the lines of air.

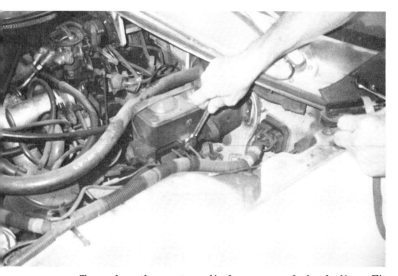

To work on the master cylinder, remove the brake lines. Fit a wrench carefully and use only enough pressure to loosen the fittings. The reservoir is usually an integral part of the master cylinder. There will usually be two lines for brake fluid.

Some cars have a metal wear indicator embedded in the pad that makes a squealing noise when the pad wears to its replacement thickness. Others have an electrical sensing unit that flashes this information to a dashboard indicator.

If you're only going to change the pads, put the car on jack stands. Remove the wheel, and the brake assembly is directly in front of you.

Remove the two pins holding the bracket that fits over the top of the pads. Disconnect any sending unit wire and lift the pads out of the calipers. Wipe out any brake dust in the unit, before slipping the replacement pads into place. Attach any electrical connection and insert and tighten the holding pins to complete the job.

Rebuilding disc brake wheel cylinders

For complete disc brake repairs, remove the aforementioned pins and disconnect the hydraulic line. Remove the bolts holding the caliper unit to the backing plate. Take it apart at your workbench, which must be free of any dirt, dust or lint that could get into the unit.

There are rebuild kits for some brake diaphragms. Clamp the diaphragm in a vise when disassembling it for rebuilding. The diaphragm is spring loaded, so take it apart slowly. You may prefer to buy a rebuilt unit or one from a salvage yard.

148

Have the correct rebuild kit on hand. Dismantle the caliper, noting the progression in which the parts come out. Clean and degrease the inside and outside of the unit before inserting new rubber O-rings, piston and dust seal. Clean and seat the antirattle spring. If there are metal backing shims behind the brake pads, be sure they're clean and in place, when you start reassembling the unit.

Clean the fluid passages within the housing, including the opening for the bleeder valve. Follow the instructions included with the rebuild kit, as you replace parts in the reverse order of removing them. Slip the brake pads into the caliper and install the rods holding them in place. Insert the bleeder valve before bolting the rebuilt unit to the backing plate. Be careful not to cross-thread the fittings, as you connect the hydraulic line.

The rotor bolts to the hub flange. If you noticed the rotor was discolored, scorched, scratched or contained concentric grooves, remove it and have it turned down at a machine shop.

Bleeding brakes

Fill the hydraulic system with silicone brake fluid. Close all but one bleeder valve. Attach a rubber hose from the valve to a bottle containing brake fluid. Have someone pump the brake pedal until fluid spurts into the bottle. Close that bleeder valve and do the same with the other three. Refill the master cylinder and repeat the process to purge the line of any air.

Repairing handbrakes

Your car's handbrake works either on a drum at the back of the transmission, or on small brake shoes on the rear wheels. On cars with rear disc brakes, you'll find a small brake drum fitted with shoes.

If the handbrake doesn't hold, first check the linkage. There is usually a take-up adjustment. If this doesn't give the desired results, the brake shoes must be replaced.

For manual shift, transmission mounted handbrakes, disconnect the linkage to the drum. Disconnect the front universal joint, as previously described, and pull the band from the drum and toward the rear of the car. Degrease the metal band and remove the lining. Buy brake lining and rivet it to the band, being careful to seat the rivets to prevent scoring the drum, or have it relined at a brake shop.

Slide the relined band into place and connect the brake linkage. Before you connect the universal joint,

You can remove the master cylinder and power diaphragm from the firewall as a unit, after the vacuum line and brake fluid lines have been removed. The diaphragm will pull away from the firewall and the brake pedal plunger.

Check the mountings of the handbrake equalizer attached to a frame member. Set the handbrake, and turn the adjusting nut until each wheel drags when turned by hand. Tighten adjusting nut and lock nut. When the brake is released, the wheels should turn easily.

If more than six clicks are heard when applying the parking brake, check the cables. They must not be stretched, frayed or stuck in their conduit. Check that the grommets through which the cables pass are in good condition and in the correct place.

turn the front U-joint slip yoke, as you tighten the adjustment on the band. When you can no longer turn the slip joint, back off the adjustment until it just clears the drum. Attach the universal joint to complete the job.

If the handbrake operates on shoes in the rear brakes, or in a separate drum, check the linkage from the brake lever, which is near the center of the car. If this doesn't do the job, you'll have to remove the rear hubs and brake drums to replace the shoes.

Buy ready-lined brake shoes. Disconnect the actuating mechanism before removing the clips holding the shoes on the pivot and positioning shafts. Disconnect the shoe positioning springs to remove the old shoes. Follow previous directions on installing and adjusting brake shoes.

Take a test drive after making brake system repairs, making a hands-off stop from about 20 mph. If the car pulls to one side, or doesn't stop as quickly as you'd like, reread the material on troubleshooting and take the necessary action. Test the handbrake on a moderate slope to be sure your linkage adjustment is sufficient. After a thirty-minute drive, feel each brake. They should all be the same temperature.

After a couple of hundred break-in miles, make a final adjustment to the brakes.

You'll find sources for additional information on brake systems and specific information on your car in the appendix.

Chapter 19

Body rebuilding and repair

For many years, US body construction has been all steel. Chevrolet's Corvette, Kaiser's Darrin and Studebaker's Avanti used molded fiberglass sections with steel bracing on a modified production chassis. Therefore, you won't find any structural wood in the car you've chosen to rescue and renovate.

Even the wood in early 1950s station wagons offered by the Chrysler Corporation, Ford Motor Company, General Motors and Packard was applied over inner steel framing with steel roofs. Chrysler's first Town and Country convertibles and sedans used wooden panels over steel shells. Later, even this wood became simulated-wood fiberglass, or printed vinyl cemented over steel body stampings.

Front and rear sheet body sections were designed to crumple on impact, providing extra passenger safety. This type of construction went hand-in-hand with the increasing use of a combined body and frame.

In the late sixties, some cars substituted molded plastic pieces for nonstructural underhood components. Later, General Motors combined the grille, headlight and bumper assembly on some Pontiac models and made them of Endura rubber, replacing certain front-end sheet steel.

Though the separate chassis and body method of building cars is still in use by some companies, unitary or monocoque construction, in which the body and frame are combined, came into wider use in the mid-1950s and spread rapidly from the small car field to

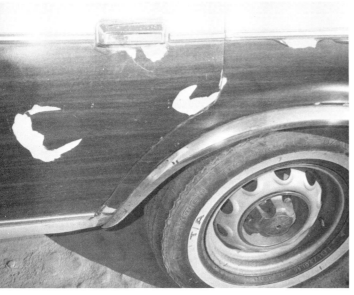

To replace damaged woodgrained sheet vinyl on the sides of the station wagons, peel off the old covering. You may need to use thinner to loosen old cement. Use a vibrator-type sander to clean the metal before applying the new vinyl. Try to match the graining.

Stub frames at the front and rear of unit body/frame cars join reinforced body cross-members. At the rear, this is ahead of the spring mounting. At the front, the stub frame joins a body cross-member near the front universal joint.

midsize models. The benefits are lighter weight, added rigidity and a lower center of gravity.

In the unit body/frame method, a strong, reinforced steel platform replaces the traditional chassis. This platform holds certain suspension and steering system components. A stub frame holds the engine and other mechanical components, and is attached to the platform. On some cars a stub frame is welded to the rear of the platform to hold rear suspension components. This strong, rigid unit gives a substantial savings in weight.

The same basic platform is often used on several makes, models and sub-models within the same family of cars.

Bodies are made up of inner and outer steel stampings. The inner shells are often used for several cars produced by the same corporation. Outer skin steel stampings are varied enough to provide different appearing bodies, to which slightly different trim pieces are added.

Made of structural steel stampings, which are crimped and corrugated for extra strength, the inner shells are welded to form the general shape of the body. These include the floor pans, cowl and firewall, door posts, roofs and roof supports. Certain stampings have cutouts, into which window opening mechanisms, radio speakers and other components fit.

Many two- and four-door sedans use common body stampings. Usually floor pans, and cowl and roof panels are the same, with only door and door post stampings differing in size, number and placement. Convertibles share many inner shell stampings with coupes and two-door sedans.

Certain areas of your car's body may need rebuilding or repair. If you discovered this only when you lifted some carpets, or removed an upholstery panel, don't panic. Aside from welding—and you may want to tackle even that yourself—you should be able to do the required work on all but the worst cases. In other words, on cars you shouldn't have chosen.

All repairs and body rebuilding, whether those required for a complete restoration, or those neces-

TYPICAL FLOOR PAN STAMPINGS

BELL HOUSING & TRANSMISSION HUMP

TOE BOARD

DRIVE SHAFT TUNNEL

FLOOR PAN

KICK UP OVER REAR AXLE

LUGGAGE AREA FLOOR

This cutaway section shows the inner and outer shell of a Dodge unit body/frame construction. Since the inner and outer skin are structurally important in this type of body, fiberglass repairs aren't sufficient. Damaged metal must be cut away and new metal welded in place.

Rocker panels and the area ahead of this Chevrolet's body are prone to rust damage. It isn't serious if it is only in the outer skin. Put the car on a lift to examine the extent of the damage. Repair these areas with fiberglass or sheet metal.

Dents, such as these in the rear fender panel of this Mercury, can sometimes be pushed out from the inside. Hit against a piece of plywood instead of against the metal to avoid stretching. Final finishing with a hand dolly and body hammer will ready it for painting.

Serious rust-through around the rear wheel cutout on this Pontiac will require that new metal be stitch-welded in place. When properly finished, it will be invisible and permanent. It could have been prevented by periodic cleaning.

A lot of work still to be done to the door and cowl of this Plymouth. Bondo-type fillers should be used only for smoothing minor dents. If a second coat is needed, it should be applied after the first coat has thoroughly dried to avoid cracking.

Out-of-line cars with unit body/frame construction can usually be brought back in alignment by powerful machines that clamp over body rails. With the car chained into place, the machine can pull and push the car's frame back to factory specifications.

sary to renovate the car, must be done to the same high standards. The car must be kept structurally strong, and no compromises allowed, which would affect the car's safety or handling.

In a renovation project you repair or replace only what is necessary, as opposed to a complete frame-off restoration, in which every component is taken to as-new condition. If only the bottom of a door is dented or rusted through, repair only that section. Often there'll be a trim piece or molding which will allow you to make an undetected break when refinishing the repair. If not, refinish the entire door.

Repair procedures are basically the same for separate body and chassis cars, as they are for those with unit body/frame construction. However, platforms are more prone to rust damage than pressed steel frames. Also, maintaining exact alignment is more difficult on cars built on a platform. Alignment of doors to cowl and side panels is also more difficult. However, a beginner should be able to make all but the most serious rust damage repairs on a car chosen for a rescue and renovation project.

Frame rail repairs

Frame rails, the stout U-shaped steel stampings that run the entire length of the body in both construction methods, are made of heavier gauge steel on unit body/frame cars, as they replace the traditional chassis. Stamped steel floor pans and braces, welded to crosspieces, form a rigid base for the body.

If the frame rails are weakened by rust, as can be the case on some early Mustangs, new metal must be welded in place. Choose the same or heavier gauge steel. Replace the entire length, or a section long enough to overlap the damaged area on both ends.

Keep the body in exact alignment when repairing the frame rails. If you don't, the doors won't close securely. This is more exacting and time consuming on unit body/frame cars, since some steering and suspension components are attached to the platform. Misalignment can change steering and handling characteristics.

Cut out rusted metal. Bolt or clamp in the replacement piece. Bolts and clamps are for positioning only during welding. Never count on bolted-in metal making a permanent repair.

Repair one side at a time, removing any mechanical part necessary to provide working room. Use a steel-bristled grinding wheel, or coarse-grit sanding disc, to clean away all rust. Cover bare metal with a rust-inhibiting primer after repairs.

Caution: Always wear safety goggles during grinding jobs.

Floor pan repairs

Unless the car has been involved in an accident, about the only damage to floor pans will be from rust that has formed under floor mats and underneath the car. In unit body/frame cars this can be a serious problem.

All surface rust must be ground away; badly rusted metal must be cut out. Weld in replacement metal and coat with rust-inhibiting primer. A followup coat of lacquer or enamel gives additional protection. Undercar repairs should be undercoated. Use the handy aerosol can for small jobs, or brush it on larger areas.

When cutting away rusted floor metal, either with a cutting torch or metal shears, be careful not to damage any underfloor wiring, cables or tubes. If any of these are beneath the area you're repairing, disconnect them and tag for later match-up.

With the carpet padding removed from the footwells in this Chevy II, the beginnings of rust-throughs are easy to see. Use a sanding disc in your electric hand drill to clean away surface rust. Any serious rust spots must be cut out and replaced with new metal.

155

If the floor has rusted through, weld in replacement steel floor pans, as done in this 1955 Chevrolet. Since an updated automatic transmission was added, the hump has been reshaped to fit. New carpets will have to be fitted to the newly shaped floor.

Before... Luggage area floor and spare wheelwell in a 1953 Packard. Cut out rusted metal in spare wheelwell and damaged areas in the floor. Grind surface rust from solid parts of the floor and coat it with rust-inhibiting primer.

Cowl and firewall repairs

The cowl and firewall, strong steel stampings that are joined to form a bulwark of strength, are welded to the frame rails and floor pans. Subject to continual racking and twisting as the car is driven, they contain the front body supports. On unit body/frame cars the stub frame holding the engine is welded to the cowl/firewall combination. The inner cowl stamping is very

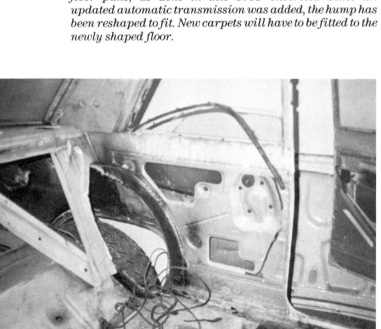

Cut away rusted and weakened metal in the floor and wheelwells to get a strong body. When welding or using a cutting torch inside a garage, have a fire extinguisher on hand for safety reasons. Do not cut through gasoline lines, brake tubing or controls.

After... Make a new spare wheelwell, with drain hole in the bottom, and weld it in place. Cut a new luggage area floor and weld it in place. Cut holes in the floor so the bolts holding the gas tank straps can be reached if necessary.

strong, giving rigidity to protect passengers in a frontal impact.

The rear of the cowl is strengthened to hold front door hinges or latching mechanism, and front roof supports.

Leaks around the windshield can cause rust damage to the upper and lower sections. Damage to the firewall may also come from leaking battery acid and corrosion.

All rusted areas must be cleaned to bare metal, or cut out and new metal welded in its place.

Remove the kick pad panels and use compressed air, or the blowing cycle on your vacuum cleaner, to loosen trapped dirt. Use the vacuum to remove remaining dirt. Apply a rust stopper, such as Chem-Solve or POR-15 to prevent future rust.

Center post repairs

Referred to as B-pillars, the center posts support the middle of the roof on all but convertibles and removable hardtops. They hold door hinges and latching mechanisms, both on two- and four-door models.

Check for rust where these attach to frame rails and to the top framing. Check any joints in the drip rails, which might let water seep into center post seams. Clean away any surface rust and protect with a rust-inhibiting primer. Any weakened metal must be cut out and replaced with the same gauge metal. Be careful to maintain body alignment so the doors will close securely.

Unless you're experienced in body repairs and have access to welding equipment, don't consider buying a car that has been in a side-swipe accident damaging the center post. An exception might be if it's in

Remove the steering wheel to allow extra working room when repairing the inner cowl and front floor area. If you remove the instrument cluster and other dash-mounted electrical accessories, tag wires for later match-up.

When cutting and welding in a new floor, fashion the drive shaft tunnel as a separate section. Weld the floor to the seat riser and sides. For easier handling, cut and fit pieces before welding. Do not damage handbrake control cables or power top tubing.

Chrysler's strongly braced cowl combined with the front door's post provides a rigid base for the door hinges. Keep drainage holes open so moisture can't collect in the cowl, rocker panels or doors and let rust start from the inside.

157

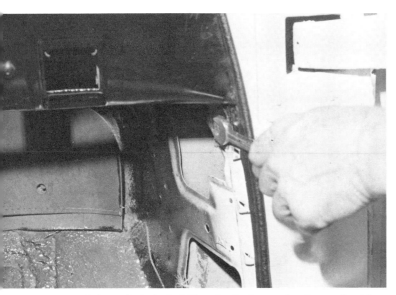

Tighten the bolts holding the dash panel to the cowl section. If you're installing welting between the door and cowl section, it should fit between the dash and cowl. Prongs on the cowl should be pried against the welting to hold it in place.

top condition otherwise, and the price is low enough to allow for professional repairs.

Roof panel repairs

Other than filling minor dents and scratches with a good grade body putty, most roof panel repairs require removing the headliner. Watch out for dome light wiring, as you remove the headliner and insulation pads.

Use a body hammer and hand-held dolly to flatten dents. You'll need a helper to hold the dolly against the outside of the roof, while you hammer on the inside. When filled and sanded, repairs won't show.

Rocker panel repairs

Rocker panels, the stamped steel panels that fit between the lower edge of the doors and curve under the body to meet the frame rails, often rust through because of trapped moisture. Though a part of the car's outer skin, they're not structural. You have several repair options, which are explained on the following pages.

With the upholstery panel removed, you can make any necessary repairs to the door's strong inner shell. Crimps and cutouts strengthen the door, as well as provide open- *ings for door and window controls, radio speakers, armrests and other bolt-on components.*

Rebuilding doors, panels and deck lids

Like other body panels, there's an inner shell and outer skin. Unless damaged by collision, doors, deck lids and panels usually pose rust problems only in the outer skin. However, if close examination shows the structural inner shells are weakened by rust, welded in replacement metal is mandatory.

In most cases, it is easier to repair doors and deck lids while they're on the car. Doors are heavy and there's a chance you'll change their contour or alignment if you remove them for repair to their inner shell. Put the car on jack stands for easier working height. Deck lids are easier to handle than doors, and the location and extent of damage should determine if you need to remove them.

You have several choices of techniques and materials when repairing rust damage to the outer skin on rocker panels, doors, deck lids and body panels. Which method you choose depends upon your ability, experience and extent of the damage. If you're restoring the car for serious show car competition, your choices are narrowed to welding and hot metal. If you're renovating the car, you can add fiberglass and double plating to your options.

Butt welding

Butt welding is commonly used by body shops. Once the old metal is cut out, a patch is cut to the shape of the damaged area and welded in place. When the weld seam is ground smooth and the necessary filling and sanding done, proper finishing will hide the repair.

Stitch welding

Stitch welding is another method used by body shops. The old metal is removed, and flanging pliers

Remove the upholstery panel and bolt-on plate to make repairs to tailgate window controls. Double-action hinges allow the door to open from curbside, or open down as a tailgate. Cement new weather-stripping in place for weather protection.

are used to indent a flange around the perimeter of the repair. A patch is cut to fit the indented area, and bolts or clecos are used to hold the patch in place until a few tack welds can be made. A weld line is flowed around the perimeter of the patch. When the bolt and cleco holes are filled, careful finishing will hide the seam.

There are drawbacks in these welding methods for the beginner, however. Certain complex shapes

Rear bumper ends have been removed from this Chevrolet for fender and luggage area lid repairs. The center section was left in place, as the car was used daily during the bodywork. Before painting, the bumper and rear light assemblies should be removed.

If the outer skin is badly dented or torn, it may be easier to replace it than repair it. Cut away the old panel and replace it with one from a salvage yard. When the section is properly finished, the replacement on this Mustang won't show.

Hammer out dents and fill minor dings and scratches on luggage area lid with a good grade filler. Sand the area smooth. Spray a light coat of different color primer to highlight imperfections still to be reworked. Make sure all contours are correct.

Cut and shape new metal to replace a badly damaged area. Use a piece of wood or clamps to hold the metal in place as you tack weld it. Run a weld seam around the replacement. When welding around the rear of a car, remember to be careful of gas fumes and sparks.

160

Measure, cut, fit and weld in new luggage area floor first. This will usually include the raised portion over the rear axle kick-up. Form the wheel arches and weld them to the floor. Make L-shaped braces to weld to the arches and body sheet metal.

and body contours may require beating and shaping the hot metal during welding.

Lap welding

Lap welding is the simplest of welding jobs. A patch, not necessarily conforming to the outline of the damaged area, is cut and welded in place. Clecos or bolts are used to hold it in place until it is tack welded on each side. When the seams are ground smooth and filler used to feather the edges, the repair is ready to refinish. Any change in body conformation will be only

Cut out old, rusted metal in the rear fender panel, and weld the replacement piece in place. The bottom should be crimped for strength in the wheel cutout. Tack weld the pieces to hold them in place, then stitch weld the perimeter. When finished, the repair won't show.

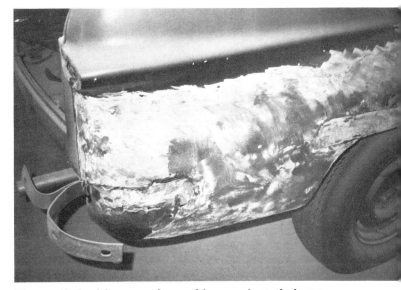

Remove the back bumper when making repairs to the lower rear areas. Cut out the rusted and weakened metal. Trim the patch metal either the same size as the cutout and but weld it in place, or cut a patch slightly larger and stitch weld it over the cutout.

161

Hot lead

Hot lead is an excellent way to fill small holes and hide seams in mating contours. The area must be heated and flux applied to accept body solder. As the heated lead melts, it must be smoothed by a wooden paddle. When the lead cools, it can be sanded, primed and finished.

It has been said that hot lead repairs are difficult, but others have said if you can spread peanut butter, you'll have no problem with hot lead. You'll probably find the method's difficulty to lie somewhere in between these claims.

Caution: Since the hot lead method requires working with a torch, there's a potential for burns, as well as fire, should there be any gasoline or solvent fumes present.

Double plating

Double plating is an easy, popular method for outer skin repairs of nonstructural rust-throughs which doesn't require welding. You work with easily trimmed, lighter galvanized sheet steel, which gives plenty of strength because you use two thicknesses.

Cut away the damaged area. Use flanging pliers to form an indentation around the perimeter, against which the outer patch will fit. Cut two pieces of galvanized steel to cover the cutout area and fit into the indented flange. Clamp them together and drill a series of $1/16$ in. holes about one inch apart around the perimeter. Hold one of the patch pieces against the car, mark and drill the holes.

Small rust-throughs are often best repaired by the hot-lead method. Use a torch to heat the area so it will accept the new metal. Spread it into the holes with a special wooden paddle.

the thickness of the metal, and shouldn't be noticeable. Lap welds can usually be made by a beginner after a little practice.

Sources for additional information on welding and welding equipment are included in the appendix.

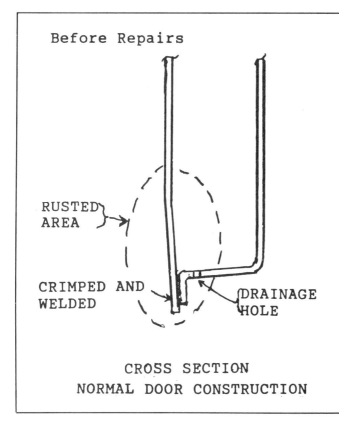

Before Repairs

RUSTED AREA →

CRIMPED AND WELDED

DRAINAGE HOLE

CROSS SECTION
NORMAL DOOR CONSTRUCTION

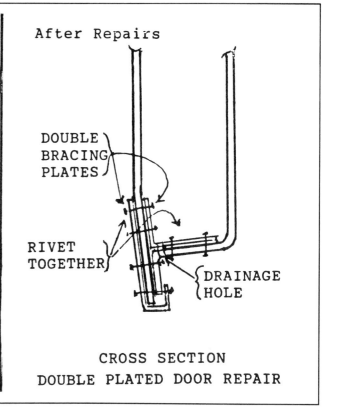

After Repairs

DOUBLE BRACING PLATES

RIVET TOGETHER

DRAINAGE HOLE

CROSS SECTION
DOUBLE PLATED DOOR REPAIR

Use dimpler pliers on the outer piece so the rivets will fit nearly flush. Use a pop-rivet gun to set the rivets. Work from side to side from the middle to avoid bunching, as you rivet through the outer patch, body metal and inner patch.

Spread epoxy filler to hide rivet heads and joints. Use two or three light coats, rather than one heavy coat. Sand lightly between coats. If properly done, there won't be any change in the outer skin's configuration.

As with other patching methods, if you can fit one edge of the patch under a trim piece, it helps to hide the repair.

Fiberglass

Fiberglass is fine for repairing curved or shaped nonstructural areas. It is easy to use, quick, permanent and inexpensive. However, your skin may be sensitive to it, so use rubber gloves.

As with other repairs, cut away the rusted metal. Clean the area with lacquer thinner. Follow directions on the container when mixing the epoxy and hardener. Mix only what you'll use at one time.

Usually, three pieces of fiberglass mesh give the needed thickness and strength. Cut the first piece large enough to extend well onto solid metal. The second and third pieces can be slightly smaller, but larger than the cutout area.

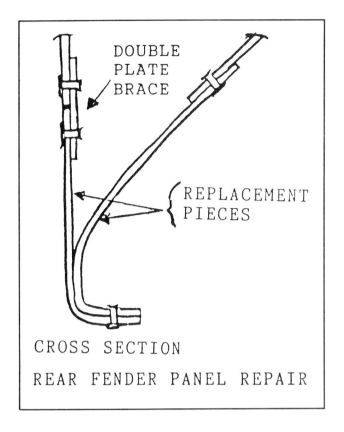

DOUBLE PLATE BRACE

REPLACEMENT PIECES

CROSS SECTION
REAR FENDER PANEL REPAIR

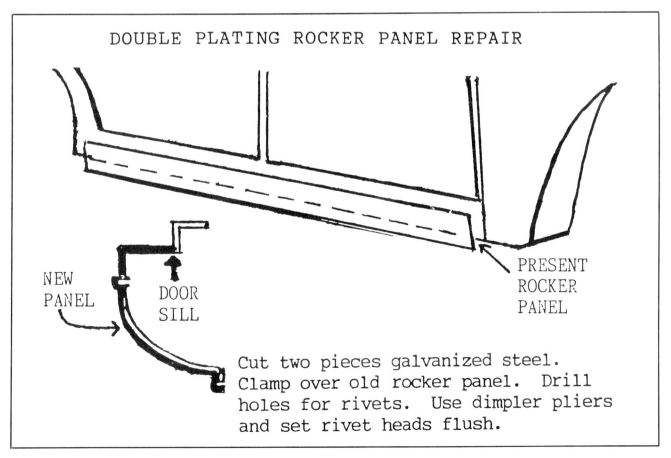

DOUBLE PLATING ROCKER PANEL REPAIR

NEW PANEL

DOOR SILL

PRESENT ROCKER PANEL

Cut two pieces galvanized steel. Clamp over old rocker panel. Drill holes for rivets. Use dimpler pliers and set rivet heads flush.

After welding in replacement metal and removing all the dents you can reach with a hand dolly and body hammer, use body filler to hide the rest. Use light coats, rather than one heavy coat, and sand between coats. Use a sanding block for hand sanding.

After grinding, hammer and dolly repairs smooth. Use a good quality body filler sparingly. Sand between coats. Normally, if it takes more than two coats, there wasn't enough work with the hammer and dolly. Repair of this fender won't show.

The resin will set fairly fast, so use the spreader to smooth the saturated material and work out any bubbles. Fiberglass patches can be filed, ground and sanded until perfectly smooth. Feather the edges, and finish as you would any other repair.

No matter which method you choose, make sure all drain holes at the bottom of the panels are open, so moisture won't be trapped between the inner shell and outer skin.

Replacement

Another option, if the necessary repairs seem too difficult, is to replace the door or deck lid. Since most car's body shells are used for two or three years with only minor changes, a replacement door or panel won't necessarily have to come from the same year car. Cars within the same family often shared the same bodies. So the part you're needing doesn't have to come from the same make, perhaps not even the same body style. Aside from color, the only outer difference may be the clip-on trim pieces.

Interchangeable body component information is covered in the appendix.

Dent repairs

Dents in fenders, doors, side panels and deck lids can often be repaired without removing the dented part from the car. Many times, even the upholstery doesn't have to be removed. If left unrepaired, a dent can invite rust, making eventual repair more difficult.

If you use the car regularly, repair dents on weekends, so you won't be without wheels when you need them. If there are several dings and dents to refinish, coat the repaired areas with primer. The final painting can be done later.

Types of dents

There are different kinds of dents, and different repair methods. Creases along the side are best removed by drilling a series of $1/16$ in. holes about two inches apart along the crevice. Use a dent puller to bring the metal back into shape. Start at the shallow end of the dent and work toward the deepest part. Ordinarily you won't have to use a hammer and dolly, but if you do, the upholstery panel will have to be removed.

Fill the holes with epoxy filler, feather the edges and prime and paint, or leave it in a prime coat and paint later with other repairs.

Torn metal

If there is a small tear in the metal, drill holes and pull the edges back together. You can make a fiber- glass patch on nonstructural skin areas. If you're restoring the car for show, you would need to weld in a patch. Large tears require welding, after the edges have been brought back into position. In these cases the upholstery panel usually has to be removed, so you can hold a dolly against the outside, while you hammer from the inside. Finish the repair with epoxy filler, then sand and prime.

Crimped edges

For crimped or bent edges at the bottom of doors or deck lids, where the space between the inner shell and outer skin is too small for a hand-held dolly, use a pry bar to force the metal back toward its original shape. You may have to weld a patch, or use fiberglass over tears in these areas. Finish and prime when the damage is removed.

Shallow dents

Sometimes shallow dents can be sprung back into position by pushing from the inside. Try using a hammer against a piece of wood covering the area. If you still are not able to reach the necessary spot, drill a hole and use a dent puller for this type of repair. In some cases you can use a suction-cup-type dent puller. You may not need to repaint the area, but if the paint is chipped or cracked, refinish it.

Use a wire-bristled brush and a putty knife to clean away any flaking coating and surface rust. Paint the inside of panels with an asphalt-based paint for lasting protection.

While the paint is still tacky, apply some insulated padding for a quiet ride.

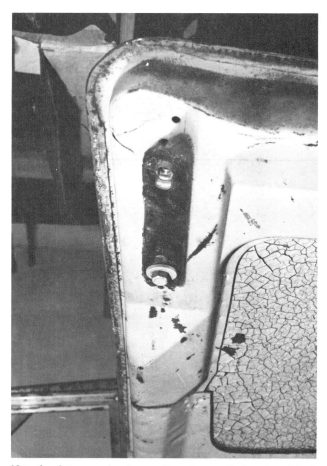

Note the slots running in one direction on the hood and deck lid, and slots running in the opposite direction on the hinge brackets. These allow you to align the hood and deck lid properly. Use new weather-stripping for a tight seal.

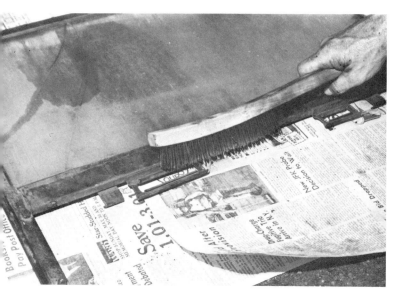

Use a wire-bristled brush to clean away scale and surface rust on window channels and the slots in which the rollers ride. When cleaned, paint with a rust-inhibiting primer before installing the frame in a repaired door.

Dented fenders

Place the car solidly on jack stands. Remove the wheel so you'll have working room. Use a bumping hammer to get the metal back into the general configuration. Then use a hand-held dolly and body hammer to smooth the remaining dents.

Start at the point of impact and work from there to the deepest part of the dent. You're less apt to stretch the metal this way. Use a power grinder, or sanding disc, to smooth the area.

If the edge of the fender is torn, as well as dented, pound it into shape, getting the torn edges as close together as possible. Weld a patch in the back to hold the torn pieces in position, then butt weld the torn edges. Butt welding alone won't make a satisfactory fender repair, however.

Use a grinding disc to smooth the weld seam. Fill any low spots or irregularities with epoxy filler. Sand and use body putty on minor imperfections. Prime and sand until the repair no longer shows. Paint is the last step, after the entire fender has been properly prepared.

Dents in contours

You may find some dents in curved areas where you don't have room to use a hand-held dolly. These could be in the windshield post to cowl, or where the roof meets the rear deck. If a screw-in dent puller won't do the job, fill the dent with epoxy. Use several light coats, rather than a heavy one. This is also a place where the hot lead method of repair gives excellent results.

If the dent is large, weld a patch over it, using epoxy filler to feather the edges, then refinish the area.

What to remove

You need what's known as "swing room," when making body repairs. This is simply enough room for you to swing the body or bumping hammer. This may mean removing a wheel. If so, be sure the car is safely positioned on jack stands, so no amount of pounding, or jarring, will topple it.

To work on the front aprons, or other front-end sheet metal and grille area, you'll have more working room if you remove the bumper and brackets as a unit. Remove the rear bumper assembly for work on the rear apron, or sheet metal below the deck lid.

The styling trend to essentially slab-sided cars, in which the front and rear fenders are just body panels, makes front fender repairs easier, but rear fender repairs more difficult. On these cars the front fender panel can be unbolted from the cowl and front-end sheet metal. However, the rear fender panel may start at the rear of the door. These panels are usually welded in place, making removal much more difficult, but not impossible.

Generally it's easier, and you'll get better results, if you remove only what's necessary to provide working room.

Sources for complete information on body rebuilding and repairs are listed in the appendix.

Chapter 20

Convertible top

You'll enjoy your convertible more if the folding roof or top is in good condition. A good top not only protects your investment against body rust and upholstery deterioration, but also adds greatly to the car's appearance, comfort and value.

If the top appears in good condition, make a careful inspection, noting minor repairs, and clean it thoroughly.

Any small rips and tears should be repaired before they become larger. Split seams can often be

Overexposure to direct sunlight has shrunk the top on this Dodge Dart, exposing the padding. The top can no longer keep rain out of the car. Water damage to the seats and door *upholstery will follow. Water seeping behind the panels will cause rust damage.*

A missing rear curtain and torn top on this Mustang will allow water to enter the car and settle between the inner and outer skin around the wheelwells and the floor. Lower rust damage to unit body/frame cars can be extremely expensive to repair.

sewn together and reinforced to prevent reoccurrence. Cuts and abrasions caused by folding arms can be repaired, but the folding arms and bows must be adjusted to prevent more damage.

Check the clamping mechanism on the front bow to the top of the windshield, making it hold the roof securely. Worn weatherstripping on the front bow and around windows can be replaced to give a snug fit.

Missing fasteners on the body or top should be replaced to keep the top from ripping. Discolored or cracked vinyl in the rear curtain must be replaced for safety reasons.

A malfunctioning power-top unit can be repaired to give dependable up-and-down movement.

The secret to a snug fitting, attractive convertible top is periodic cleaning and inspection, with prompt repairs.

Patch repairs

Patches should be applied to the inside of the roof. Cut the patch larger than the area it is to cover. Coat the top of the patch and underside of the roof. Stick the patch in place. Put wax paper between the patch and pieces of wood, and clamp tightly in place.

When sewing a patch to the underside of the top, match material, graining and thread to make it inconspicuous. Sew the perimeter first, then more lines of stitches until you're as near the tear or rip as possible. Clip loose threads and coat the exposed part with a sealing coat of cement.

Avoid the so-called special convertible roof paints, as most of these dry out and crack the material.

Faded tops

If your car has a faded black top in good condition, you can re-dye it. Brush and vacuum dirt from the top. Apply a heavy coat of wax to parts of the car, where some dye may run off.

Buy black fabric dye and mix as directed. Use a two-inch brush to apply the dye in long, even strokes, avoiding overlaps. Let the roof dry for twenty-four

Make a new rear curtain. Repairs to the roof and rear-bow molding can make this Buick's top last for a while longer. Vinyl and canvas roofs will mildew if they're not kept clean and stretched tight. Avoid using top dressings on folding roofs.

Patch a torn roof only as a temporary measure to protect the car's interior until you can make a new roof. It is usually impractical to make only a new center section, as you're apt to tear the side pieces as you remove them.

hours, before spraying the top lightly, to rinse away excess dye. Wash the car to remove excess wax and any dye that dripped. Don't lower the roof for forty-eight hours.

Vinyl roofs

Repair kits for convertible and hardtop vinyl roofs include patching compound, cleaner, solvent and coloring. Rent a heating iron with graining head and variable heat control switch to bond the material. Cut frayed edges with a sharp blade. Use vinyl cleaner to remove dirt, grime and wax. Mask off the area to be repaired. Then heat the iron to the temperature given in the directions.

Apply patching compound with a spatula or putty knife, spreading until smooth and filling the damaged area; remove any excess. Press the graining head back and forth over the area to bond the patch tightly with the rest of the top.

Ordinarily, the roof won't have to be removed for this repair, but you may need someone to hold a piece of wood under the area you're working on to give support.

Convertible roofs shouldn't be painted, but vinyl roofs on hardtops can be. Mask off the windows and use a handy aerosol vinyl paint for this job.

The folding arms and roof bows must operate easily and not bind when opening or closing. The covering must fold free of the mechanism so it can't bind or tear. Make any necessary repairs to the top irons to postpone making a new roof covering.

When you've repaired the roof bows and folding arm mechanism, paint the bows for protection as well as for their looks. Either clean plated parts, or have them replated. If you're saving money, paint any rusted plated parts you don't want to replate.

Check where the front roof bow meets the top of the windshield, and where the folding side rails meet vent windows. These must be tight if the roof is to keep rain out of the car. Plan on replacing rubber weather-stripping if it is worn.

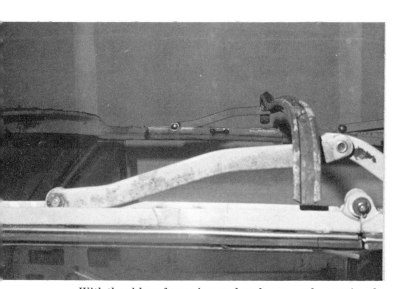

With the old roof covering and pads removed, examine the folding arms and roof bows. Straighten any bent bow or arm. Check pivot pins to make sure they don't bind. Open and close the roof a few times to check that everything works before making the new top.

Roof padding

To remove the roof covering and replace worn padding, pull tacks or staples from welting, along the front bow, rear bow and around the body line. Lift the roof from the framework, handling it carefully to avoid damage.

Take measurements from the old padding, or from the front bow over each bow down to the body. Indentations in the roof bows indicate padding width.

Cut covering material to three times the padding width, so it can be folded over from each side. Cut two lengths of polyurethane or latex padding for each pad, since these won't hold moisture like the original cotton.

Put one piece of padding in the center, and fold the covering material over it and sew a seam. Put the second strip over the first one and fold the remaining covering over it and sew a seam. Sew reinforcing seams on each side and across each end. Padding is attached only at the front and rear bows and to the body.

Webbing

To avoid the "starved cow" look between bows, webbing supports the weight of the roof covering. It

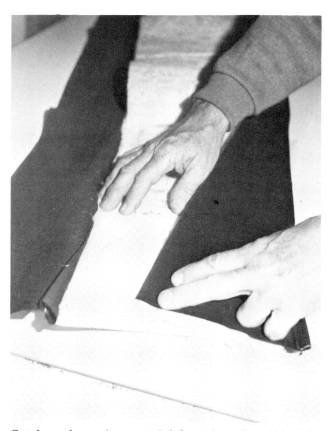

Cut the pad covering material three times the width of the pad. Use polyurethane foam when making new roof pads. Lay the padding in the center of the covering. Fold one side and sew a seam. Fold the other side and sew a seam. Sew reinforcing seams.

must be tight and firmly attached and is installed on the roof framework before the padding. Buy replacement webbing in upholstery outlets, fabric shops and auto trim stores.

Block the front bow about one inch from the windshield and measure from front to back. Attach webbing to the front bow, then attach to each bow and to the body. Remove the blocking at the front, and clamp the front bow to the windshield to stretch the webbing even tighter.

Power-operated tops

Power-operated convertible tops are either electrically or hydraulically operated, the latter being the most popular type during these years. Repairs to the operating mechanisms are within the capability of the average beginner and should not be postponed if needed.

Hydraulic

On hydraulically operated tops, a reversible electric motor powers a rotary pump connected to two hydraulic cylinders. The pump and its reservoir are mounted on the firewall, or behind the rear seat. A dash-mounted, double throw switch controls the action.

Hydraulic cylinders on each side of the rear seat are hidden by quarter panel upholstery. To raise the top, the pump forces fluid to the bottom of the cylinders, pushing up the pistons and rods attached to the main roof bow. Fluid above the pistons returns to the

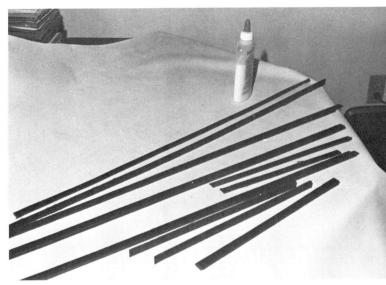

Either use clean, used fan belts, or cut pieces of hardwood to make new tack strips. Glue hardboard strips together to get the right depth. Remove the old strips and clean the channels in which they fit. Some restorers prefer rope for this job.

reservoir through lines at the top of the cylinders. To lower the top, the fluid is pumped to the top of the cylinders, forcing the piston down and returning the fluid at the bottom of the cylinder to the reservoir, where it recirculates through the system.

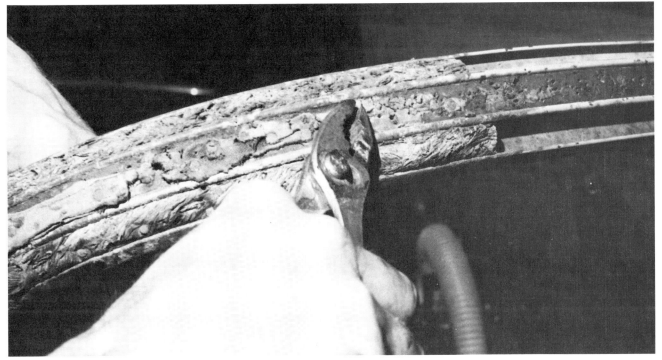

Examine the tack strips in the main roof bow, to which the roof pads and top covering are attached. Use pliers to remove old tacks or staples, which could damage the new top covering. Make sure there is room on the strip for new tacks or staples.

171

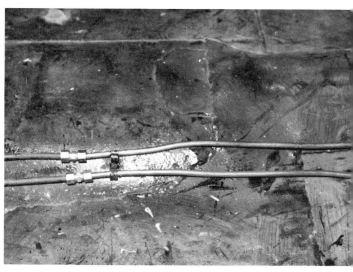

Be sure all the small brackets that hold the top's hydraulic tubing are in place. Make sure there are no crimps in the lines that could impede the flow of the fluid. Leave a dry piece of paper under newly fitted joints overnight to check for leaks.

The pump and reservoir for hydraulically operated tops may be on the firewall, under a fender panel or behind the rear seat. Tubes carry the fluid to and from the reservoir to hydraulically operated pistons attached to the main roof bow.

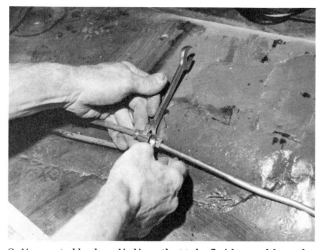

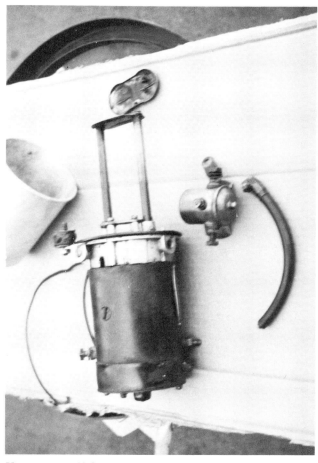

Splice rusted hydraulic lines that take fluid to and from the pump to the actuating pistons in the quarter panels. Use two wrenches on the fittings so you'll get a tight fit, without putting stress on the lines. Cut and flare the copper lines to avoid leaks.

Use your test light to check the electric motor. Disassemble and clean the pump, filter and canister. Check the dashboard switch, solenoid and tubing. Auto supply and some hardware stores carry parts with which you can rebuild the simple pump.

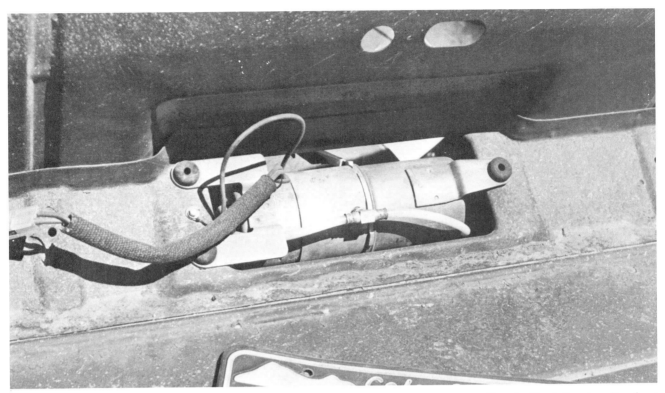

Remove the rubber plugs holding the reservoir and pump assembly low behind the rear seatback and accessible from the luggage area. Disconnect the tubing, and make necessary repairs at your workbench. Check the circuitry from the switch to the pump.

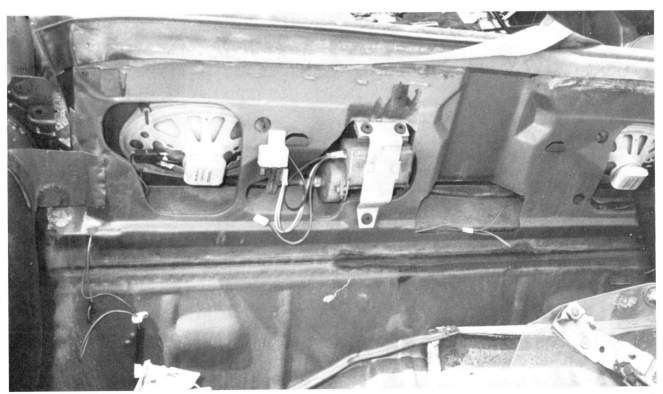

Remove the rear seatback to service electrically operated tops. A reversible motor, connected to a gear reduction case, drives flexible cables in conduits to gears connected to each side of the main roof bow. A dashboard switch gives control.

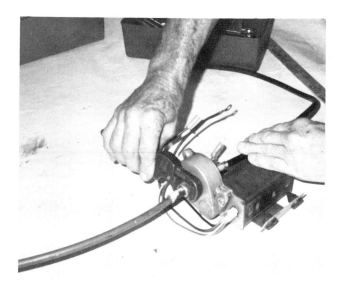

Remove the rubber plugs holding the motor and gear case in position. Uncouple the flexible cables attached to the gears at the main roof bow. Tag and disconnect the wiring. At your workbench, uncouple the cables from the gear case.

Electric

On electrically operated tops, a reversible electric motor, attached to a gear reduction unit and controlled by a dash-mounted switch, is positioned behind the rear seat cushion and seatback. Flexible drive cables, attached to each side of the reduction unit, are connected to actuators mounted on each side of the pivoting main roof bow.

There are internal reduction gears in each actuator, which increase the motor's power. When the control switch is moved to the desired position, the motor turns the cables attached to the reduction unit and the actuators. These raise or lower the top.

Troubleshooting power tops

If the top won't operate, check the fuse or circuit breaker, and look for a faulty ground. Next, test for a short in the circuit between the switch, pump or motor; test for a faulty switch; and check for a defective pump or motor.

If the top operates only one way, check the dash-mounted control switch; look for a short in the circuit between the switch and motor or pump; check the

Use your circuit tester when checking the operation of retractable hardtops. A dashboard switch operates a series of solenoids which control the action of the motor and folding arms that raise the lid, move the top, fold part of the roof and tuck it all in place.

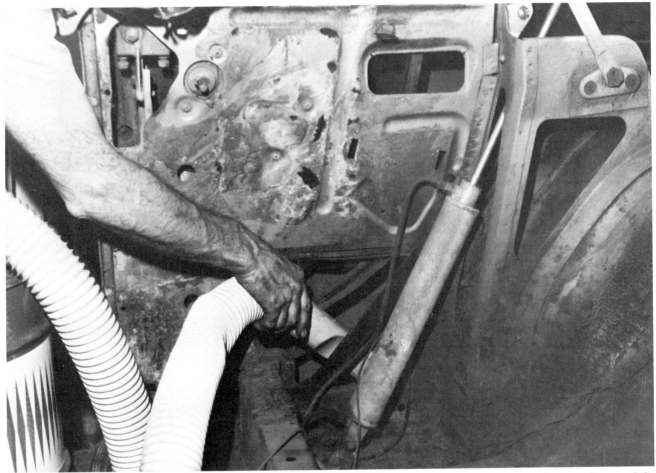

Use the blowing cycle on your vacuum cleaner to loosen dirt and debris from areas around the top's hydraulic cylinders. Switch to the suction mode to pick up the loosened dirt.

Put a few drops of oil on the bottom pivots and around the piston rod.

Check the connection of the piston rod to the main roof bow. It must be free of play, yet must not bind. Pivots on arms connected to the roof bows must move easily, yet must not have side play. A few drops of light oil is usually all these need.

You may have to cut into the sheet-metal top piece of the front roof bow, if the mechanism is stuck or won't clamp the bow securely. Overhaul the gear case and locking arm mechanism. Use double nuts on the bolts holding the arms to the fulcrum ends.

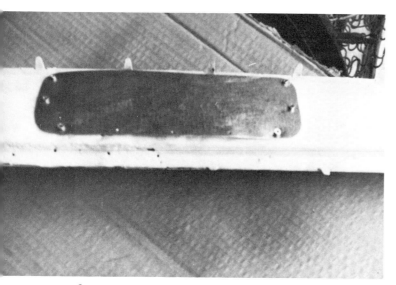

Cut a piece of galvanized sheet steel to cover any opening you had to make in the top portion of the front roof bow. Either rivet it in place, or use self-tapping screws. Fit it snugly so it won't show or rub against the cloth top covering.

fluid in the reservoir; look for a defective or crimped cable, or a crimped hydraulic line; and check for a defective actuator on electric tops.

If the top operates slowly, check for a defective motor or poor ground; check the pump for insufficient pressure, leaks or a crimped hydraulic line; look for debris in the actuator or hydraulic cylinder area which could impede their movement; and check for bent or corroded actuating rods.

Repairs to power units

A defective fuse on a power unit must be replaced. Trace electric lines for shorts and replace the faulty wire, replace any defective control switches, and check all electrical connections, making sure they're tight.

Remove and clean the reservoir filter. Replace any crimped or damaged hydraulic tubing. Disconnect one hydraulic line at a time and blow through it. Then run a wire and pour kerosene through a plugged line. After cleaning the lines, free them of air, as you do brake lines. Replace any dried or brittle plunger in the cylinder, and clean and lubricate the actuating arms.

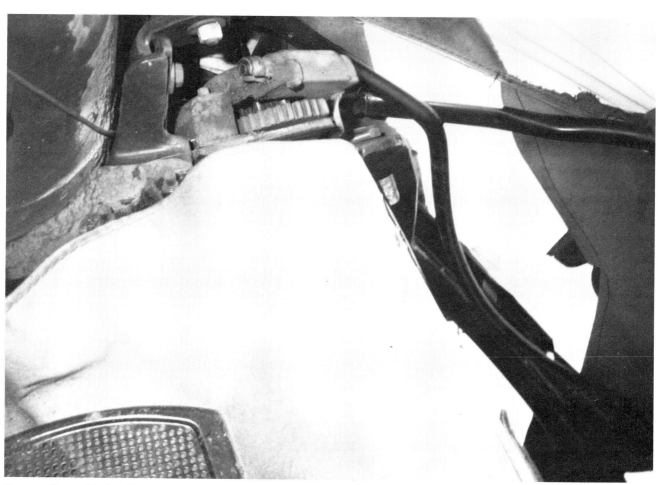

Remove the molded rubber cap covering the gear case at each end of the main roof bow. This should be done routinely to keep the gears free of dirt and debris that can hinder their smooth operation. Use light oil to lubricate the gears.

The rubber grommets, through which the rods extend, must fit snugly.

To repair or replace a defective motor on electric tops, disconnect the motor relay wires and uncouple the threaded cable connectors from the actuator unit. Remove the screws holding the unit in place. Take it to your workbench for any repairs.

To remove and repair the actuators, lower the top, if possible. Remove the rear seat cushions. Disconnect the threaded drive cables from the actuator, and remove the screws attaching the actuator to the pivoting arm. Loosen the seating screw in the side rail actuating link and remove the shoulder bolt connecting the sector arm to the actuating link. Take the unit to your workbench for repairs.

Buy repair or replacement parts at auto supply stores, or pick up serviceable parts at a wrecking yard.

Rear curtain repair

When removing the rear curtain, be careful not to rip it. Loosen tension at the front bow to make this easier. Use a seam ripper on the vinyl insert to cut the stitches.

Remove the bolts holding the reduction gear cases to the main top bow. Uncouple the flexible cables from the gear cases and take them to your workbench for cleaning and disassembly. Put a cloth under the cases to catch nuts that could drop out of reach.

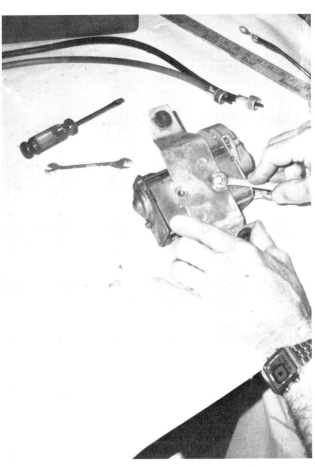

Remove the holding bracket from the motor and gear case. Use your tester to check the operation of the electric motor. Long bolts running through the motor housing hold the back plate and the reduction gear case together. Clean each part as you go.

Disassemble the bracket and gear case carefully. Mark mating gear teeth for correct match-up during assembly. Lift the sector gear and shaft and the worm gear from the housing. Replace any chipped or worn gears. Clean and lubricate gears before assembly.

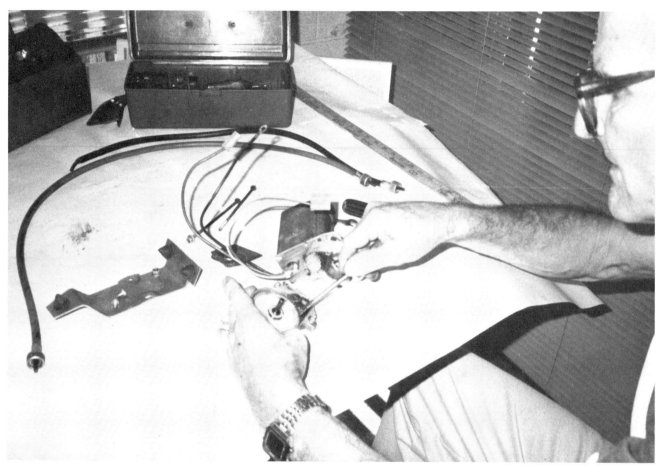

Remove the reduction gear case from the motor. Be careful not to chip any teeth while prying out the nylon gears. Replace any chipped or stripped gears. Clean the gears and case and lubricate with white grease. Mesh gears carefully when reassembling the unit.

Measure and trim replacement vinyl and pin it to the curtain. Use a #16 needle and cotton-wrapped polyester thread in your sewing machine. Stretch the vinyl to remove wrinkles. Sew reinforcing seams about ⅛ in. apart. Knot the threads at the end of each seam.

If the zipper is sewn directly to the vinyl, procedures are the same. Check both sides of the zipper, making sure the binding tabs are in place.

When installing the repaired curtain, center it on the car correctly. Tack or staple as you stretch it tight.

Making a new top

If the present top has shrunk, and the material is brittle or weak and torn, you need a new top.

Ready-made convertible tops are available for many cars and they fit fairly well, but they're expensive. You may be able to find a trim shop to install it for you. This is an added expense. Otherwise, you'll have to remove your old top and install the replacement yourself, which is a large part of the overall job.

If you can locate an auto trim shop that still makes convertible tops, you can have one made and installed on your car. This is very expensive, especially if there is only one shop in your area doing this kind of work. It may take a lot of time, if the shop plans to fit your job in with their regular upholstery work. If you plan on having a top made for you, ask for names of other customers, so you can check their work. Be sure to get a firm quote on the cost.

Your best bet is to make a new top yourself, install it and save a bundle. Buy replacement materials from local trim and upholstery shops, or from ads in car publications. Sew the pieces on a regular home sewing machine, or rent a machine. You can install the top and have the satisfaction of having made it yourself.

Choice of materials

Roof materials have changed since the 1950s, 1960s and 1970s. Some cars used woven, rubberized fabric; others used lighter-weight vinyl material. Choose either, but the original will be judged better in car shows.

You'll have to sew the vinyl material, instead of heat bonding it, as was done originally. Both coverings can be sewn on a regular sewing machine.

Making the pattern

Remove the old roof, saving what you can for a pattern. Use a seam ripper to separate the old top into its parts. Unfold the material along seam lines to get the correct measurements; correct these in areas where the old top may have shrunk. Mark measurements on a drawing and transcribe them on the back of the material.

If there's not enough of the old top for measurements, take them directly from the roof bows. Start at the windshield and measure to the rear bow, then down to the body. The width has to be measured across the front bow; from the window tops on one side, to the window tops on the other; across the rear bow; and the distance from the bottom of the rear window on one side, to the corresponding position on the other side.

To check your measurements, draw them on an old sheet or piece of unbleached muslin. Cut and pin the pieces, making a practice roof. Slip this over the framework to see if it fits. Correct any problems.

As the sectional illustration shows, there are usually seven pieces in the average roof. These should be cut individually, making sure weaving and graining runs in the same direction.

Center section

The center section, number 1, is basically a rectangle, but the front may be pointed or rounded, depending on the shape of the windshield. It usually extends from the front bow to the back of the rear bow. On some cars it goes to the body.

Rear curtain

You'll probably make the rear curtain, number 2, of heavy-duty clear vinyl, or use vinyl as an insert in a panel made of roofing material. Use the old zipper if you can, or buy a heavy-duty one in the correct length.

Reinforcing pieces

Numbers 3 and 4 are reinforcing pieces that follow the window line from the windshield to the back of the side windows. These are from three to four inches deep. They'll be sewn to pieces 5 and 6, placed so the finished edges are inside the car.

Side sections

Numbers 5 and 6 are mirror images of each other. They run from the front along the top of the windows down to the body line. They follow the curve of the body from the window around the rear deck, where

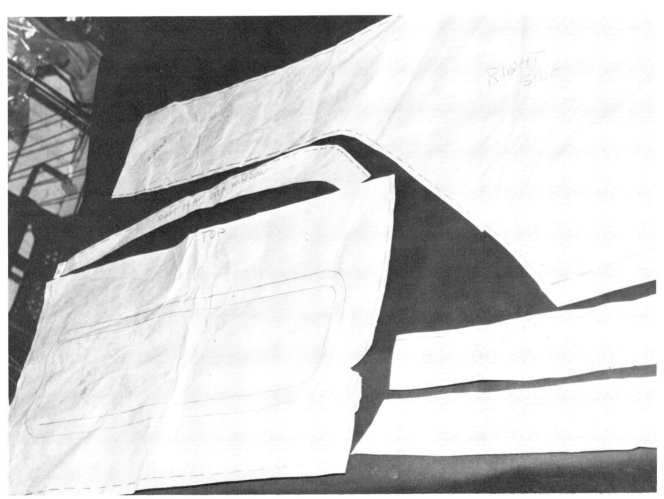

Make a pattern from pieces of the present top, or take measurements from the roof framework. Lay the pattern pieces on the roofing material in the most economical way before cutting. Be sure to keep the graining of the material in mind before cutting.

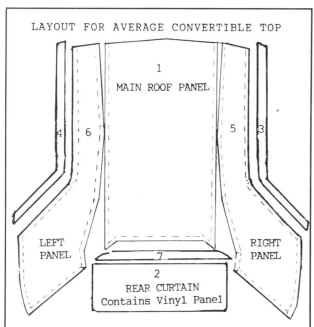

LAYOUT FOR AVERAGE CONVERTIBLE TOP

1
MAIN ROOF PANEL

4   6   5   3

LEFT   RIGHT
PANEL   PANEL

7

2
REAR CURTAIN
Contains Vinyl Panel

Install #2 first. Join #3 and #5, then join #4 and #6, before joining #5 and #6 to Main roof panel #1. Panel #7 is installed after the new roof has been fitted to the car.

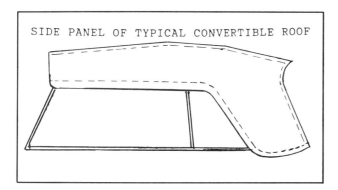

SIDE PANEL OF TYPICAL CONVERTIBLE ROOF

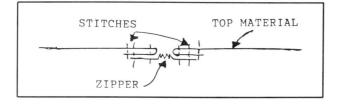

STITCHES   TOP MATERIAL

ZIPPER

TOP AND SIDE PANELS JOINED

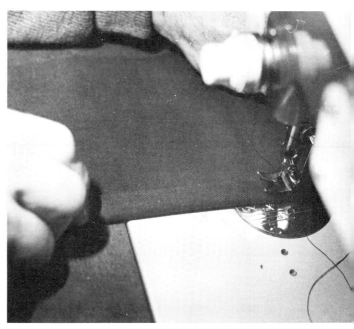

When sewing roof covering material, examine it to determine any discernable pattern or weave, and which is the inside and outside. To avoid any raw edges, fold the material back against itself and sew seams. When joining material, lay it face to face.

they overlap the rear curtain opening by about an inch.

Rear valance

Piece number 7 fits across the rear bow, hiding where the top and portions of the side pieces are attached to the bow. It's three to four inches in depth and straight across the lower edge. The front edge will be trimmed slightly, when it's installed on the rear bow.

Joining the sections

Because of bulk when sewing the sections, it's easier to sew pieces 3 to 5 and 4 to 6, before joining them to the main panel. The outside of 3 and 4 should face inside the car. Sew back to back 3 to 5, and 4 to 6. Cover the bottom seam with binding.

Thumbtack each side assembly to the roof bows to check alignment around the windows. Lay the main panel in place, and mark and pin at each bow. This is to check future fit, while there's still time for changes. Use tailor's chalk for marking on the roof, as it can be wiped off with a damp cloth.

Remove pins on one side and lay the center panel on the floor or table with one side still attached. These pieces must be face to face, as you pin every few inches along the seam. Sew a seam that joins the panels, stretching the material ahead of the sewing foot to avoid bunching. Follow the line carefully, removing pins just before you get to them. Sew a second, reinforcing seam. Knot threads at both ends.

Follow the same procedure with the other side and main panel to have a nearly complete roof.

Before installation, lay it over the bow assembly to check the fit. Match center lines front and back.

Some manufacturers installed a snugging cable through pieces 3 and 5, and 4 and 6. These run from the front bow to the body in back of each side window.

Installing the new top

Align center marks and staple the front center and rear bow center. Work each side on the back bow, using staples about every inch, until you've covered the area over the rear curtain opening.

Stretch the panels that extend to the body. Start at the rear curtain opening and work toward each side until about a foot from the side window. Move back to the rear bow again, stretching upward and stapling each side panel to the rear bow and stretching the material. Complete stapling the main panel to the rear bow.

Attach the snugging cable to the body, leaving the unstapled side panel as it is for the moment.

Block the front bow about one inch from the windshield and stretch and staple the main panel to the front bow. Work each side of the center, stretching toward the front and side to get a tight fit. Attach the snugging cable at the front.

Remove the blocking and clamp the bow to the windshield header. If there are cams on the bow to change its position against the windshield frame, adjust for a snug fit.

To keep the top from tearing when folded, some cars fitted three or four snap fasteners to a lip on the body just behind the side windows. The threaded part attaches to the body, the mating part to the roof. Rub chalk against the fasteners on the body. Press the fabric against these, and the chalk mark indicates where the top portion of the fasteners should be attached. Work one at a time to ensure a wrinkle-free fit.

Make the rear curtain separately. Close the zipper joining the vinyl insert and zipper tab. Measure, draw and cut the insert's outline on the curtain. Double seam the insert and the trimmed curtain. It is easier to install the curtain before the top.

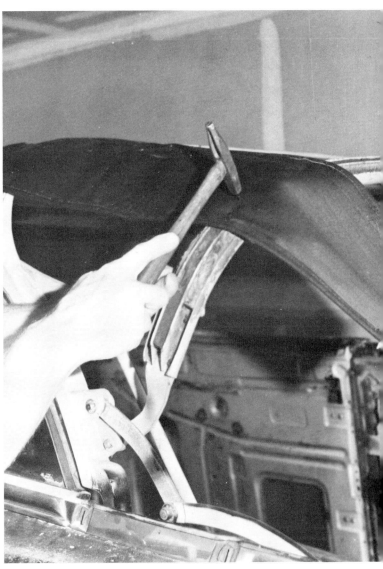

Staple or tack the new padding to the front bow. Lay a one-inch piece of wood between the top of the windshield and the bow. Stretch the material to the main rear bow and tack it in place. Remove the wood to stretch the padding. Trim any excess padding.

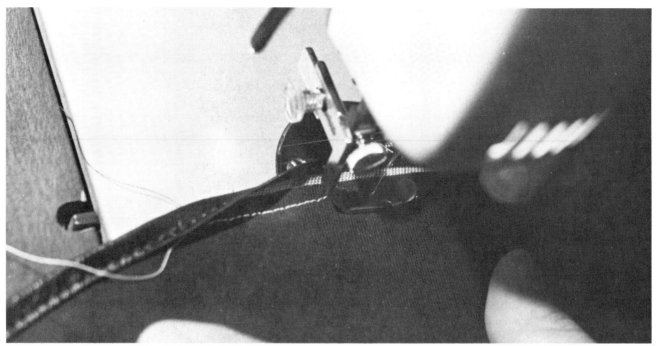

Because of the stress the binding takes when the roof is stretched tight, sew a hidden seam attaching the binding to the roof material. When sewing the finished binding seam, the reinforcing seam won't show. Use cotton-wrapped polyester thread.

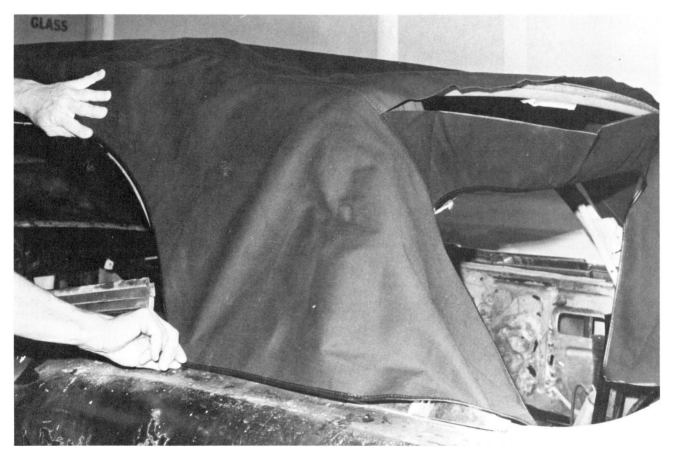

Stretch the newly sewn top over the frame to check its fit. If any alterations are necessary, they should be made before attaching the roof. The roof covering attaches only at the front bow, main rear bow and to the body.

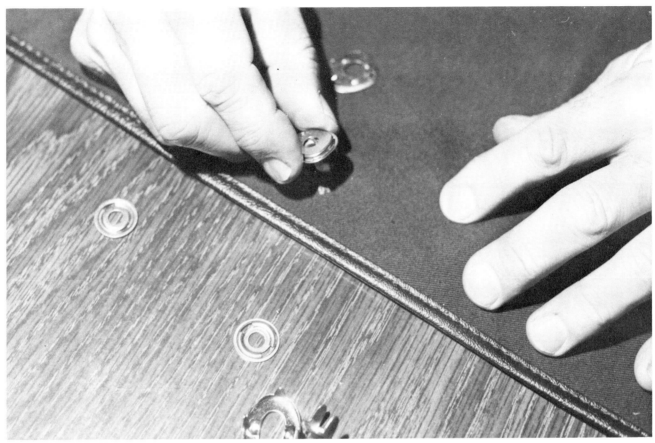

Measure the distance between fasteners on the car's body. Mark these on the finished top and punch a hole. Press the base, or pronged portion of the fastener into the fabric. Turn the material over and attach the other part.

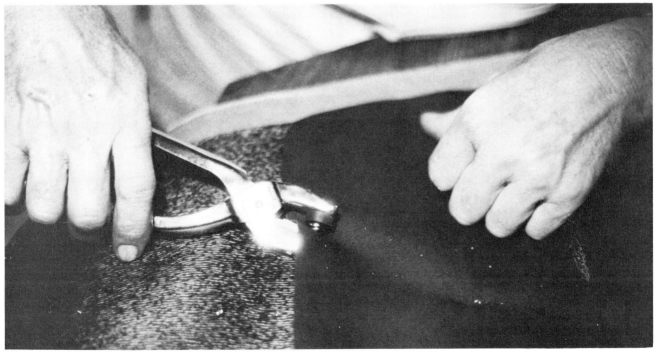

Use the handy pliers-like punch and clamp to install snap fasteners to the material. There's also a concave metal cup that will hold the outer part of the fastener, while you tap a matching rod fitted into the inner part of the fastener.

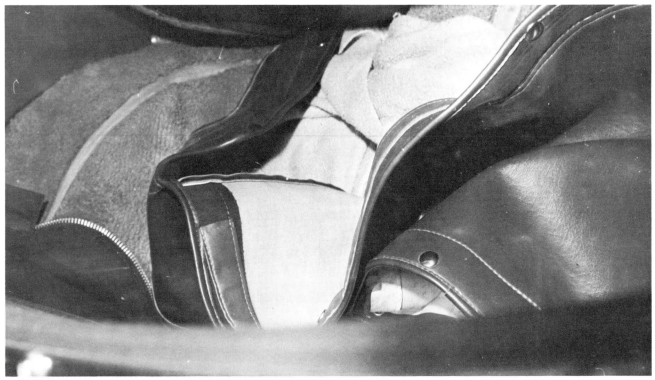

Make the convertible top boot from material matching the car or upholstery color, or from the same fabric as you used for the top. Take measurements from the old boot, or from the car.

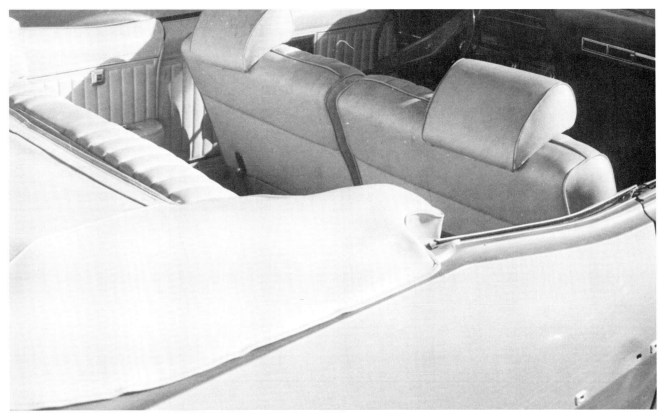

You may find the top boot is held in place by small pieces of fabric fastener attached to the car's body and boot. These pieces of fastener are cemented in place and don't show when the boot is fitted.

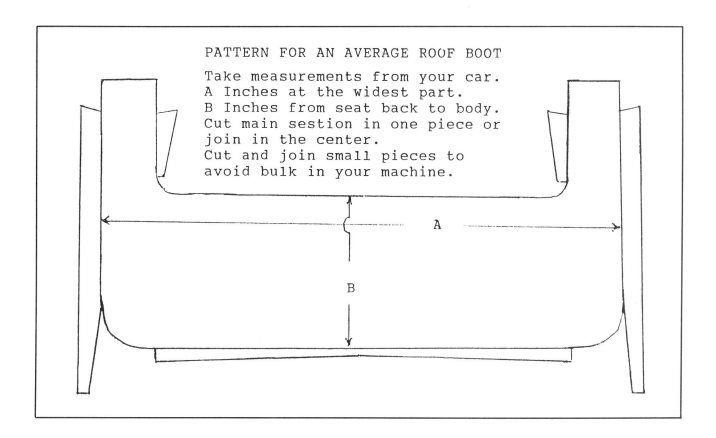

PATTERN FOR AN AVERAGE ROOF BOOT

Take measurements from your car.
A Inches at the widest part.
B Inches from seat back to body.
Cut main sestion in one piece or
join in the center.
Cut and join small pieces to
avoid bulk in your machine.

A

B

Welting

Some cars used a plated molding where the body joins the top; others used welting. Attach welting over the staples attaching the roof at the front and to the body. Use plated caps at each end of the welting.

If there are major wrinkles in the roof, pull staples in that area and stretch the roof tighter. Minor wrinkles can be removed by soaking the top and leaving it in the sun.

Buy top welting by the yard for a lower price. Pry open spring-loaded welting and use tacks or staples in this area. Welting will snap back, covering the tacks. Use brightmetal caps at each end of every section of welting.

Chapter 21

Upholstery

Most cars of these years had colorful, comfortable and durable upholstery on seat cushions and side panels. Cloth or vinyl were commonly used, with leather seat facings on some top-of-the-line models, or as an added cost option on others. In many cases these can be cleaned and repaired to give more years of satisfactory service.

You may have noted some needed upholstery repairs when you got the car home and made a close inspection of just what you'd bought, and what needed repair or replacement. If not, do it now. Check each seat cushion, side and door panel, as well as the headliner.

Upholstery repairs are usually best made with the panel or cushion removed from the car.

Cleaning it

You'll be surprised what a thorough cleaning can do. Use a whisk broom and vacuum cleaner on cloth to get the dirt out of creases and pleats. Once you've removed all you can, give it a good scrubbing.

To clean cloth or vinyl, mix a strong solution of household detergent and water. Use a soft-bristled brush or sponge to rub the suds into the material. Rinse with clear water and let dry. There are excellent upholstery cleaners to remove oily stains. When cloth upholstery is clean and dry, spray it with Scotchgard or a similar product for lasting protection. Armor All is great for protecting vinyl.

Leather can best be cleaned by using one of the fine leather cleaners, such as Connollys, Fiebings and

Direct sunlight and heat can cause serious damage to cloth, leather and vinyl upholstery. Foam padding will become brittle, rot and break apart, as on this Buick. Take measurements from the cushion or from a similar car to make a replacement covering.

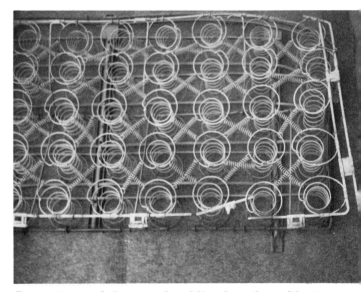

Remove torn upholstery and padding from the cushion to determine damage to the springs and framework. Buy a salvage yard cushion and remove coils, which can be twisted around weak or broken coils and wired or welded in place. Weld necessary repairs to the seat frame.

Lexol. These clean away dirt, grime and wax and leave the leather softer for you to work on. Directions are on the container.

One caution; don't use a stiff-bristled brush to clean dirt out of upholstery seams. You risk breaking the threads.

With all the products available for cleaning cloth, leather or vinyl, there's no excuse for dirty upholstery.

Repairing seats

Remove the upholstery covering to examine the condition of the springs. This is usually held in place by pig rings or clips. If individual springs are broken or sagging, they should be repaired. The easiest way to repair a broken or weak coil is to buy a replacement cushion. Even if the cushion is worse than the one you have, you can remove the good coils and wind them into place in your present cushion. Twist thin wire around the new and old coils to hold them in place. If the cushion's framework is broken, attach a replacement section to give the necessary strength.

Once springs and framework are repaired, protect these with rust-inhibiting primer, or any leftover spray paint.

Fit new webbing over the springs, wrapping it over one side of the framework and stretching it to the

Use pig rings to hold replacement webbing in place. Weave it over and under webbing running in the other direction. Cut indoor/outdoor carpet or jute padding to fit. Add a layer of polyurethane or latex padding for softness before installing the upholstery.

Use a hose to clean old seat cushion springs. When they are dry, stack them for painting, so the overspray from one may cover another. Use leftover spray paint to protect the springs. Make sure your repairs are strong enough to meet weight requirements.

187

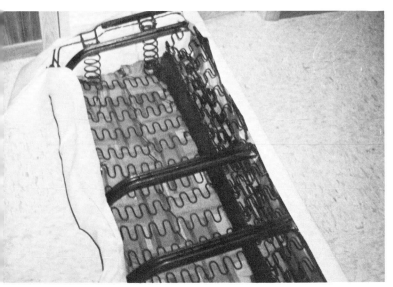

When you have repaired and painted the springs and seat framework, and installed the webbing and padding, make and fit a practice cover of unbleached muslin. If it doesn't fit as you want, correct your pattern before cutting expensive upholstery material.

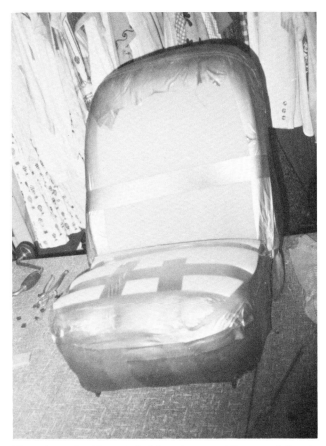

Do not use duct tape to hold replacement foam padding in place when repairing seat cushions. It can't be smoothed on compound curves and will pull loose in time. Also, foam padding isn't a satisfactory repair for weak and broken seat springs.

other. Use pig rings to hold the webbing to the framework at each end. When all the webbing in one direction is in place, weave webbing in the other direction, over and under, and fasten at each end with pig rings.

Replace worn original jute padding with indoor/outdoor carpet, bought as remnants. Fit polyurethane or latex foam padding, and spread household glue between the two to hold them in place. To keep the padding from slipping out of place, secure the perimeter with pig rings or clips.

Make a basic cover of unbleached muslin, taking measurements from the original covering, and fit it over the repaired cushion to protect the upholstery.

Repairing cloth seat cushions

Have patching material on hand, either from a cushion found at a salvage yard, or taken from a side riser. If you have to use other material, match the color and pattern as closely as possible.

Clip any frayed edges on the original covering. Cut a patch larger than the damaged area. Glue the patch on the underside. Clamp pieces of wood with waxed paper between the cloth and wood to prevent the material sticking to the wood. When the patch is thoroughly dry, use a curved needle and matching thread to sew it in place.

Seams that have pulled apart can often be sewn together, using a reinforcing piece underneath wide enough to bridge the weakened area. Because of the bulk involved, the seam may have to be hand sewn, with a second, reinforcing seam sewn close to the first.

Repairing leather cushions

Often, neglected leather appears to be more than a beginner dares tackle, causing some to substitute

Cut and fit a new polyurethane or latex patch to repair original worn or cracked cushion padding. Use latex adhesive, available in aerosol cans from auto supply stores or upholstery shops. Use the spray only in a well-ventilated area.

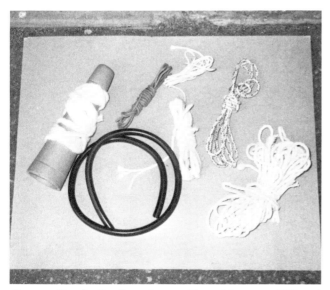

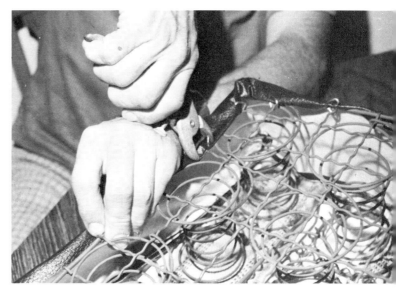

Buy cording in the diameter you'll need for your different applications. This can be rubber or plastic tubing, clothesline, venetian blind cord or common twine. Match the original diameter as closely as possible to keep things original.

Use pliers-like tool to pinch #1 pig rings through a double thickness of material holding the covering to the seat frame. Each ring should be attached to loop around metal, holding the covering firmly in place. Avoid extra bunching on corners.

vinyl for leather repairs. This isn't necessary, as leather cushion facings usually can be repaired.

You can buy replacement leather, in a wide variety of colors, from leather supply stores and firms advertising in car publications. An inexpensive source is to pick up a cushion from a car salvage yard. Choose

one as near to the original graining and color as possible.

Remove pig rings or clips holding the covering to the cushion. Turn it inside out to determine the extent of the damage. If the seams have pulled out

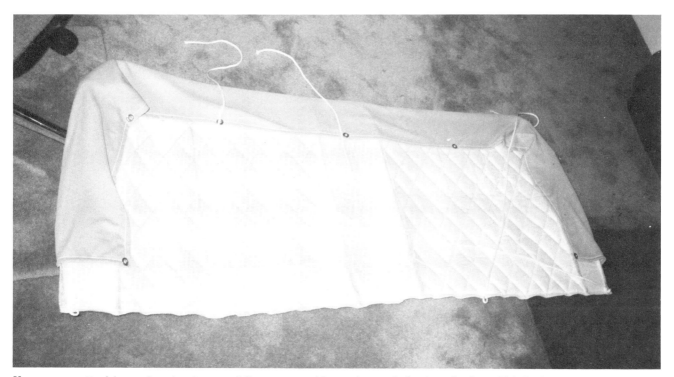

You can sew attaching strings in place, and fit grommets, if you want to tie the seat upholstery to the framework,

instead of using pig rings. This isn't as smooth fitting, nor will it duplicate the original fitting methods.

and the leather isn't torn, knot the threads to stop more pull-out. Sew the seam, either by hand with a curved needle, or on a home sewing machine using a #16 needle and cotton-wrapped polyester thread.

If the thread has torn through the leather, you may be able to hand stitch it by sewing between the original stitch holes. Many splits can be repaired by sewing the edges back together, then cementing a patch on the underside to relieve the tension on the repaired area.

In some bad splits, the panel can be cut away and a replacement panel sewn in place. Cut the replacement large enough to extend beyond the original piece. In addition to sewing along the original seam line, sew reinforcing seams on each side. After sewing, cement the parts that extend beyond the seams to the covering. If you cement the piece before you sew, the cement may clog the sewing machine.

A small patch cemented to the back will keep burn holes from developing into something worse.

Color Plus markets Flex-fill, which fills and hides small creases and wear marks. It will not repair large cracks and splits. There are excellent dyes in a variety of shades and colors. All leathers don't dye evenly, so you may not get an exact match. In this case, dye the entire cushion to hide repairs.

Dyeing leather

Leather can be dyed if you prepare the surface properly. First, it has to be cleaned to remove dirt and grime. Use a mild household detergent and water solution and a soft-bristled brush or sponge. Clean one panel at a time and rinse with clear water. Do *not* soak the leather.

After the initial washing, wipe on a leather cleaner and conditioner, following directions on the can. This will make the leather soft and pliable, prevent cracks and remove some stains. Use a surface preparation cleaner to remove wax and excess dye so the leather will accept new dye evenly.

Take a piece of leather with you to match the dye. If you can't get an exact match, plan on using the next darker shade. You can't change black or dark blue to white or light beige. You can, however, dye a light color to a darker color or shade.

Work on one pleat, panel or section at a time. Use the dauber that comes with the dye. Take short, uneven strokes so there is no visible break line. Be sure the dye gets into seams and around weltings or bindings. Don't be discouraged after the first coat, as it often takes several light coats to give the desired finish.

When the surface has dried, give it a light coat of the correct color wax for protection. Plan on using a

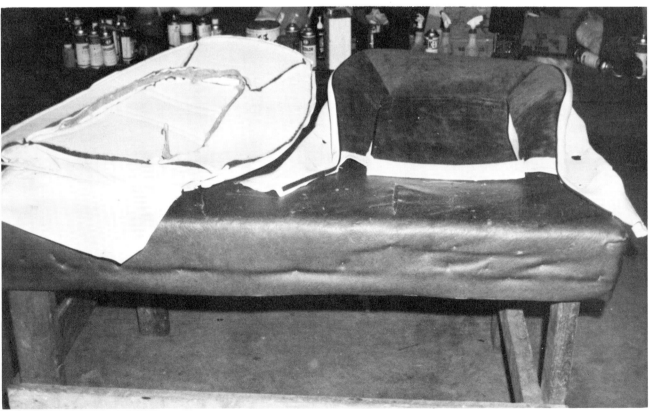

Measure carefully when making a pattern using two or more colors or different materials. Make a practice cover of inexpensive material to check the fit. Make any necessary changes to your pattern, and group pieces to avoid bunching in your machine.

leather cleaner and conditioner periodically to keep the surface soft and pliable.

Repairing vinyl-covered seats

Repairing torn vinyl-covered seats is easier than repairing either cloth or leather. Vinyl can stretch more than leather and won't fray as easily as cloth.

Choose a replacement vinyl close to the original in color, pattern and thickness. Remove the old covering from the seat and make any necessary repairs to the springs and framing. Cut a patch piece for small tears or splits, and cement it to the back of the material. Use a curved #16 needle and cotton-wrapped polyester thread. If you use your sewing machine for this job, don't cement the patch in place.

To replace a pleat or panel, cut the replacement piece larger than the original. Use a seam ripper to remove the old piece and knot the ends of threads. Sew seams, attaching the new piece to the old and a second, reinforcing seam close to it. Small burn holes can be repaired by cementing or sewing a patch to the underside.

Remove damaged welting from seat edges with a seam ripper. Cut strips of vinyl about one inch wide and join them on the bias to provide the length you need. Choose the correct thickness cord and using the cording foot on your sewing machine, run a seam to make the welting.

Lay the riser and top panel face to face, with the welting between them, and pin these together. From the back side of the material, sew a seam close to the edge of the welting, joining the pieces. Sew a second seam for added strength. When the material is righted, only the welting shows where the pieces were joined.

Mark the center of the covering and cushion at the front and back, and attach these points first.

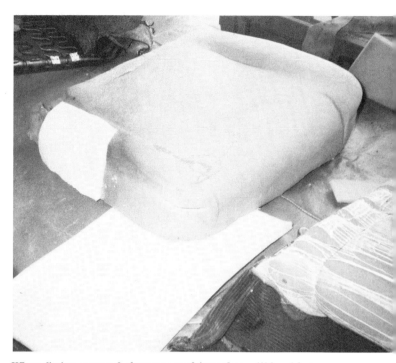

When fitting new upholstery to cushions that will be side to side, take pains to see that color breaks are in alignment. The cushion on the left will have to be removed, additional padding fitted to the top and the covering attached for proper alignment.

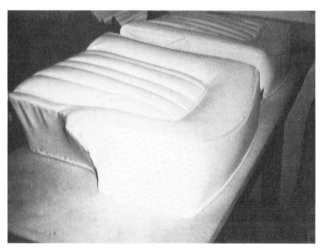

When sewing light color leather or vinyl, choose the thread color carefully. For the deep pillow effect, allow ½ in. extra on the seams. Use spray adhesive to hold extra padding strips to the back of leather or vinyl. Sew padding on cloth upholstered seats.

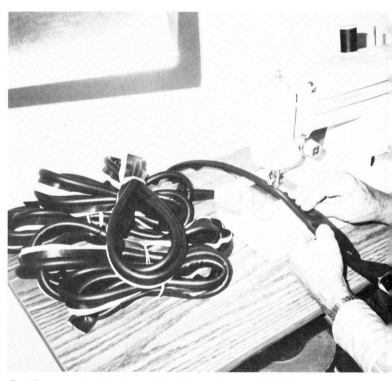

Cut the covering for the welting into strips and fold them around the cord. Fit the cording foot to your machine. Use cotton-wrapped polyester thread and a #16 needle for upholstery cloth, leather or vinyl. Press the material against the cording foot.

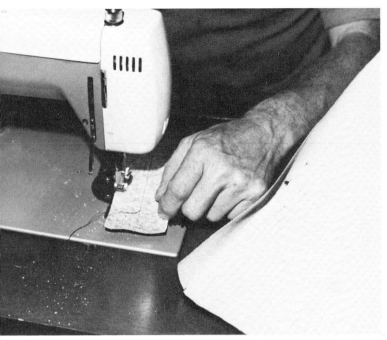

To make straight seams, draw a seam line on the back of the material and sew along this line. Lay material face to face, so there will be no raw edges showing. In areas where there'll be extra strain, sew a reinforcing seam close to the first.

For a padded or quilted effect, buy backing material with seam lines showing in the width you want. Lay the material on the back of the covering and sew along the lines. The padding will compress along the seam lines, giving the effect you want.

Stretch the material from front to back and side to side, as you attach the pig rings through a double thickness of material.

Repairing panels

Remove door and window hardware. Panels are usually held in place by clips hidden by the upholstery, and brightmetal screws at certain points. Use two thin blades, or a handy tool made for this use, and pry the clips out of the door or body.

Examine the pressed fiber backing. Often trapped moisture will have rotted and warped the bottom. Backing material is available in large sheets from auto trim shops or building supply stores. Some stores will cut sheets into easier-to-handle sizes.

A good scrubbing with a detergent and water solution usually will clean soiled panels. There are a variety of household upholstery cleaners that will do a good job removing spots and stains.

Often only the bottom portion of the backing panel needs to be replaced. Measure first, then cut out the damaged piece and replace it with a new section, which can be held in place by duct tape. When the upholstery is stretched over it, the repair will be strong and won't show.

Remove the covering and any scuff pad from the panel. Cement a patch behind any small holes. Cut away frayed threads and sew a patch behind small tears. If the bottom of the covering has been damaged by moisture, you can cut a new piece and sew it in place, using welting where the new piece joins the old.

Repair small holes in molded vinyl upholstery panels with a repair kit made for this purpose. Follow the included directions. Be sure the heating tool is at the correct temperature to bond the vinyl paste. You can smooth and paint the patch to make it invisible.

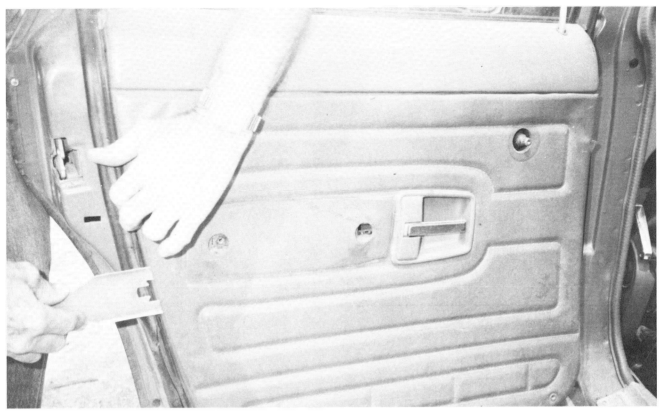

Remove the window crank, armrest, door latch handle and any visible screws to remove upholstery panel. Use handy tool, or twin blades to slip between the frame and panel to

pry the clips from the framework. Pull the panel down from the window molding.

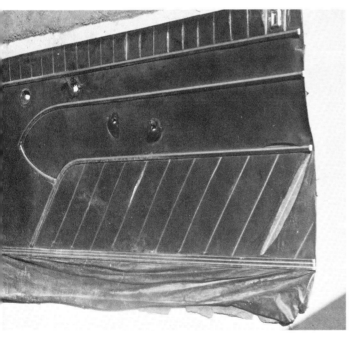

Before discarding the old panel, remove any metal molding and trim pieces. Take careful measurements of each section. Plan to duplicate the original pattern and design as closely as possible. Plan on making a new backing panel if there is serious rot.

Check the backing on panels for deterioration. You can cut away small rotted areas and attach a new section with duct tape, if you don't need to replace the entire panel. Try not to break rusted prongs holding trim pieces to the panel.

Remove the curved metal panels in convertibles that hold and hide the top-operating mechanism. Remove any attached hardware and rotted upholstery. Clean away any rust, and spray with a rust-inhibiting primer before attaching new upholstery.

If the carpet scuff pad is rotted away, buy similar carpet, and cut and bind it as a replacement.

If the covering is worn around door or window hardware, it's best to replace that section. Many times, different color or pattern materials on panels are separated by plated trim pieces. Remove the trim pieces, and using them as a guide, cut a new piece to cover a worn one. When trim pieces are installed, the repair won't show.

Making new panels

Use the old panel for a pattern. If this isn't possible, take measurements from the car. Measure and mark holes for door and window controls, speakers and armrests. Backing panels are too thick to cut with shears. Use a sharp blade against a straightedge for cutting and trimming.

Reupholstering

If your inspection convinced you the upholstery needs more than cleaning and repairs, you have some choices.

Sure, you can buy a high-priced upholstery kit for some cars that'll give you a like-new appearance, but you'll have to install it yourself.

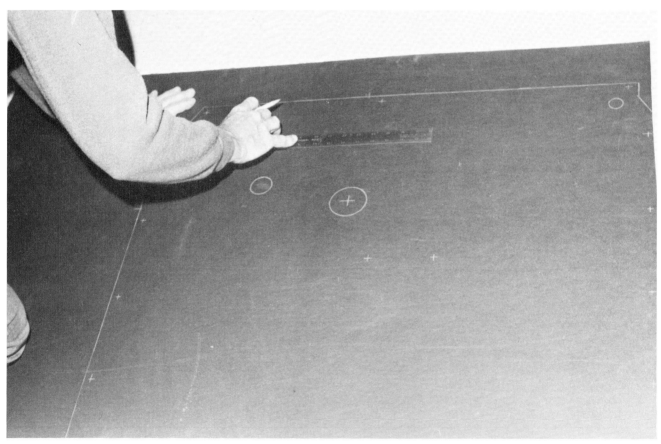

Take measurements directly from the car's body when making new backing panels. Use a white marking pencil and straightedge to draw exact measurements. Mark in holes for door and window hardware and lock. Punch holes for armrest screws and fastening clips.

You can take your car to a trim shop and have it reupholstered, *if* you have the time and money.

You have a third choice, one that will save you money and give you a lot of satisfaction. You can reupholster the car yourself. This is usually work you can handle, driving the car between jobs. It doesn't have to be done at one time, if you're budgeting money and time.

You have a choice, too, as to whether you want to redo it to original colors and standards, so you could show it in serious show car competition, or if you want something other than original, though thoroughly acceptable.

Upholstery is available in a wide choice of materials, colors, patterns and weaves at a number of sources. You'll find cloth and vinyls at local fabric stores or upholstery shops. Buy leather from leather specialists, or from firms advertising in car publications. In most cases you can duplicate the original.

When measuring for upholstery, be sure to take weave, pattern and graining into consideration, so the finished product will have these properly matched.

Upholstery panels should fit smoothly without any wrinkles. If the covering has pulled loose from the backing, and the material has wrinkled in places, the panel must be removed and the material stretched and glued in place, as on this Chrysler door.

The lighter weight fabric and vinyl yard goods for headliners are also easy to locate, as are bindings, welting and cording, matching thread, latex or polyurethane padding and luggage area coverings.

Seats

You'll get a better upholstery job if you make a trial cover of unbleached muslin. Remove the old cover and use it as a pattern. Otherwise, take measurements directly from the cushion. Measure, cut and sew, just as you'll have to do with the more expen-

Use either a band saw, or sharp blade against a steel straightedge when cutting a backing panel from a large piece of hardboard. You cannot cut this material with shears. Drill door and window control holes with a circular saw blade.

Remove the screws holding the armrests to the door. Disassemble the unit, taking the padding and covering from the framework. Make a pattern by tracing the frame, allowing extra material to fold over and cement to the framework.

Mark the center of each cushion and cover. Match these marks when fitting the new cover. Start at the front center of lower cushions and stretch newly made covers tightly over the cushions toward the back and sides. Align side welting on seatbacks.

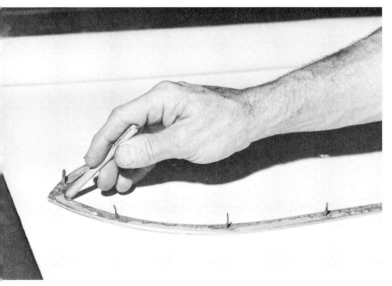

Lay brightmetal trim pieces against the material and trace the outline, when using a different color or pattern. When cutting this material, trim just short of the outer edge, so the material won't extend beyond the trim.

sive material. Attach webbing and padding to the cushion, as previously described, and slip the muslin cover over the cushion and secure with pig rings.

Lay the new material face down and draw the pattern lines on the back. Allow ½ in. extra for sewing. If there are pleats, allow ¾ in. on each side of the seam line for sewing. The seam will be ¼ in. above the center line, allowing ½ in. above for the padding.

Make the top part of the cushion first, then sew the welting around the perimeter of this section. When you complete this, measure and cut the pieces that cover the front riser, sides and the part that tucks under the seatback cushion. Lay the pieces face to face, so no raw edges will show. Be sure you have a double thickness along the bottom, through which the pig rings fit.

On visible seams, such as on each side of the front vertical riser, lay material beyond the seam back against itself and sew a seam ½ in. each side of the main seam.

When joining the side and top pieces, mark the middle of both and pin together. Lay the pieces face to face. Start an inch before the midpoint where the pin

196

is inserted and sew to just beyond the midpoint at the rear of the cushion. Reposition the material in the machine. Start about an inch from the pin and sew in the opposite direction. This ensures centering the cushion top on the riser and double stitching at these points.

Stretch the covering over the frame, making sure front and side edges line up evenly. Start from the front center, stretch and attach the tucked under bottom edge to the frame. Work front to back and side to side, stretching it as you install the pig rings.

The seatback cushions have hooks on the top that slip into seat framework, and screws through tabs to hold the bottom of the cushions in place. Follow the same directions as for bottom cushions, when reupholstering seatbacks.

Side panels

Often door and side panel coverings are made of two or more materials and in different colors. They're usually separated by welting or brightmetal trim pieces.

Remove the door and window hardware, armrest and any other attachment. If your car has electric windows, tag and disconnect the wires. Follow previous directions to remove the panel.

Use a seam ripper to separate upholstery pieces. Measure each piece and draw seam lines on the back of the material. When cutting, allow at least ½ in. extra material for seaming. Trim any excess material later.

Before joining the pieces, use the cording foot on your sewing machine to make the necessary welting. For thick cording, use plastic or rubber tubing, or clothesline, with the covering material cut accordingly.

When joining different panels that make up the covering, plan on joining small pieces first to avoid

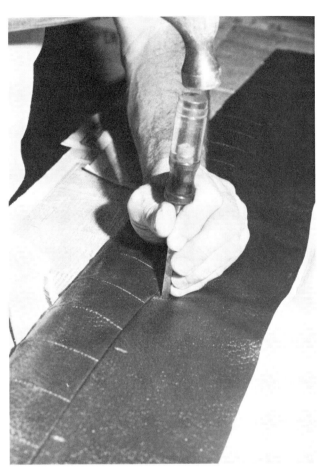

Straighten prongs on the trim pieces and mark where these go through the upholstery. Use a sharp blade to slit upholstery at these marks. Tap against a sharp chisel to make a slit in the backing plate. Fit the trim piece prongs through these slits.

Cut holes in the backing panel to align with holes in the door or inner panel. Use pliers to fit the spring clips into these holes. If the originals weren't rusted or weak, reuse them. However, if any have lost their tension, replace them.

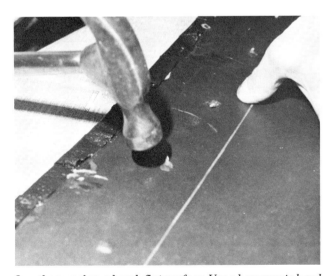

Lay the panel on a hard, flat surface. Use a hammer to bend the prongs against the backing plate. Bend prongs in alternating directions to keep the trim piece from moving. Prongs must fit flush with the panel to ensure a tight fit on the car.

197

Sew the various sections of the upholstery together and lay them on the backing panel. Make sure any insert and all trim pieces will line up with those on the adjacent panel. If the color scheme is also carried over to seatbacks, they must align.

feeding too much bulk through the sewing machine. Tie loose thread ends.

If there's thin padding on the front of the panel, cement it in place. Lay replacement covering on the panel and align it carefully. Use duct tape to hold the top side of the overlapping material to the backing. Stretch the remaining overlapping material and tape it in place. Turn the panel over. If you're satisfied with the fit, turn it back again and glue the overlap in place, removing the tape. Clamp against pieces of wood on each side of the panel.

When the covering is secure, use a sharp blade to cut an X in the center of the material covering the holes through which the hardware fits. Use a sharp blade to make slits through the upholstery and backing panel for the attaching prongs of brightmetal trim pieces.

Many door panels have scuff pads at the bottom that match the panel or carpeting in color. When replacing these, measure carefully, as most are bound and don't have the material turned back over the edge of the panel.

You may have to trim some of the tufting or pile, to attach the binding and keep it flush with the outer edge of the material. Usually, scuff pads are glued to the panel with brightmetal screws at the corners.

When replacing the reupholstered panel, fit the door and window hardware shafts through the Xs cut in the material. Match and connect any electric wiring. Attach the armrests before aligning the clips with the holes in the door framing. Turn in the plated screws, making sure the panel is correctly placed. Attach the door handle and window crank. If there's a

Fold excess material over the back of the panel and glue it in place. Put pieces of wood between the material and the clamps to avoid marks. Spray an adhesive on the back of the carpet scuff pad and position it. Fit and attach trim strips last.

Measure and cut carpet scuff pads for doors, side panels and kick pads. Sew a matching color binding around the perimeter to give it a finished look and keep the carpet from raveling. Use spray adhesive and brightmetal screws to hold it in place.

metal frame for the window, or a sill at the bottom of the window opening, attach these to complete the job.

Replacing headliners

If you couldn't clean or repair the headliner, you can make a replacement. Though they're bulky, they aren't overly difficult because the material is lighter weight.

To remove the old one for use as a pattern, you may have to remove framing for the windshield and rear window. Some ribs holding the headliner are sprung into receptacles above the doors and windows. Others are held in place by screws. Remove the ribs and headliner as a unit.

Mark the ribs from front to back, so they'll go back into the same position, before you slip them out of their sleeves. Use a seam ripper to remove the threads so you can spread the headliner out flat.

Lay the new material face down and draw in a center line from front to back. Mark the distance from the windshield to the first bow and on to each of the other bows. Lay the front rib on the first seam line facing it toward the front. Trace the curve on each end. Turn the rib facing the rear and trace the curves

When installing the re-covered panel, make small X slits in the upholstery where shafts stick through the covering. Attach the door and window cranks. Use a long nail to line up holes for the armrest and other screws that go through the upholstery.

Clean the back of the molded upholstery cover and use a spray adhesive when fitting it on the backing panel. In the *1960s, armrests became an integral part of door and side panels on some cars, making repairs more difficult.*

again. Do the same with each rib at the appropriate position.

Allow an extra inch on the overall front-to-back and side-to-side measurements for tuck-in, before cutting the material. Pin along the sleeve lines you drew in and sew along the pinned line. Sew a second seam slightly larger than the diameter of the rib, forming the sleeve through which the rib will fit. Trim extra material above the second seam to remove bulk and have a smooth-fitting headliner.

Slide the ribs through the correct sleeve and attach them to the body. Feel where any lights fit and cut an X in the material at that spot. Trim to the correct size and attach the lens.

Use a putty knife or curved blade to tuck the liner under welting above the doors or windows. Stretch it tightly toward the front, where it is held in place by the windshield molding. Do the same at the back window for a wrinkle-free headliner. To help keep the headliner looking like new, spray it with Scotchguard.

Sources for further information on working with leather and upholstering techniques are listed in the appendix.

Steel bows, conforming to the contours of the car's roof, fit into channels on the inside roof rails to hold the headliner in place. The bows fit through the sleeves in the headliner.

The bows may be insulated in some cars to provide a quieter interior.

Chapter 22

Carpets

Interior styling changes, including carpeting, followed changes in exterior styling during these years. Instead of somber or neutral shades, carpeting compatible to seats and upholstered panels made interiors more colorful and attractive.

Easier to clean latex-backed nylon carpeting, in loop or cut pile, gained widespread use. Though a few top-of-the-line cars were still fitted with thick, tightly woven wool carpets, many times these were color keyed to the upholstery.

Take measurements from the old carpet or directly from the car. Lay carpeting face down on the floor. Use a straight- *edge and draw the outline with chalk, as on this front, left-hand section. Mark where any cutouts must be made.*

Rubber floor mats in front were replaced by carpeting, with rubber or vinyl inserts for heels. One-piece mats, molded to fit over increasingly large transmission humps and drive shaft tunnels, replaced the former three-piece mats.

Fitting and installation methods changed, too. Less binding was attached, as carpets were often fitted under doorsill plates and left unbound under front seats and where they tucked under firewall insulation panels.

These changes were economy moves on the manufacturers' part, but the colorful carpeting gained public acceptance.

Inspecting

To determine what needs to be done to refurbish your car's carpets, you should make a careful inspection. This may require your removing seat cushions, and in some instances seat framework and doorsill plates. Perhaps a thorough cleaning will be all that is necessary. You may find a few worn spots that can be repaired or covered with a mat. You may decide the carpeting is beyond repair and should be replaced.

Carpeting on the driver's side may be stained by gasoline or oil from gas stations. Wet carpeting will collect dirt, keeping it damp, eventually causing it to rot. Tears that are not repaired can become larger, stains that aren't cleaned properly can set and become permanent and carpets that aren't secured in place by snaps, seat tracks or doorsills can wrinkle, even shrink.

Cleaning

There are several excellent carpet shampoos available at supermarkets and other stores. If there are oil or grease stains, choose one recommended for that use. You can clean most carpets with a sudsy detergent and water solution.

Remove the carpets for best results. Sweep or vacuum thoroughly, before applying any liquid. Use a scrub brush to work in the suds. Use a sponge and clear water to rinse out excess suds. When it is dry, sweep or vacuum to raise the pile before installing it.

Repairing

Small rips or tears can often be repaired by gluing a patch on the back. Hand sew small patches and reinforce by gluing canvas to the back. Use a large, curved needle and strong thread, matching the color if possible. Make small stitches. If you pull the thread

When drawing measurements for the center section of a front, three-piece carpet, work from a center line on the carpet, as each side may not be the same. Mark the cutout for a floor-mounted gearshift. Recheck each measurement before cutting.

tight enough it will disappear into the pile and hardly show, if at all.

Parts worn thin by the driver's heels can often be covered satisfactorily by cementing or sewing a vinyl piece over the worn spot, after cleaning the carpet. Get a close color match, and sew a similar size piece on the passenger's side to give uniformity.

Don't overlook the possibility of finding a suitable carpet from a similar car in a salvage yard. Because many manufacturers used similar carpeting in many of their offerings, a carpet you could use doesn't necessarily have to come from the same marque or year.

Carpeting sources

You have some choice of carpeting sources. Ready-to-install carpet packages are available for some cars, as are exact duplicates of original equipment carpeting by the yard. Similar cut or loop pile nylon carpeting, in a variety of colors and sizes, can be found in department or discount stores.

Your choice depends on what you want in your refurbished car. Duplications of original carpets are required for serious show car competition. A trim shop will make new carpets for you. Or you can make them yourself . . . and save a lot of money.

Making new carpets

Remove old carpets for patterns. They're held in place by brightmetal screws, by front seat tracks if they're unbound, under doorsill plates and by push-clips to the firewall. You may need to remove a console or plate on floor-mounted shifts. Try to get worn

Use heavy shears to trim carpeting for a clean cut. When cutting pieces to be joined, take any pattern or tufting into consideration for a better looking finished job. Run a line of glue on any raw edges that won't be bound to prevent raveling.

carpets out in one piece, so you can take measurements. Otherwise, you could take measurements from carpets in a similar type car.

Draw measurements on the back of the carpet, remembering these will be reversed, when the carpet is righted. If the carpets are to be bound, you may have to trim a small portion of the pile, so the binding will fit flush. Use cloth, leather or vinyl for the binding, depending on what was used originally.

Some carpet pieces will be irregularly shaped so they will fit around contours and brackets. Measure carefully with a straightedge for short sections, and with a tape measure for curved surfaces. Allow up to one inch extra for seaming.

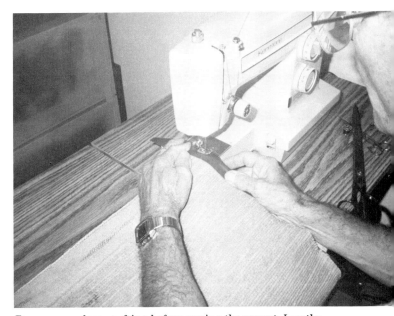

Remove any loose tufting before sewing the carpet. Lay the binding and carpet face to face and sew a seam at the correct distance from the edge. Turn it over and sew a second seam bordering the edge of the folded-over binding. Tufting will hide the thread.

203

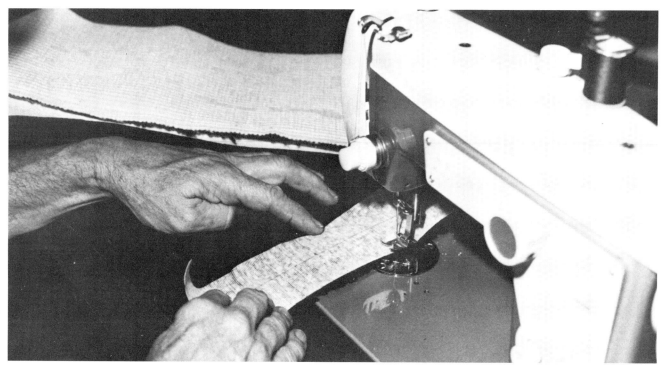

Adjust the sewing foot on your machine to accommodate the thicker, rubber-backed loop pile carpet and binding. Use a #16 needle and cotton-wrapped polyester thread. Knot threads at each end of the seam. Fold attached binding over and sew or cement it on the underside.

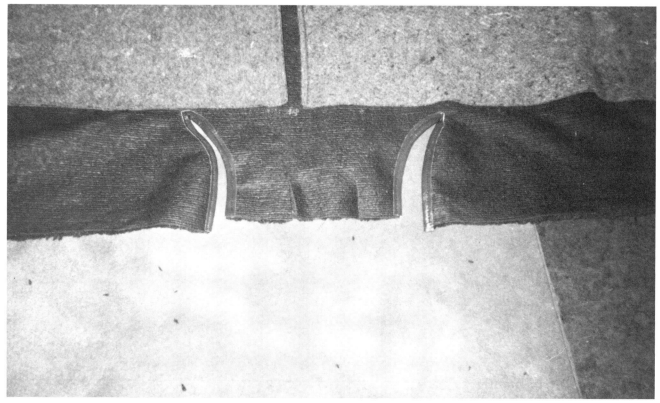

When sewing bindings in cutouts on carpets, cut small Vs on the underside of the binding to avoid bunching. Because of the bulk, join smaller pieces before the larger ones. In some cases, you may have to have the larger pieces joined at a carpet shop.

204

Though you should keep the carpeting as close to the original as possible, you may want to make front carpets in two or three sections, rather than in one piece. If you do this, make a pattern for the bell-housing/transmission hump, and a pattern for each side. Don't assume the floor on each side of the hump will have the same dimensions, as there can be differences. This will take additional binding.

Draw your measurements on an old sheet or piece of unbleached muslin and cut along your lines. Pin these together to check the fit. Make any necessary corrections before cutting the carpeting. If you're using one piece to cover the entire front floor, you'll have to use canvas or vinyl pieces to reinforce the seamed material.

Cut binding material about 1½ in. wide and to the correct length. Lay strips face down along the outer edge of the carpet. Sew a seam along what will be the correct width of the binding. Fold it back over itself and onto the back of the carpet. On the underside the binding should extend beyond the seam you've already sewn. Sew a seam just beyond it; the carpet pile will hide the stitches. If you prefer, you can

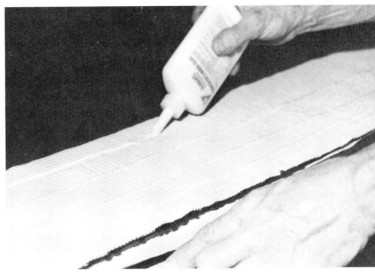

Use either a spray adhesive or household glue to hold carpet to scuff pads, back seat risers or to the bottom of front seatbacks and sections between doors. Let it get tacky before pressing the carpet in place. Wipe any drips before they dry.

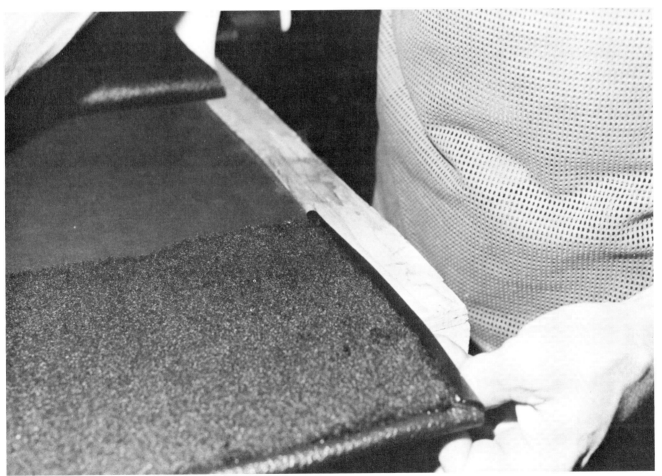

When sewing the binding on scuff pads, take time to check the fit after seaming the bottom, before you start on the sides. Pin the side binding in place, and fold the binding to be sure you have it right. Remove the pins just before you reach them.

1. It may be necessary to clip some of the pile so binding will be level with top of carpet.

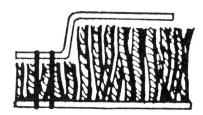

2. With binding face down on carpet stitch in at least two places.

3. Fold free end of binding over the stitched end and glue to underside of carpet.

cement the binding along the carpet backing, to avoid sewing a second seam.

Front carpeting, because of the hump, may be made in three pieces and sewn together. A center piece, often with Vs cut out and sewn together to make it fit over the hump, is the most difficult to sew. Side pieces that extend from the firewall to under the front seat, and from the hump to the outer edge have to be sewn to this. Any binding that fits on these three pieces should be sewn in place, before joining the sections. This cuts down on the bulk passing through your sewing machine.

You may decide to cut the pieces and take them to a shoe repair or upholstery shop to have them joined. You'll still save a bundle.

If pedals or the shift lever extend through the carpet, mark and cut these slits or holes before joining the pieces. In some cars, these openings need be bound to follow original installation.

Rear carpets may be in one piece, fitted from side to side, or there may be a center section covering the tunnel, with a piece of carpet on each side. On many cars, the part that fits under the front seat, and the portion that covers any rear cushion riser won't be bound.

Unless you have the old carpet to use as a pattern, draw the measurements on muslin or an old sheet. Pin the pieces together to be sure your finished product will fit correctly.

When joining pieces, lay the material face to face to avoid any raw edges. If your car has separate pieces on each side of the tunnel, fit the tunnel section first. Bind the edges that meet the tunnel, and back edges that don't fit under the rear seat cushion. Bind the outer edges, if they don't fit under the doorsill.

Padding

You'll get more enjoyment and longer use from your new carpets if the padding is in good condition, as it protects the carpet from direct contact with the steel floor. Padding also repels some moisture that would otherwise reach the floor, and gives better underfoot feeling and insulates against heat, cold and noise.

Buy replacement padding by the linear foot from carpet shops, home furnishing and discount stores. Polyurethane or latex padding will repel moisture that would be absorbed by jute padding.

Measure and cut the padding, just as you did the carpet pieces, making any holes or slits for pedals and controls. Be exact in your measurements.

Before installing the padding, clean the floor thoroughly. If there are rust spots, use a wire-bristled brush and sandpaper to clean to bare metal. Use an aerosol can of rust-inhibiting paint for lasting protection.

If the padding or carpet fits under seat tracks, clean with solvent and lubricate lightly with graphite. Remove and clean the doorsill plates. Use new screws through the plates and carpet when you install them. Make sure seatbelt anchors are secure.

Even though the carpeting should hold the padding in place, you may want to cement areas under the driver's and passenger's heels to keep padding from bunching.

Install the carpets, stretching them tightly and use brightmetal screws with washers to hold them in place. They should fit wrinkle-free, without any padding showing.

Rejuvenating or replacing carpets are jobs the beginner can handle evenings or weekends. The car doesn't have to be out of service during these jobs. The time and money spent will increase your driving pleasure and the value of your car.

Chapter 23

Trim items

A lot of changes in the composition and style of many interior and exterior trim pieces took place during these years. The increased use of plastic and molded foam cause the most headaches.

You'll enjoy your car more and its value will increase, if you pay attention to interior and exterior trim pieces. These plastic or brightmetal pieces have little to do with the car's operation, but add to its appearance and your driving pleasure.

Exterior pieces include window and windshield moldings, hood ornaments, script insignia, side and rocker panel strips and other attached, decorative pieces.

Inside trim includes instrument clusters, window and windshield moldings, visors, ashtrays, dashboard knobs and controls, and other items that add to driver and passenger comfort and convenience.

Intense sunlight and heat are the biggest problems with molded plastics and vinyls. Dashboard and window trim often crack. Steering wheels often split along the rim and at the hub. Plastic lenses on dome and courtesy lights crack and discolor because of heat.

There are ready-made replacements for the foam covering on dashboards for many cars. Carpet-like pads to hide the damage and prevent further deterioration are also available, if you don't want to make one.

The chrome-plated plastic knobs and other decorative pieces can be replated, if not in your town, by firms that advertise in automobile publications.

Many plated and plastic interior and exterior trim parts can be cleaned, satisfactorily, by soaking and scrubbing in a strong household detergent and water solution.

Steering wheel

Many cars have composition steering wheels, which can be repaired to like-new with a two-part epoxy paste. Remove the wheel by pressing and turning the horn button counterclockwise. Remove the holding nut and lift off the steering wheel. Rent a wheel puller for this job, if necessary.

Use a hacksaw to cut away material on each side of the crack. Use solvent to clean each cut. Follow directions, when mixing the epoxy, and overfill each cutout area. Dip your fingers in solvent to smooth contours where the spokes meet the rim. Let repaired areas cure for twenty-four hours.

Sand each filled cut, using progressively finer grit paper. Sand between spokes on banjo-type wheels. Mask all plated parts and spray with the correct color lacquer, using several thin coats, lightly sanded between coats. Finish with clear lacquer. A final rubbing with fine steel wool, or pumice stone will produce a glass-like finish. A source for more detailed informa-

Loose trim parts can soon become missing trim parts. Inspect and fasten these loose pieces that detract from the car's appearance and value. Replacement clips and fasteners are readily available at auto trim shops and are easy to install.

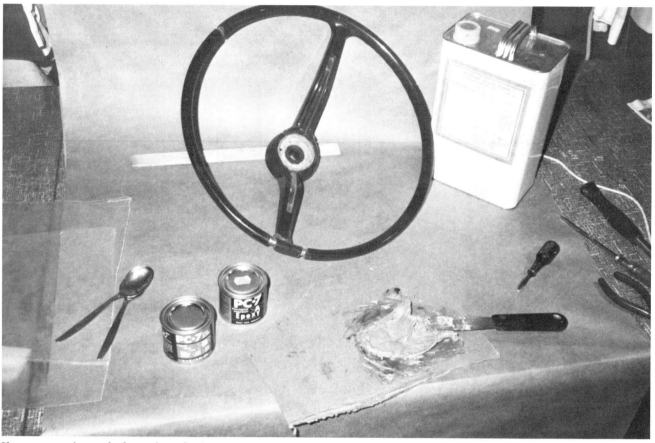

You can repair cracked steering wheels to like new. Rent a gear puller to remove the wheel. Use a hacksaw to enlarge cracks in the hub and rim. Use PC-7, following directions on the cans. Handle flammable lacquer thinner very carefully.

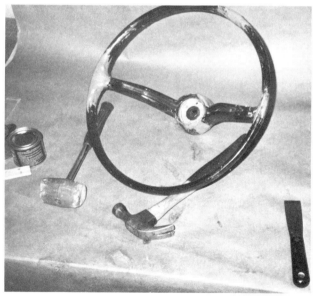

As the directions suggest, overfill the cutouts with the PC-7 mixture. Use your finger and lacquer thinner to smooth filled spots in the hub and the contours where cross-members join the rim. Any additional contours can be made later.

Clamp the wheel, with the cuts filled with PC-7 mixture, in a vise. Place boards on each side of the rim to avoid damage. It takes twenty-four hours for the mixture to cure. It can then be filed, sanded and painted. Properly made repairs won't show.

tion on rebuilding and refinishing steering wheels is included in the appendix.

Window moldings

If these are plated, they can often be cleaned satisfactorily; otherwise, they must be replated. If the paint has worn off in some areas, the whole molding should be repainted, as it's impossible to finish just the worn spots.

Though woodgraining isn't overly difficult, it is time consuming. Specialists in this work advertise in the auto hobby publications.

If you'd like to give it a try and have had some experience with hand painting, have a few samples of woodgrained shelf paper on hand to use as a guide. Apply a base coat as near to the desired color as possible. Apply two or more contrasting colors with a coarse brush, imitating the graining on the shelf paper. These colors are not intended to cover the base coat completely, and should leave parts of each preceding coat showing through.

When you're satisfied with the graining effect, apply several coats of clear lacquer, rubbing after each coat with progressively finer sandpaper and finally extra-fine steel wool or pumice stone.

If the vinyl window moldings are cracked, try to find replacement moldings at a salvage yard. Remember, these don't necessarily have to come from the same make, or year, as your car. Take one with you for match-up. Many moldings in the same car family are interchangeable. If you locate some in good condition, but a different color, use handy aerosol lacquer to make them all the same color.

Tag wires for match-up, and remove the instrument cluster from the dash to clean the individual dials. Use cotton-tipped swabs and alcohol to clean dial faces and protect figures and graduations. Don't forget to clean the inside of the glass lenses.

Repair kits are readily available to repair all but the most severe cracks and splits. Follow the detailed directions on the container, choosing a color and graining pattern similar to the original.

Dash knobs

Many plastic dash knobs can be repaired in the same manner, and with the same epoxy compounds, as used for steering wheel repairs.

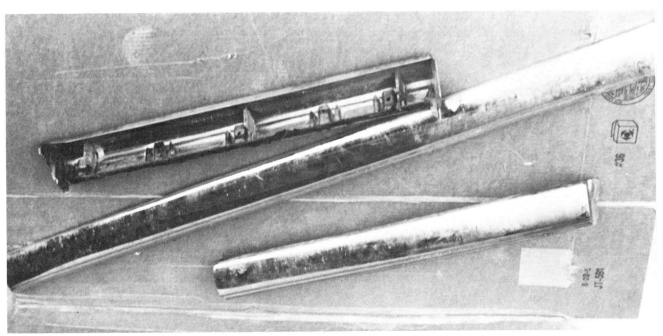

Remove screws holding plated window trim pieces for initial cleaning. These are often pot metal castings and require careful handling. If you have many items for replating, group them for a better price. Compare quality of work and price before choosing a plater.

Trace around a good visor to make the pattern for a new covering for those without a firm backing. Allow ½ in. extra for seaming. Cut a series of small Vs around curved edges to avoid bunching. Hand sew the top, where your stitching won't show.

Salvage yards are a good source for replacement knobs. Occasionally you'll find a knob molded to the rod or cable. In this case, replace the cable and knob. To keep a matching set, especially in orphan makes, you may have to substitute a complete set of knobs from another car. If so, choose knobs that are as compatible as possible.

A source for detailed information on repairing molded knobs is included in the appendix.

Instrument clusters

During these years, most cars grouped instruments in clusters. To repair or clean an instrument, you must remove the group. Remove the bolts or clamps holding the instrument in place. On some cars

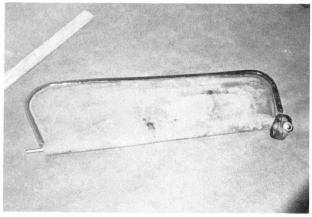

This soiled, cloth-covered, fiberboard-backed visor has a plated channel-type frame for stiffness. Pry the trim loose and peel away the soiled cloth covering. Some thin rubber padding may tear away. Use the old covering as a pattern.

the cluster is held in place by plated screws, which can be removed from the front of the dashboard. Tag and disconnect all wires before removing the cluster.

It is usually easier to replace an instrument than trying to repair one. You can remove individual instruments from the cluster. In some cases the dial can be removed from individual instruments, so you'll only be replacing the works. Remember, many cars within the same family used the same instruments, though dial faces may differ.

Use cotton-tipped swabs, dipped in alcohol, to clean instrument faces. Do not use solvents, as they may wipe off numerals and graduations on dial faces. Radio dials and clock faces should be cleaned in the same manner.

Visors

Excessive heat and ultraviolet rays from the windshield may have cracked, discolored, shrunk or warped the visor. These usually have a hardboard inner panel, or a stiff wire framework supporting foam padding.

If the visor appears hopeless, look for a replacement in a salvage yard. Remember to look in the same family of cars, so the mounting bracket will fit. Paint both visors if you can't get an exact duplicate.

If you believe it can be repaired, remove the visor from the car and the panel from the holding bar. If the inner piece is warped, try dampening it and leaving it overnight under weights to straighten it. If this

Trace and cut the visor's outline on new latex padding. Use spray adhesive to hold the padding to the fiberboard. Draw your seam lines on the back of the material. Seam only the portion surrounding the rod. Do not cement the cloth covering.

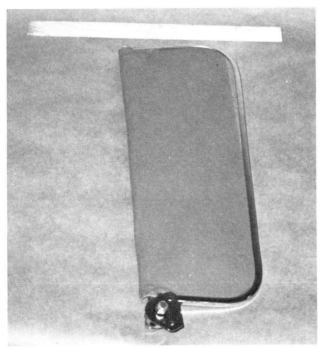

Slip the new covering over the fiberboard panel. Fit the metal edging in place and crimp the upper ends to be sure they stay attached. Spray with a fabric protector to keep it clean. Tighten the nut so the visor will hold its setting.

If you have broken or missing door or window cranks and can't find exact replacements, consider changing the entire set. You can buy these from cars sitting in salvage yards. Most shaft diameters and lengths are the same. Look in cars from the same auto maker.

doesn't work, slit and remove the covering along the top. Cut and install a replacement panel and refit the covering. You can glue or hand sew the edges.

Interior hardware

Door handles, window cranks and lock buttons can usually be cleaned by soaking and scrubbing them in a strong household detergent and water solution.

Most interior hardware is made of pot metal, which can't be brazed, welded or cemented.

If you have trouble finding individual replacements, consider changing the whole group for a matched set. Shaft size and mounting methods should be the same within the same car family, though the car may not be the same make, model and year as yours.

Ashtrays, door and panel trim pieces and similar plated pieces are usually held in place by clips, which

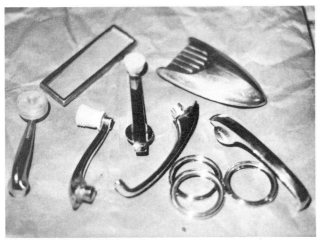

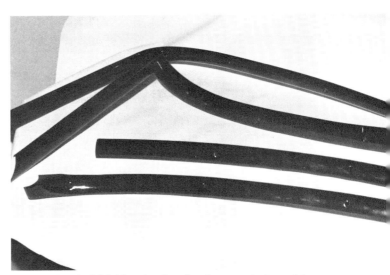

Remove small trim parts and group them for cleaning in a strong household detergent and water solution. A light scrubbing with fine steel wool will usually make them shine again. If there are scratches and rust remaining, they'll need to be replated.

If plated windshield trim is pitted or rusted, making replating expensive, you can save money by refinishing it in your car's interior color. Clean, fill, sand and prime, as you would any other car part. Use thinned lacquer for best results.

All three plastic trim inserts looked alike before two were soaked overnight in a strong detergent and water solution and scrubbed with fine steel wool. A light coat of wax, applied periodically, will keep them looking like new. Find replacements at car club flea markets.

are easily removed for refurbishing. In some cases, an upholstery panel may have to be removed when replacing trim pieces.

Escutcheon plates, dome light rims, script nameplates and other trims can usually be cleaned satisfactorily, once they're removed.

Exterior trim

During these years many cars had a wide variety of plated trim pieces bolted or clipped to hoods, front and rear fender panels and rear decks. Some of these were functional, others were simply decorative. Some trim pieces were added to adapt panels used on other nameplates and camouflage their common use. Other trim pieces were used to update the previous year's models. It was common to use body shells for a two- or three-year period, with only grille and ornamentation changes during these years.

Trim pieces can be removed for refurbishing. In many cases, soaking and scrubbing in a strong detergent and water solution is all that will be necessary. Dented pieces may have to be replaced; some pieces will have to be replated. Before you go to this expense, try to find replacements in a salvage yard.

Though a beginner can't replate trim pieces, there are some things that can be done to ready the parts to be plated and save money. These are jobs that would otherwise be done at a plating shop.

Plating preparation
Degreasing

Clean the article with perchloroethylene, which is available at pharmacies or dry cleaning shops. It is less volatile than carbon tetrachloride. You can also

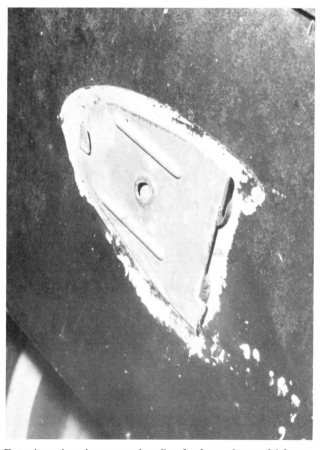

Exterior trim pieces are often fitted to base plates which are bolted to the body. Remove the item from the base plate for plating. Remove the plate from the car, so the metal beneath it can be properly prepared for painting.

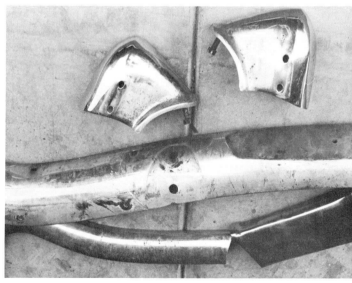

Disassemble the bumper for easier handling, as well as for cleaning and degreasing. This is work the plater would have to do later, so you should get a lower price on the overall job. Get a receipt for the number of pieces you leave at the shop.

use the hot alkali solution, commercially known as Oakite. Careful use of these, as previously described, will clean the parts to be plated.

Stripping

The mechanical method of stripping the old plating is by sanding and using a grinding wheel. This must be done carefully to give an even surface. Use a sanding block to distribute pressure evenly. When using a grinding wheel, take it easy, so you won't remove anything beyond the old plating.

Smoothing the surface

If you don't remove pits from the parts before plating, you'll have a part with shiny pits, once it is replated; plating won't remove pitting. If the metal is thick enough, pits can be ground out. You may try your hand at flowing silver solder or brass into the imperfections and sanding them smooth. Badly pitted items will have to be professionally repaired, and it is expensive. This adds to the importance of finding suitable replacement parts.

Sources for information on the chemical method of stripping and plating are included in the appendix.

Removing the grille

Parts of the grille may be combined with the front bumper on some cars, and once the bumper is removed, these can be unbolted for cleaning and preparation for plating. Other grilles and grille parts are attached to front-end sheet metal by bolts or self-tapping screws. Some of these must be removed from under the car, others from the top, with the hood propped open.

Though the grille may appear to be one piece, you'll often find that once it has been removed from the car, it is made of several smaller castings or

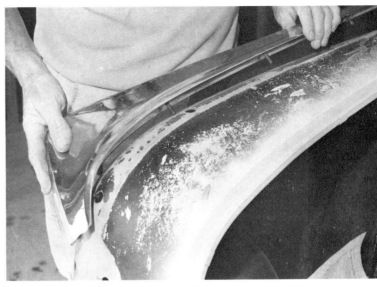

Plated fender trims and other bolt-on pieces should be removed so the entire body can be cleaned, sanded and painted. You may need to remove plating from threads on bolts and nuts that have been plated. Use a steel nut or bolt to do this.

stampings, which can be separated for lower plating costs.

Side trim

The long side trim strips are held to the body and fenders by clips. Some clips simply push into holes, others are bolted to the body. Trim strips snap over the clips.

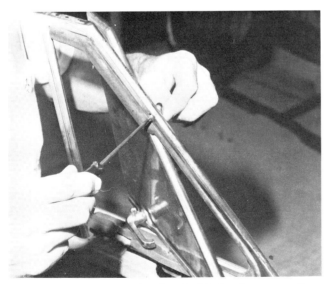

Window frames cannot be plated with the glass or weather-stripping in place. Remove vent windows from the car, and remove the glass from the frames at your workbench. A little glycerine will help soften the weather-stripping for easier removal.

Remove the lenses from taillights when plating the units. Tag wires for later match-up. Sealed beams can be masked when the car is painted, but any plated rim or bezel should be removed. Save all screws and clips for easier reattaching to the car.

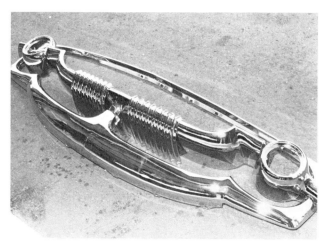

Remove the bolts holding the grille to the front-end sheet metal and remove it as a unit. Most grilles are made up of several parts. Disassemble and clean these to get a better and lower-cost plating job. The money spent on the grille is a good investment.

Remove bolts holding headlight assembly to front-end sheet metal. Disassemble further at your bench. If plated parts have only light surface rust, a good scrubbing with a strong detergent solution may make replating unnecessary.

Small decorative pieces, in the form of simulated air scoops, louvres, top of fender trim, nameplates and script logos bolt in place.

Larger trim pieces, such as plated headlight bezels, taillight housings and large, center-mounted luggage lid handle and license plate light combinations are bolted in place. Nuts can be reached from under the fender, the underside of the hood and luggage area lid, or inside the luggage area. Tag all wires for later match-up.

Plated moldings around the windshield and rear window, as well as where vinyl tops and convertible roofs join the body are clipped in place. Some pieces slip over the clips and have a screw at one end to secure them. Use a thin blade to pry trim from the clips. Be careful not to bend it. Plated trim on rub strips, rocker panels and the lower edges of doors and body panels snap over clips bolted or pushed into

After having the grille and other parts replated, you may need to repaint lettering and other indentations. Mask the plated parts for protection. Use a small brush for painting intricate areas the same color as originally used. Work slowly for perfection.

Bolt-on plated pieces usually have no function, but are only for style. During the fifties and sixties, many trim pieces were attached to give the appearance of a rear-mounted engine. Other trim was added to differentiate deluxe from standard models.

holes in these panels. Pry them from the clips for repair or replacement.

Mounting plated trim

Mount newly plated trim pieces carefully, after cleaning the surface to which they attach. Replace any rusted clips and be sure all pieces are in place firmly. Use a rubber mallet to tap pieces over clips. If you're going to paint the car, store plated pieces in old towels, or soft wrapping until you're ready to mount them.

Shop around

You'll often get a lower price by having all the plating done at one shop at one time, if this is convenient for you. See samples of the plater's work and get price estimates, telling exactly what will be done, before leaving any parts to be plated. Get a receipt, showing every piece you're leaving, so you can be sure to pick up everything. If nuts and washers are included, be sure these are listed. Bolts and nuts may not fit, until you knock off the thickness of the plating. Either use taps and dies to do this, or turn in an unplated bolt or nut.

Though your car may not be as attractive with some trim pieces removed, the time taken for plating doesn't necessarily keep you from driving it.

Sources for information on plating are included in the appendix.

Most of the fancy trim on dashboards of cars of the 1950s and 1960s can be easily removed for servicing. Stainless steel and plated parts can be cleaned satisfactorily or replated. Many dashboard knobs can be rebuilt as good as new.

Many interior trim pieces on doors and dashboards can be removed for cleaning without removing the upholstery or instrument panels. Often a thorough scouring is all that is necessary to make the pieces like new again.

Before having wheel discs replated, try polishing them with a buffing wheel in your hand drill. Wash them first, then use a fine rubbing compound or jeweler's rouge to buff them to a high shine. Use a fine-bristled brush and lacquer for painted parts.

Chapter 24

Preparing for painting

Unless you're painting only a small repair or one panel, preparing your car for painting should be done only when all mechanical and body and fender work are complete. Give yourself plenty of time to prepare the surface. Shortcuts taken on preparation will result in a less than perfect job and decrease the car's value.

The spray gun is not a substitute for bodywork. Though there have been great improvements in fillers, primers and sealers, they cannot hide a poorly made body repair.

Badly rusted metal parts should be taken to a dip shop for cleaning by the alkaline immersion process, then they must be thoroughly rinsed before priming.

You can rent small, hand-held sandblasters, which not only remove rust down to the bare metal, but recycle the sand. These are ideal for in-garage

For the best paint job, remove the front bumper and bumper arms as a unit. Plan to paint the bumper arms later. Remove the grille, which may include parking lights and turn signals. Spray flat black on front-end sheet metal. Keep spray dust from radiator core.

216

sanding of small parts. Always wear goggles and a respirator for protection.

On rust-prone areas, such as the bottom of the cowl and door and rocker panels, use a zinc-rich cold galvanizing compound, which is available in spray cans. These form a ninety-five percent pure zinc film over rust, shutting out oxygen, giving protection equal to the hot-dip method. POR–15 is easy to use, and does a fine job. Oxy-Solv is another excellent product.

Headlight, parking light, turn signal and taillight trim should be removed. Cover lenses with paper and masking tape. Protect wiring contacts with plastic tape. Bolt-on and clip-on trim pieces should be removed and the areas underneath sanded and cleaned like the rest of the panel.

You should paint the doorjambs and drip channels around the hood and luggage area lids. Remove weather-stripping and doorsill plates and clean underneath.

If you're going to remove paint from various panels or the entire car, POR–15 stripper, or one offered by the major automotive paint companies, makes the job easier. Spray on these clear liquids, which work on old paint in seconds and won't hurt aluminum, chrome, fiberglass or rubber. Rinse thoroughly and cover bare metal with a metal conditioner, such as Metal Prep or Chem Grip before priming.

Paint specialists agree that a car shouldn't have more than one paint job after the original, as the surface gets too thick. Your car's paint was four to six millimeters thick when it left the factory. Each repaint adds more thickness, making the finish prone to chipping and cracking. If your car has had several

Remove the tack strip in the channel where the convertible top meets the body. Clean away rust and scale. Use compressed air to blow away dust before painting the area car color. Install a new tack strip, which may be cemented in place, or held by tabs.

paint jobs, you should strip it to bare metal and start from there.

Use glazing putty to fill minor dings and scrapes, and feather the edges so they'll blend with the surface.

Then use a power sander. The vibrator type is easy to use. You should be able to spot any small

Remove old or torn weather-stripping. Use a wire-bristled grinding wheel in your hand drill to clean the rain channels around the luggage area and the hood. These must be free of rust and scale. Paint them car color and install new weather-stripping.

If there's any sign of rust in the doors, remove the door-latching and window-operating mechanisms. Clean and spray with a rust-inhibiting primer. Once they are installed in the doors, a light coat of graphite will keep them operating properly.

It is sometimes easier to remove a front fender panel from the car to prepare the surface for painting. After all hammer and dolly work and grinding are done, fill minor imperfections with a light coat of body filler. Use a sanding block to smooth the panel.

scratches the sander didn't remove. Fill these with a good grade body putty, and when dry, hand sand for smoothness. When hand sanding, use a sanding block for evenness.

Choose a polyester-base catalyzed primer. It won't shrink, and minimizes gloss dieback.

Once a panel has been repaired, it should be primed before getting a color coat. For best results, give the area at least two prime coats, sanding between each coat. It is better to prime and paint the entire panel, than to try to match only the repaired area.

PPG's (Ditzler) K-200/K-201 Primer Surfacer, DuPont's URO Prime Filler 1120S or Sherwin Williams' Ultra Fill II will help you prepare the surface for an excellent paint job with minimal work. These can be sprayed in a heavier coat, without undue worry about runs or sags. They'll fill in most sanding scratches, allowing you to build a smooth surface. Sand between coats with #220 grit paper.

Body filler is not a substitute for hammer and dolly work on doors or panels. It should be used only to cover slight dings or dents, or to feather the edges of welded-in metal patches and areas that have been ground after shaping.

After the damaged areas have been repaired, primed and sanded to your satisfaction, use compressed air to clean sanding dust from seams and crevices. Wipe the surface with a tack cloth to remove any dust or lint before spraying a prime coat.

218

Remember . . . the less subcoats the better. Don't expect spraying to remove blemishes that should have been worked out with a hammer and dolly.

When you think the surface is smooth, spray a light coat of a different color primer. Use a sanding block with #400 grit paper, and minor imperfections you missed will pop out at you because of their different color.

Fill these imperfections, hand sand, feather the edges and give a final coat of primer. Use #600 grit wet sandpaper to provide the glass-like surface you need for color coats.

Visit the major automotive paint stores, study their literature and ask advice on the use of their products. You'll probably choose an acrylic polyurethane paint. These are very durable, give full gloss, are easy to apply like lacquer but don't require rubbing out like lacquer. You'll learn the amount of each product you'll need for your renovation, along with other helpful information.

Use masking tape to hold newspapers or wrapping paper over the windshield, windows and parts you don't want painted. If you're planning a two-tone job, paint the upper part first. This prevents dragging the air hose over the new paint.

When installing masking tape, use a blade to press the edges firmly, so paint can't seep under the tape. Later, when you paint the lower part, use a sharp blade to cut along the edge of the tape. This prevents paint from being lifted with the tape when it is removed.

When masking for a two-tone job, remember that the newly painted section must be covered by a plastic

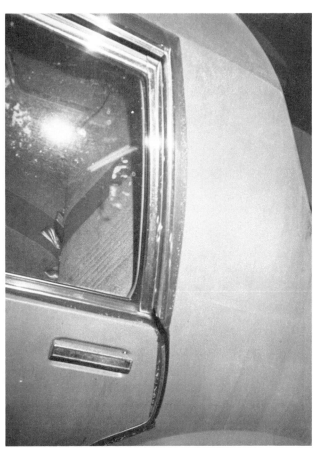

To prevent paint peeling around door or luggage lid edges, you may want to apply paint remover by brush to these areas. Wash the old paint away and rinse thoroughly with clear water before priming. Sand the area carefully to feather the edges.

You'll get a much better paint job if the entire car is given a prime coat, rather than using a color coat over various colors. After priming, the car should be sanded lightly and the finish inspected for blemishes. Wipe with a tack cloth before the final painting.

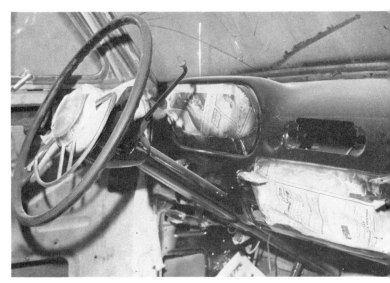

When painting the dashboard, steering column and pedals, mask the instrument cluster, radio speaker and all knobs and levers. Mask plated parts of the steering wheel. Leave car doors open for ventilation and aim the gun to avoid spray dust under the dash.

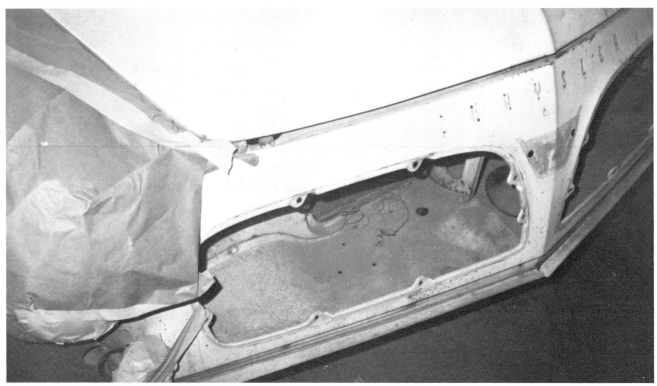

Remove all nameplates, badges and lettering from the car before painting. Some plated pieces will be held in place by bolts, others by clips. Tag any wires you disconnect for later match-up. If the car is a two-tone, mask the bottom and paint the top first.

Remove all lid-mounted trim items and wash the area. Choose one of the new, easy-to-use paint removers that will take cracked paint off in minutes, right down to the bare metal. Rinse the area with clear water before building the surface with filler and primer.

drop cloth, held to the dividing line with masking tape to protect it from overspray. If your car isn't a two-tone and you'd like to change it, two-tones are best separated at a body crease or under the middle of a trim strip.

If the wheels are on the car during the paint job, drape plastic drop cloths or paper wheel covers over them. Be sure to mask off the radiator so overspray won't clog it. If the firewall is to be painted, cover the engine with a drop cloth. Mask off all mechanical parts attached to the firewall.

Do any underfender painting and undercoating before the rest of the car. Clean off anything that gets on the exposed part of the fender lips or rocker panels.

An important part of preparation is a *thorough* cleaning of the area in which you'll paint. Move the car out of the area and clean the rafters, walls and floor to remove sanding dust, which could settle on the freshly painted car. Hose the floor to wash away dirt, dust and metal filings. If you're painting in half a garage, be sure the other car is out and any bikes, snow blowers or mowers are covered.

Prime body repairs as soon as you finish them, so rust won't start on bare metal. If you're making body repairs a few at a time, priming each will give protection until you've completed them all and can paint the car.

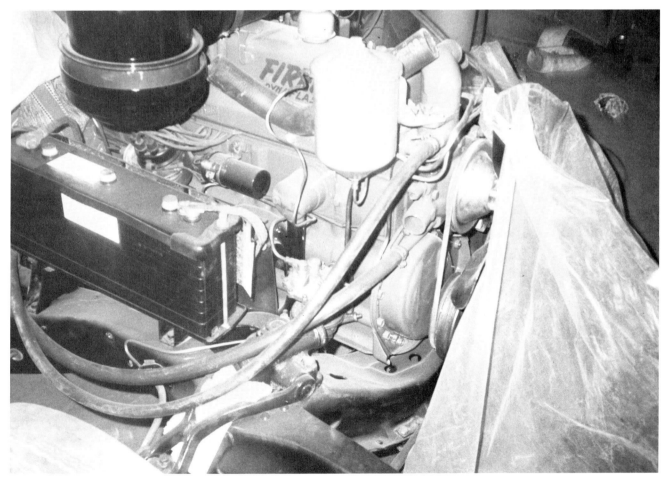

To avoid sanding and spray dust from entering the cooling system or air cleaner, as well as getting primer or paint on the engine, cover it with plastic sheeting or a drop cloth.

Always wear a mask when spray painting and change the filter regularly.

When repairing a nonstructural panel with several contours, fiberglass is easy to use and makes a permanent repair. Follow the directions on the package. Fiberglass can be sanded, primed and painted like metal. Wear gloves for protection.

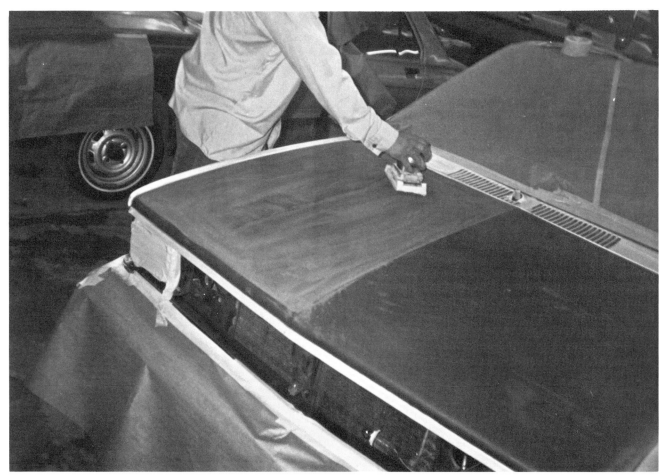

An electric vibrator-type sander is excellent for flat surfaces. You can change from medium to fine grit for the second time over an area. Ready-cut pads are handy, but you can save money if you buy sandpaper by the sheet and cut it to size.

The temperature should be at least seventy degrees Fahrenheit for best results. Leave a window open a few inches and fasten a damp towel over the opening to catch incoming dust. Block the door open a little and use a slow-moving fan to push out the spray dust. *Never* paint in a completely closed area.

Wheels are best painted off the car. Always paint both sides, with tires and decorative trim removed. On many cars it's best to remove bumpers to get complete body coverage.

The time and effort you take in preparing your car for painting, and the area in which you'll paint it, will be reflected in your finished renovation project.

Sources for additional information on painting techniques are included in the appendix.

When applying priming coats, it's often necessary to use a wet-type sandpaper or emery cloth between coats to get a glass-smooth finish. Keep the emery cloth wet and rub in even strokes in one direction, then at right angles.

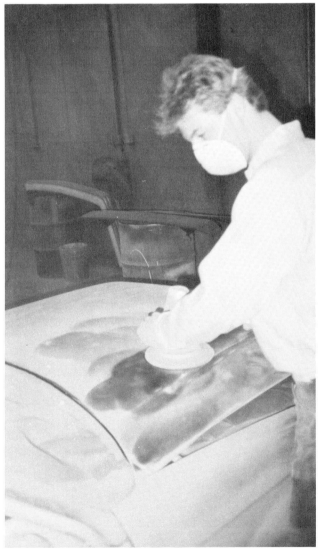

A grinder with sandpaper pads is easy to use and does a good job if you keep it moving. If you keep it in one spot more than a few seconds, however, it will remove too much primer. Change discs as soon as one clogs, and wear a respirator mask when sanding.

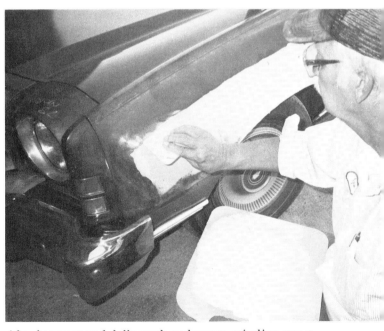

After hammer and dolly work and power grinding, use a plastic spreader to cover the repair with a good-grade body putty. It's better to use a couple of thin coats, rather than one thicker coat to hide the repair. Sand area between coats.

Use a find sanding disc between coats and after the final coat of body filler to produce a smooth finish. Feather the edges to hide the repair. For the best results, remove any trim pieces and prime and paint the entire panel.

Use a wire-bristled grinding wheel to knock away rust and scale around wheel cutouts and other hard-to-get-at areas.

If you look at the dirt and dust trapped in the filter after this type job, you'll always wear a mask.

Chapter 25

Painting

You have reached the last part of your rejuvenation process to make a real creampuff out of that old clunker you started with—painting. After all the time, work and money you put into renovating and repairing the various components, you want the paint job to reflect those efforts.

If you want to keep the car strictly original, you should paint it in one of the colors or combinations originally offered by the manufacturer. Several paint companies carry color chips cataloged by make, model and year, so you can choose the correct colors.

If authenticity isn't important, choose colors you like. If you want a two-tone, choose colors that complement each other and determine where you want the break. On most cars this will be along a molding or trim line.

Many cars of these years offered upholstery keyed to the car's color. When repainting your car, choose a color that will go well with the interior. Hopefully you considered this if you reupholstered your car.

Pebbled and textured finish paints are available for tops or lower parts of rocker panels. Stick-on vinyl striping in a variety of widths and colors makes hand striping unnecessary.

Equipment

Unless you already have equipment, it's better to rent it. Specify at least a ½ hp compressor. The more power, the more pressure you'll have, along with a more even and steadier force at the gun. Get a spray outfit that will deliver at least 30 psi (pounds per square inch). It should deliver at least 4 scfm (standard cubic feet per minute). These are important, as they guarantee you ample and sustained pressure for an even paint job.

Determine where you'll put the compressor, and get enough lengths of hose to reach all around the car. This will keep you from having to pass the air hose over the hood or rear deck. It's better to use extra lengths of hose, than a long extension cord.

When choosing a spray gun, be sure the needle that fits into the nozzle is clean and the orifice in the nozzle is also clean. There must be nothing in the

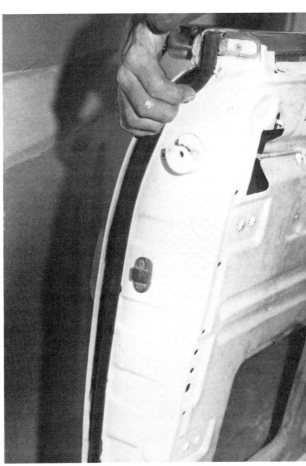

For the best paint job, you should paint the doorjambs and the rain troughs around the luggage area lid and hood. To avoid overspray onto your finished job, it's better to paint these parts before you do the rest of the car. Apply new weather-stripping.

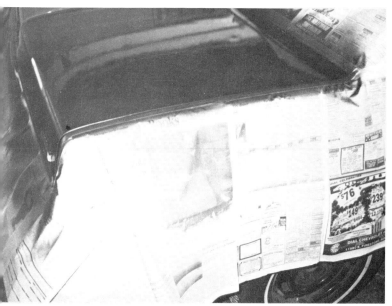

If you're painting a repaired luggage area lid, mask the rear window and the fender panels on each side. Newspapers are fine for this, and should cover the rear bumper. Use a flat blade to press the masking tape firmly in place to avoid paint seepage.

spray gun that alters or impedes a steady, even flow of paint. The gasket at the top of the container must seal tightly, so paint can't drip as you tip the gun in use.

Spraying techniques

If you've never used a pressure spray gun before, get suggestions from the person at the rental shop, and from knowledgeable people at the paint store. Ask friends who have painted cars for suggestions and tips. Talk with professionals at auto paint shops. The more information you can get on handling a spray gun, the easier and better your paint job will be.

Experiment on a large piece of cardboard, or a piece of scrap metal, such as a deck lid or hood picked up at a wrecking yard, before you start on your car. This will give you the feel of the gun.

The nozzle should be adjusted so it sprays an oval pattern about six inches in height and three inches in width. When spraying synthetic enamels, hold the gun about eight to ten inches from the surface. If you're using lacquer, hold it six to eight inches from the car. If you hold the gun too far away, the paint will start to set before it reaches the surface, giving a sandy or dusty finish. If you hold the gun too close, you'll get too thick a coat, which is apt to cause runs and sags.

Keep the gun perpendicular to the surface at all times, spraying in a horizontal pattern. Go back and forth, aiming the gun at the bottom of the previous stroke to get the slight overlap you need.

Peel away damaged sections of vinyl roof covering that detract from the car's appearance. Remove the molding around the rear window to get at the narrow strips on the sides. Paint the top car color, or match the color of the vinyl on the front section.

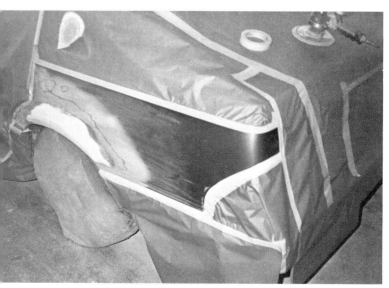

Cover the wheels for protection from overspray. Try to break the paint line at a trim strip or molding. Buy masking paper by the roll for big jobs. Run a sharp blade where the paint meets the tape before peeling the tape off to avoid lifting the paint.

Start at the top of a panel and work across and down. It may be necessary, from time to time, to use a vertical stroke on door and panel edges for proper coverage. When spraying, it's better to give a couple of light coats, rather than one heavy one.

Once you get the feel of the gun and are comfortable with it, you're ready for the car. Go over it with an air hose to blow the dust out of all crevices, making sure the surface is absolutely clean. Be sure the paint is mixed to the right consistency and that it has been stirred thoroughly to avoid settling. Finally, go over the car with a tack cloth to wipe away any last minute dust that may have settled on it.

Press the trigger when starting a panel and hold it. As you reach the other end of the panel, release the trigger, but continue the stroke a couple of inches before pressing the trigger and coming back on the reverse stroke. Be sure to keep the strokes smooth and easy so you'll spray enough paint to cover the area. Keep the gun moving to avoid runs and sags.

When painting a large, hard-to-get-at panel, such as the roof, start at one side and spray only to the distance at which you can hold the gun perpendicular

Resist the urge to attach plated trim pieces as soon as you remove the masking tape. Let the car stand at least 24 hours before attaching trim. Take care not to scratch the new paint doing this. Wait a month or more before you wax the car.

Replacement vinyl roofs are available for many cars, but they're expensive. You can remove a damaged roof and paint it car color, or use a textured paint that looks much like vinyl. Clean, sand and prime the area formerly covered by vinyl before painting.

227

Cellulose lacquer paint jobs must be rubbed down after painting to bring out the shine. Wait at least 24 hours before using a fine-grit rubbing compound or pumice stone and water for this job. You can spray a clear coat for a lasting shine.

to the surface. Vary the distance as you work from one end to the other to avoid a noticeable overlap, when you start on the other side.

On the hood and deck lid, start at one side and work toward the other, beginning at the windshield or rear window. This makes any overspray land on a dry surface, rather than on a newly painted area.

Once you've completed the top portion of a two-tone, let it stand until the paint is thoroughly dry,

before you remove masking tape. Run a sharp blade along the edge of the tape to separate the tape and paint. Peel off the tape slowly, making sure you don't lift off any paint with it.

Let the already painted portion of a two-tone stand about twenty-four hours before you apply masking tape to hold protective paper or a plastic drop cloth in place.

Before you start on the lower portion, wipe the area to be painted with a tack cloth, making it absolutely free of dust. Use the same spraying techniques as on the upper part. To keep the spray gun perpendicular to the surface, you may have to squat or kneel when painting rocker panels and front and rear aprons below bumpers.

When you've finished the lower part of the car, use the same precautions when removing masking tape. You may be tempted to start attaching trim pieces and accessories you removed before painting. Wait at least twenty-four hours before doing this, however, and be careful not to scratch the car. Avoid attaching any stick-on striping or decals for a few days, in case you make a mistake and have to lift it off for repositioning.

Painting wheels

Paint the wheels either before or after you paint the rest of the car. Before may be more practical, as you can leave them covered with a drop cloth, but can push the car from the garage if necessary.

With the wheels thoroughly washed, sanded and primed, lay them on cardboard or paper, with blocking in the center to keep the rims elevated. Spray the

PPG (formerly Ditzler) products allow the beginner to make a professional paint job. Their literature describes each of the products and how to use them. They also carry color ships showing original colors for most cars. Ask advice from the salesperson.

DuPont offers a complete line of car paint products, which will remove the old paint and fill many surface imperfections. Their primers and fillers are easy to use. Centari acrylic urethane enamel gives a tough finish. It is available in a wide choice of colors.

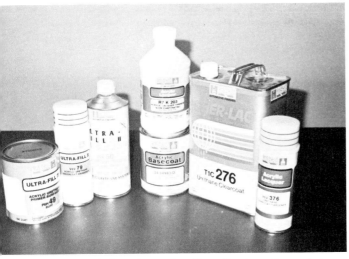

Sherwin Williams' complete line of automotive paint products can provide you with everything necessary to do a top-notch job. Their acrylic basecoat produces a good surface on which to start. Acrylic lacquer doesn't need rubbing down to produce a shine.

With dings and dents filled and the edges feathered to hide the repairs, spot-spray primer on these small areas to cover any exposed metal and prevent bleed-through on the color coat. Use a sanding block and #320 grit (fine) paper after spot–priming.

Use masking tape to hold paper around windshield and glass to protect it from overspray. Remove plated molding and other trim pieces. Adjust the nozzle on the spray gun to cover an oval-shaped area about nine inches at the widest spot.

inside of the wheels, following the circumference. They may take two or more coats. Sand between coats with #320 grit paper.

When you've finished one side of all wheels, turn them over and follow the same procedures.

Let the wheels dry thoroughly before mounting the tires. Use a little soapy water on the rims to help the tires slip on easier. Attach wheel rings before mounting the wheels.

Either have the wheels and tires balanced before mounting them on the car, or let it be one of the first trips you make in your newly painted car.

Let the car wait a week before washing or waxing it. Lacquer paint should stand twenty-four hours, before you rub it down with rubbing compound or pumice stone.

Caution: Always wear a respirator mask when spray painting, and change the filter frequently during the job.

If any paint seeped under the masking tape on trim pieces you didn't remove, use a little lacquer thinner to remove it. Don't let the thinner touch the new paint.

Take pictures of your creampuff. When they're compared with pictures of the clunker you started with, your friends will be amazed at what your rejuvenation accomplished.

Sources of additional information on painting techniques are included in the appendix.

When repainting the entire car, give it a complete coat of primer, so the color coat will be covering only one color. Choose the lighter, gray primer for light colors and the darker, red-brown primer to go under dark colors. Sand lightly after priming.

Chapter 26

Serious show car restoration

As you worked on your rescue and rejuvenation project, perhaps you decided you'd like to go all-out for a complete restoration; one that will qualify your car for serious show car competition.

Perhaps you found also that repairing and rejuvenating a car of these years isn't as difficult as you first thought. As you became more familiar with automotive construction and design, you may have found there were no secrets you couldn't fathom. You may have gained confidence in your ability to handle the necessary mechanical and body work to bring the car to tip-top shape.

Or it could be your desire to excel in all you do, that has changed your mind about the extent of your project. Perhaps seeing cars similar to yours brought to perfection by persons no more competent than you, has challenged you. It's the old "if they can do it, so can I" syndrome.

The car you chose may have been in better condition than you originally thought. Your comprehensive, after-purchase inspection may have indicated it wouldn't take much more effort, expense and time to make a complete restoration.

Whatever the reasons, if you decide to go for a show car restoration, you must realize the differences will be far more than just looks. There could be a considerable degree of difference in the amount and scope of mechanical work and bodywork.

This 1951 Buick convertible body was disassembled and removed from the chassis for a complete rebuild. Trim was removed for plating; cushions and panels were removed for reupholstering. With the body remounted on the rebuilt chassis, the car will be like new.

While the body was off the chassis for rebuilding, the engine, drivetrain, suspension, steering and brake systems were completely rebuilt. Every part must be brought to as-new condition for the car to compete in serious show car competition.

231

Rejuvenation versus restoration

There can be no compromises in structural integrity between a rejuvenation or restoration project. Neither can there be any lessening of safety standards. A car that has been rejuvenated must be just as safe and sound as one that has been completely restored.

Following the continuity of this book, the differences between the two projects start with chapter 6, but only after the general troubleshooting procedures outlined in chapter 4 have been completed.

In a frame-off restoration, the car would be completely disassembled, leaving only the chassis supported on jack stands, before that would be sandblasted or dipped in a stripping vat. On unit body/frame cars the body cannot be separated from the basic platform frame, but all mechanical components would have to be removed for a complete show car restoration.

The procedures outlined in chapters 6 and 7 would be included in a complete engine rebuild. Depending upon wear, additional machine shop work might be necessary. These could include reboring the cylinder block, regrinding and balancing the crankshaft, fitting oversize pistons and rings, milling the cylinder head(s) and completely rebuilding the valvetrain.

In a rejuvenation project, you would adjust, repair or replace only what is necessary. You would define the degree of performance acceptable to you. A completely rebuilt engine could well exceed original factory performance criteria, because of increased cubic inch displacement and machine shop work on the cylinder heads and valvetrain.

The engine swap outlined in chapter 8 would be made in a car intended for show car competition only if the replacement engine was offered as original equipment, or as an option. This wouldn't be the case in a rejuvenation project.

In a complete restoration you would replace any worn electrical components with new, rather than rebuilt parts, or make the repairs and adjustments covered in chapter 9. This could mean new wiring harnesses, coil, alternator or generator, distributor components and starter.

The differences between a rejuvenation and restoration project, as far as the fuel system (chapter 10) is concerned, would be substituting an electric fuel pump for a mechanical one in certain cases. This wouldn't be allowed in serious show car competition, as the cam driving the mechanical pump would have to be replaced so the mechanical pump would work.

Concerning the cooling system (chapter 11), the radiator core and collecting tanks would have to be boiled out and repainted in a restoration project, whether they needed it or not. In a rejuvenation project this would be done only if you discovered an overheating problem that couldn't be cured by a cooling system flush. The water pump, hoses, belts and other cooling system components would be brought to as-new condition in a complete restoration.

Everything must be removed, so the instrument panel can be completely refinished to original condition. Individual instruments, dials and the radio must be repaired and refinished. All plated trims must be replated before installation.

Fender panels, luggage area lid and the hood must be removed, repaired and repainted. After this fender has been repainted in an original color, it will receive a coat of clear lacquer so it will keep its new-car luster and shine.

Because of safety standards and some states' emission laws, there should be no difference in rebuilding an exhaust system as described in chapter 12, other than discarding still usable parts, instead of replacing only what's necessary.

If you decide to make a complete restoration, you would dismantle and inspect the bearings and gears in a manual transmission, and replace everything that shows wear. In a rejuvenation project you would do this *only* if you had a problem shifting gears, or one of the gears was noisy. The clutch (chapter 13) wouldn't be touched in a renovation project, unless it slipped, and even then possibly an adjustment would suffice.

The standards on automatic transmissions, other than minor adjustments, would be the same for each project. For show car competition, an automatic transmission could be replaced only by an identical unit, and could not be updated, as could be done in a rejuvenation.

In a complete restoration project, the differential and rear axle assembly (chapter 14) would be disassembled and checked for wear. New gears or bearings would be installed to bring the assembly to as-new condition, and axle housings and differential case would be painted.

For safety reasons, all work on rear suspension systems (chapter 15), front suspensions (chapter 16) and the steering system (chapter 17), would be the same for either type of project, except for painting the components for show car competition.

Rare when it was new, and extremely rare today. This Chrysler Town and Country convertible, with wood trim gleaming as the day it was delivered, is like new in every respect. The frame-off restoration included every mechanical component.

Keeping safety in mind, there would be no appreciable difference between a rejuvenation and restoration project, as far as the brake system (chapter 18) is concerned. You might reuse brake tubing and rubber grommets, if they were in good condition, when reju-

Stylish and trim, this 1954 Mercury convertible shows the results of a basically sound car completely restored to as-new condition. Though the job took many hours to search out and install NOS parts, the finished car is worth the effort and expense.

venating your car. You might opt not to repaint the brake backing plates and drums, as you would for a complete restoration. Important parts would be replaced in each project.

Body repairs (chapter 19) would be strictly welded-in steel and hot lead. The fiberglass or double plating options wouldn't be used in a complete restoration. Procedures for repairing dents would be the same.

There would be no differences in making and fitting the convertible top (chapter 20), though on a show car project, you wouldn't repair a damaged top, you would replace it.

If you make a complete restoration you would have to bring seat cushions, side and door upholstery and headliner to as-new condition. If this means reupholstering these items, you would have to do it in the same style, color and type of material that was used originally. The rejuvenation project covered in chapter 21 might not qualify your car for serious competition.

As with upholstery, the carpeting (chapter 22) would have to be replaced with duplicates of the original in a complete restoration, instead of repairs and substitutions, as allowed in a rejuvenation project.

Concerning trim items (chapter 23), every piece of inner and outer trim would have to be in as-new condition. This could mean replating to bring all components to show car quality.

When preparing the car for painting (chapter 24), you would have to remove all the old finish, either with paint remover, or the dipping process. You would use fillers and primers, just as in a rejuvenation, except you would start from bare metal and it would take more time and materials to build up the surface for painting.

Keep in mind that the car would have to be painted in an original color, or combination of colors. Any striping would have to duplicate the original.

There would be no differences between a restoration and rejuvenation, as far as painting the car (chapter 25) is concerned. All methods and techniques would be the same.

Your choice

Consider the differences between rejuvenating and restoring a project. Weigh the pluses and minuses of each type of project—there may be plenty of these.

Many times a restorer will invest more money in a complete frame-off restoration than the completed car will be worth. However, that person has a "new" old car. It is difficult to put a price on the personal satisfaction and sense of accomplishment you'll get from completely restoring the car of your choice to as-new condition.

It is not the intent of this chapter to influence your decision, simply to outline some of the major differences for your consideration.

It's your choice.

This completely restored Dodge Coronet sedan, its chrome-trimmed fins highlighted with a contrasting color, is an excellent example of a medium-priced family sedan re- *stored to show car condition. Inside and out it is restored to factory specifications.*

Chapter 27

Caring for your car

When your rescue and rejuvenation project is completed and you've made a creampuff out of that old clunker, you'll want to drive and enjoy it. You should also protect your investment so it will continue appreciating.

You'll enjoy your car more if you join one of the car clubs, preferably one for your marque. National, regional and local branches of these clubs plan tours, and hold interesting technical events and enjoyable social programs that include the whole family. They're also a good source for buying, selling or swapping parts. Many clubs distribute periodic publications that invite owner participation. Information on car clubs is included in the appendix.

Follow state laws on licensing and any periodic vehicle inspection. Some states issue antique or collector plates, but there may be some restrictions as to the car's use. Your motor vehicle bureau can advise you on this.

If you plan to use your car regularly, it should be licensed and insured accordingly. However, if it will only be used occasionally, different insurance cover-

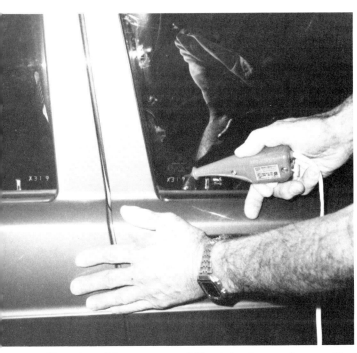

There is a risk your car could be stolen for resale or parting out. This handy engraving tool allows you to mark a code on windows, radio, wheel discs and other parts. Some insurance companies give a discount if this is done. Many police departments loan them out.

Install a simple disconnect switch on the battery if your car is used infrequently. This prevents it from being drained by an electric clock or other electric appliance. It can also foil a would-be thief, who hasn't time to look for the cutoff.

Keep leather and vinyl upholstery supple and looking like new with periodic applications of specially formulated cleaners and conditioners. Pay special attention to those areas that get direct sunlight. Armor All is fine for vinyl upholstery and padding.

After washing your car, keep the finish in tip-top condition by regular applications of a fine-quality cleaner and polish. After the initial applications, plan on waxing one panel at a time to maintain the protection a good wax can provide.

age may save you money. Check costs on collision damage to your car, and fire and theft. Certain segments of your insurance may cost more, because of the scarcity and expense of replacement parts on certain cars. Some cars are more attractive than others to thieves, either because of their popularity or for parting out. Where and how you store your car may make a difference, too. Discuss these points with your insurance agent. Sources for special insurance coverage for cars of these years are also included in the appendix.

Many police and sheriff departments lend engraving devices to mark an identifying code or number on windows, radio, tape deck, wheel discs and other easily removable parts. You can buy this type machine

at hardware stores for about what you'd save on the first year's premium, as some insurance companies offer a discount if this is done.

Keep your car locked and stored in a secure place where it is protected from weather. If it will only be driven occasionally, buy a ready-made car cover, or make a simple cover of unbleached muslin. This material breathes and lets air circulate freely, giving better ventilation than vinyl.

An assortment of household cleaners, available at any supermarket, will help keep upholstery, carpets and wood trim in tip-top condition. Use a fabric protector for cloth-upholstered seats and panels. Protect woolen carpets and upholstery against moth damage.

Either leave the dashboard fresh air vent open, or lower one window just enough to let air enter. Cardboard sun shields help protect dashboard padding, steering wheel and front seat upholstery, as well as tops of the rear cushion.

Wash and wax the car periodically. Be sure to clean the underside of the fenders, keeping dirt from accumulating in the area over headlights and in fender curl-unders. Areas where aprons meet the body require extra cleaning and waxing from time to time. A light coat of wax on plated parts helps prevent surface rust.

Glycerine or a silicone spray helps keep rubber gaskets and moldings around windows supple and prevents cracking.

Sweep or vacuum the interior as necessary. If the car has woolen upholstery or carpeting, use a spray to protect against moth damage, as well as stains. Lift the carpets periodically to look for damp spots, indicating trapped moisture. Remove seat cushions from time to time and vacuum out any dirt and debris that has accumulated.

Use a leather cleaner and conditioner two or three times a year to keep leather supple. Use a vinyl cleaner to preserve vinyl and molded foam.

Make sure there are no openings under the car, through which destructive mice could enter and take up residence.

If your car wasn't equipped with seatbelts, by all means install a set. Buy these from an auto supply store, or pick up a good set at a salvage yard.

The best protection for a convertible top is to keep it clean and dry. Use a soft brush to remove dirt from seams, bindings and weltings. Check snap fasteners, making sure the top is stretched tightly. Don't store the car for long periods with the top folded, as you're inviting cracks and mildew. Don't use abrasives on the rear curtain.

Keep a 50:50 mixture of permanent-type anti-freeze in the cooling system and add a can of water pump lubricant. Check battery water from time to time, as you check the oil, brake and power steering reservoirs. Also, check the garage floor from time to time, looking for signs of a leaking radiator, or other components.

If the car is to be unused for more than a few weeks, disconnect the negative terminal to the battery, to keep the electric clock from draining the battery.

Keep the tires, including the spare, to the correct pressure. Use powdered graphite on locks and door latches.

Keep a box containing an extra set of belts, radiator hoses, windshield wiper blades, ignition points, fuses and other minor parts, along with a quart of oil, a filter and can of transmission fluid in the car, if you plan to drive any distance from home. You should also take along a set of the most commonly used tools. Make sure a jack and wheel wrench are stored with the spare.

You may have some extra parts left from your renovation. If any of these are parts you feel you might use some day, identify each and store them in an out-of-the-way place. Metal parts should be protected by a light coat of oil. Trim pieces can be protected by regular car wax. Cloth pieces may need spraying with Scotchgard, while vinyl can be protected by Armor All, and leather by a good leather conditioner.

You may have some parts you can sell or swap. All unrepairable parts should be thrown out.

So, drive and enjoy your creampuff, realizing that it is increasing in value every month.

Appendix

Throughout this book there are references to the sharing of many body and chassis parts, as well as interchangeability of engine, powertrain and suspension components. You'll find that information in the following publications, which may be available at your public library, or can be ordered from firms advertising in car publications, and from the following sources.

Parts interchangeability
Hollander's interchange manuals
23rd edition, 1946-1956
32nd edition, 1954-1966
40th edition, 1964-1974
   Available at Dragich Discount Auto Literature, 1500 93rd Lane NE, Minneapolis, MN 55434.

Parts interchange manuals
1938-1954 All US cars
1950-1962 Ford, Lincoln, Mercury
1963-1974 Ford, Lincoln, Mercury, Mustang
1950-1965 Chrysler, DeSoto, Imperial, Plymouth
1950-1965 Buick, Cadillac, Chevrolet, Oldsmobile, Pontiac
   Available at the Auto Book Center, 50 Aleppo St., Box 37, Providence, RI 02909.

Standard Catalog of American Cars 1946-1975
   Available at Krause Publications, Book Order Department, 700 E. State St., Iola, WI 54990.

Technical information
   For an easier renovation, you may need owners manuals, parts books, factory specifications, shop service manuals and other materials on US cars of these years. Such resources are available from:

Motorbooks International
P.O. Box 2
Osceola, WI 54020

Dragich Discount Books
1500 93rd Lane NE
Minneapolis, MN 55434

Discount Book Co.
P.O. Box 3150
San Rafael, CA 94912-3150

Auto Book Center
50 Aleppo St., Box 37
Providence, RI 02909

Chenning's Auto Literature
P.O. Box 727
Broadway, VA 22815

Periodicals
   You'll save money, time and a lot of frustration if you keep current with the hobby. These publications are a quick source of information. They contain a variety of well-written articles, timely advertisements and are good reading, too.

Cars & Parts, Box 482, Sydney, OH 45637
Car Collector, P.O. Box 171, Mount Morris, IL 61054
Hemming's Motor News, Box 380, Bennington, VT   05201
Special Interest Autos, Box 196, Bennington, VT   05201
Old Cars Weekly, Iola, WI 54990
Skinned Knuckles, 275 May Ave., Monrovia, CA 91016

General restoration books
Auto Restoration, from Junker to Jewel, Burt Mills, Motorbooks International.
How To Restore Your Collector Car, Tom Brownell, Motorbooks International.

Power accessory repairs
Chilton's Power Accessory Manual, Chilton Book Company, Radnor, PA 19089.

Multi-car mechanical information
Chilton's Auto Repair manual
   Editions for 1940-1953; 1954-1963; and 1961-1971; Chilton Book Company.
Motor Repair Manual, 2nd Edition, 1953-1961, Motorbooks International.

Additional sources by chapter
Chapter 1
American Car Spotter's Guide, 1940–1965 and 1966–1980, Tad Burness, Motorbooks International.

Chapter 2
Standard Guide to Cars & Prices, Krause Publications.
How To Buy or Sell a Car by Long Distance, Adams Hudson, Motorbooks International.

Chapter 9
Electrical and Ignition Systems, Peter Wallage.
Automotive Electrical Handbook, Jim Horner.
    Both available from Motorbooks International.

Chapter 10
Carter Carburetors, Dave Emanual.
Holle Carburetors, Urich & Fisher.
Rochester Carburetors, Doug Roe.
    All available from Motorbooks International.

Chapter 13 and 14
Clutch & Flywheel Handbook, Tom Monroe.
Automotive Manual Transmissions & Power Trains, Crouse & Anglin.
How To Restore Gearboxes & Axles, Ivan Carroll.
    All available from Motorbooks International.

Chapter 15
Handling and Roadholding, Jeffery Daniels.
How To Make Your Car Handle, Fred Puhn.
    Both available from Motorbooks International.

Chapter 16 and 17
How To Restore Suspension & Steering, Roy Berry.
Steering Wheel Restoration Handbook, Jack Turpin.
    Both available from Motorbooks International.

Chapter 18
Brake Handbook, Fred Puhn, Motorbooks International.

Chapter 19
The Welder's Bible, Don Gray.
How To Replace Metal with Joining Techniques, Tony Fairweather.
The Key to Metal Bumping, Frank Sargent.
Auto Body Solder Book, T. Cowan.
How To Restore Fiberglass Bodywork, Miles Wilkes.
    All available from Motorbooks International.

Chapter 21
How To Restore Upholstery, Tony Fairweather.
Leather Work for the Restorer, Dan Post.
    Both available from Motorbooks International.

Chapter 22
How To Restore Car Interiors, Peter Wallage.
Car Interior Restoration, Terry Boyce.
    Both available from Motorbooks International.

Chapter 23
Electric Plating for the Amateur, L. Warburton.
Auto Detailing for Show and Profit, David H. Jacobs, Jr.
    Both available from Motorbooks International.

Chapter 24 and 25
Custom Painting: The Do-It-Yourself Guide, Motorbooks International.

Chapter 26
If you're considering restoring your car for competition, write to the owner's club for your marque requesting judging standards, or contact Classic Car Club of America, P.O. Box 2113, Dearborn, MI 48123.

Chapter 27
Your regular insurance company may not cover your car. The following companies specialize in insuring your type of car.

American Collectors Insurance
P.O. Box 8343
Cherry Hills, NJ 08034

Condon & Skelly
Suite 203, 121 E. Kings Hwy.
Maple Shade, NJ 08052

The Collector Vehicle Program
The Grundy Agency
501 Office Center Dr.
Fort Washington, PA 19034

J. C. Taylor Antique Auto Insurance Agency, Inc.
320 S. 68th St.
Upper Darby, PA 19082

Tax information
Because your creampuff will increase in value, you may have a tax liability when you sell it. This readable book gives valuable information on recordkeeping and other pertinent subjects:
Tax Savings on Antique, Collector and Investor Automobiles, A. S. Foner, Motorbooks International.

Automobile companies
When rejuvenating or restoring a car of these years, it is helpful to have information from the manufacturer. This is no problem with companies still in business. However, through mergers and consolidations, some respected names have been discontinued and these cars are now considered orphans. You should be able to get needed information on most cars by writing to the auto maker's home office.

Chrysler Corporation
Chrysler Historical Collection
12000 Chrysler Dr., CIMS 416-02-46
Highland Park, MI 48288-1919
    Information on Chrysler, DeSoto, Dodge, Imperial and Plymouth. Also on AMC cars, including Hudson, Nash and Jeep vehicles.

Chrysler Motors
Owner Relations
P.O. Box 1718
Detroit, MI 48228
    Restoration information and guides.

Ford Motor Company
Ford Archives
The Edison Institute, Henry Ford Museum
Dearborn, MI 48121
    Information on Ford, Lincoln, Mercury and Mustang.

General Motors Corporation
Buick Division
Customer Service Department
Flint, MI 48500

Cadillac Division
Customer Service Department
2860 Clark Ave.
Detroit, MI 48232

Chevrolet Division
Customer Assistance Center
Hobby Shop
P.O. Box 7047
Troy, MI 48007

Chevrolet Division
Central Office
Public Relations Department
30007 Van Dyke Ave.
Warren, MI 48090

Oldsmobile Division
Research Department
Lansing, MI 48900

Pontiac Division
Public Relations Department
One Pontiac Plaza
Pontiac, MI 48053

Lincoln Division, Ford Motor Company
Customer Relations Department
One Park Lane Blvd.
Suite 1220 West
Dearborn, MI 48121
   Additional information on Lincoln and Mercury.

Navistar
Public Relations & Research Department
401 N. Michigan Ave.
Chicago, IL 60601
   Information on International Harvester vehicles.

Studebaker National Museum
Archives Department
120 S. St. Joseph St.
South Bend, IN 46601
   Information on Packard and Studebaker cars.

The Society of Automotive Historians, Inc.
c/o the National Automotive History Collection
Detroit Public Library
5201 Woodward Ave.
Detroit, MI 48202
   Information on US cars of these years.